For my pal,
Joe —
thanks for the
introduction to Elliott!

Love you,

Terry

For Neil Mahoney

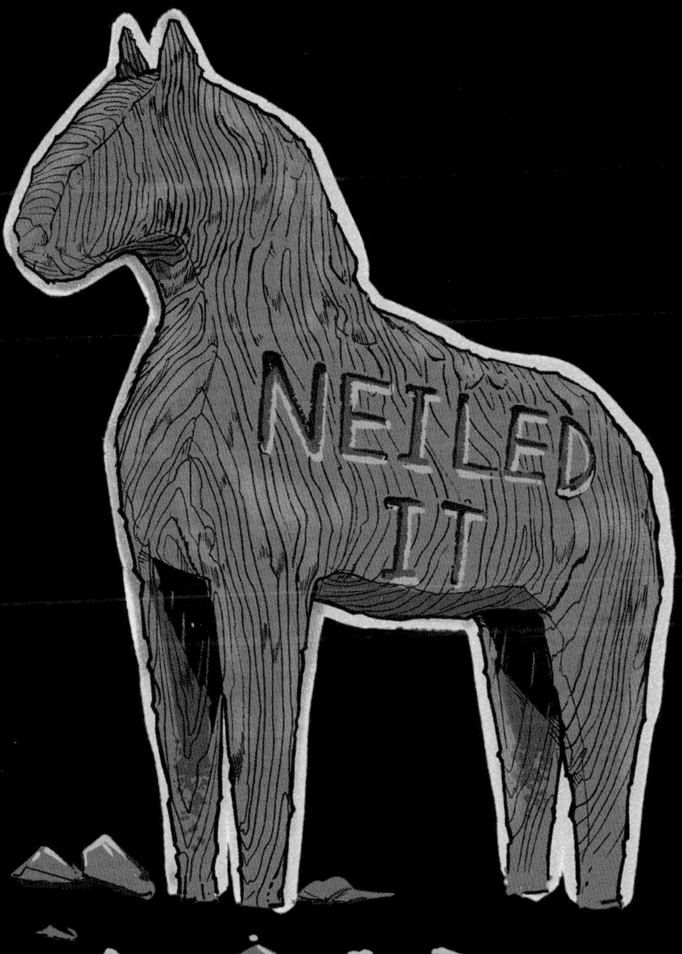
NEILED
IT

THE DARK ROOM

WORDS
GERRY DUGGAN

ART
SCOTT BUONCRISTIANO

COLORS
TAMRA BONVILLAIN

LETTERS
JOE SABINO

DESIGN
ELLIOTT GRAY

THE DARK ROOM. First printing. June 2022. Published by Image Comics, Inc. Office of publication: PO BOX 14457, Portland, OR 97293. Copyright © 2022 Gerry Duggan & Scott Buoncristiano. All rights reserved. "The Dark Room," its logos, and the likenesses of all characters herein are trademarks of Gerry Duggan & Scott Buoncristiano, unless otherwise noted. "Image" and the Image Comics logos are registered trademarks of Image Comics, Inc. No part of this publication may be reproduced or transmitted, in any form or by any means (except for short excerpts for journalistic or review purposes), without the express written permission of Gerry Duggan & Scott Buoncristiano, or Image Comics, Inc. All names, characters, events, and locales in this publication are entirely fictional. Any resemblance to actual persons (living or dead), events, or places, without satirical intent, is coincidental. Printed in Canada. For international rights, contact: foreignlicensing@imagecomics.com. ISBN: 978-1-5343-2118-2.

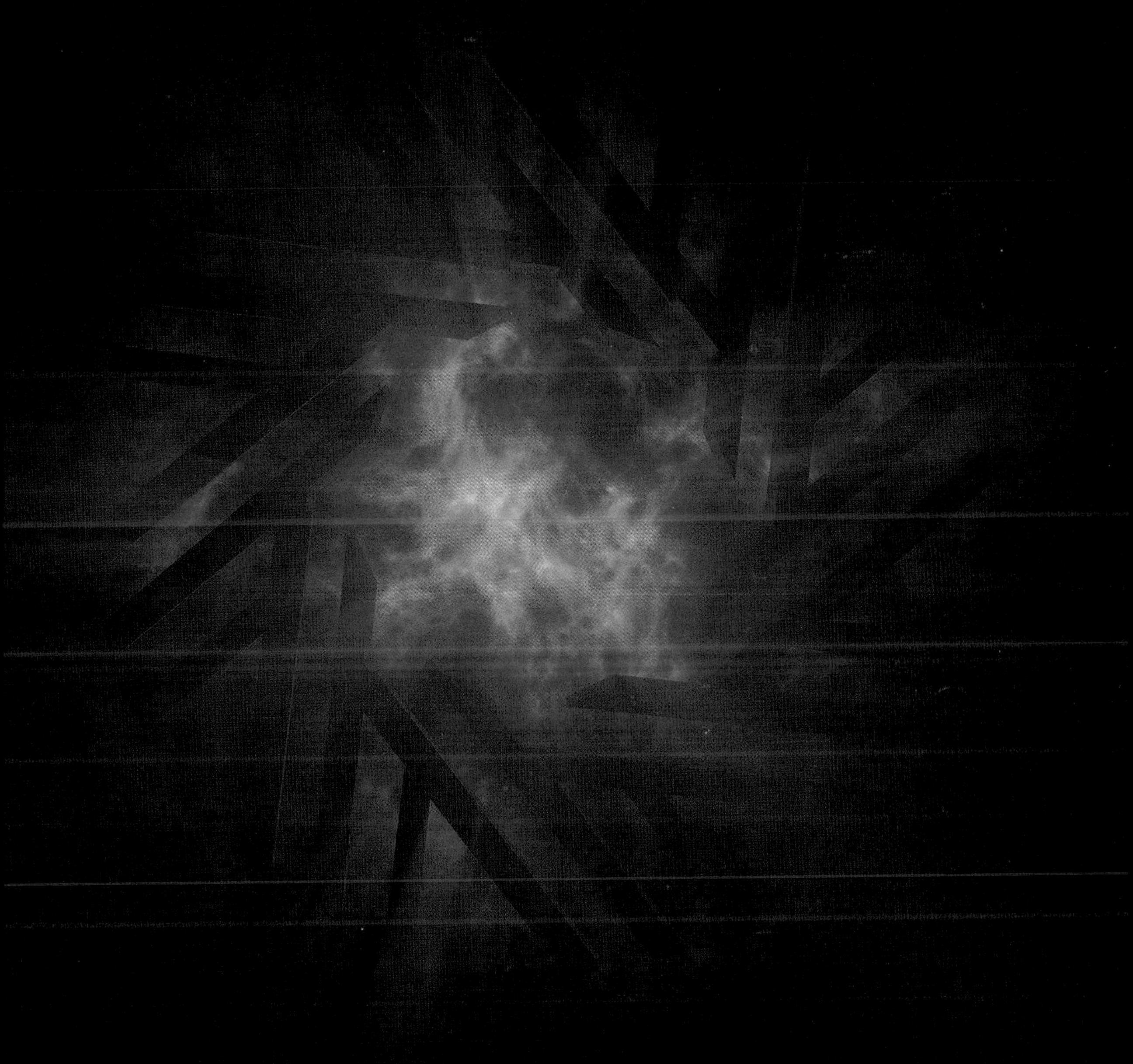

VOLUME ONE

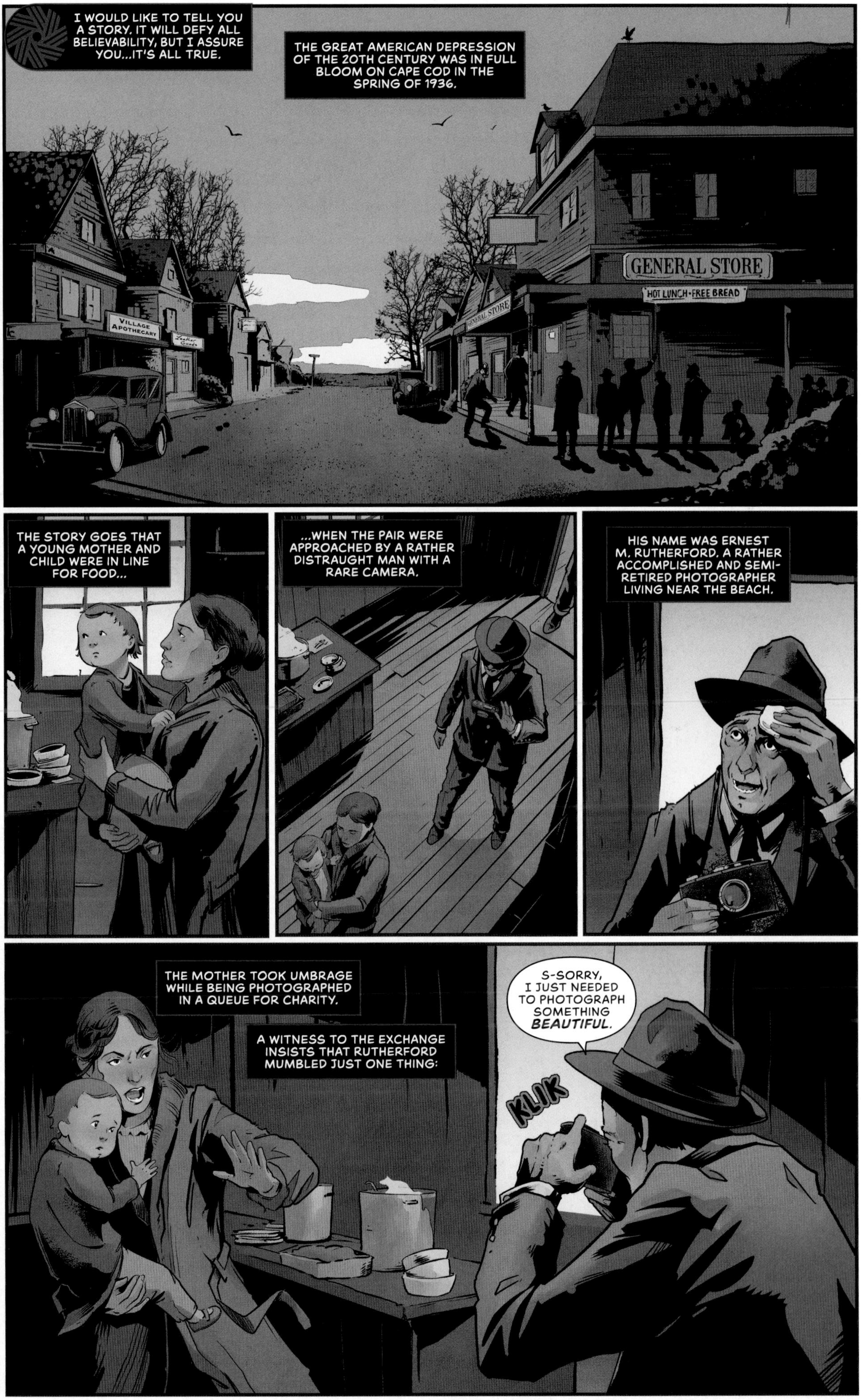
I WOULD LIKE TO TELL YOU A STORY. IT WILL DEFY ALL BELIEVABILITY, BUT I ASSURE YOU...IT'S ALL TRUE.
THE GREAT AMERICAN DEPRESSION OF THE 20TH CENTURY WAS IN FULL BLOOM ON CAPE COD IN THE SPRING OF 1936.
VILLAGE APOTHECARY
GENERAL STORE
GENERAL STORE
HOT LUNCH·FREE BREAD
THE STORY GOES THAT A YOUNG MOTHER AND CHILD WERE IN LINE FOR FOOD...
...WHEN THE PAIR WERE APPROACHED BY A RATHER DISTRAUGHT MAN WITH A RARE CAMERA.
HIS NAME WAS ERNEST M. RUTHERFORD, A RATHER ACCOMPLISHED AND SEMI-RETIRED PHOTOGRAPHER LIVING NEAR THE BEACH.
THE MOTHER TOOK UMBRAGE WHILE BEING PHOTOGRAPHED IN A QUEUE FOR CHARITY.
A WITNESS TO THE EXCHANGE INSISTS THAT RUTHERFORD MUMBLED JUST ONE THING:
S-SORRY, I JUST NEEDED TO PHOTOGRAPH SOMETHING *BEAUTIFUL*.
KLIK

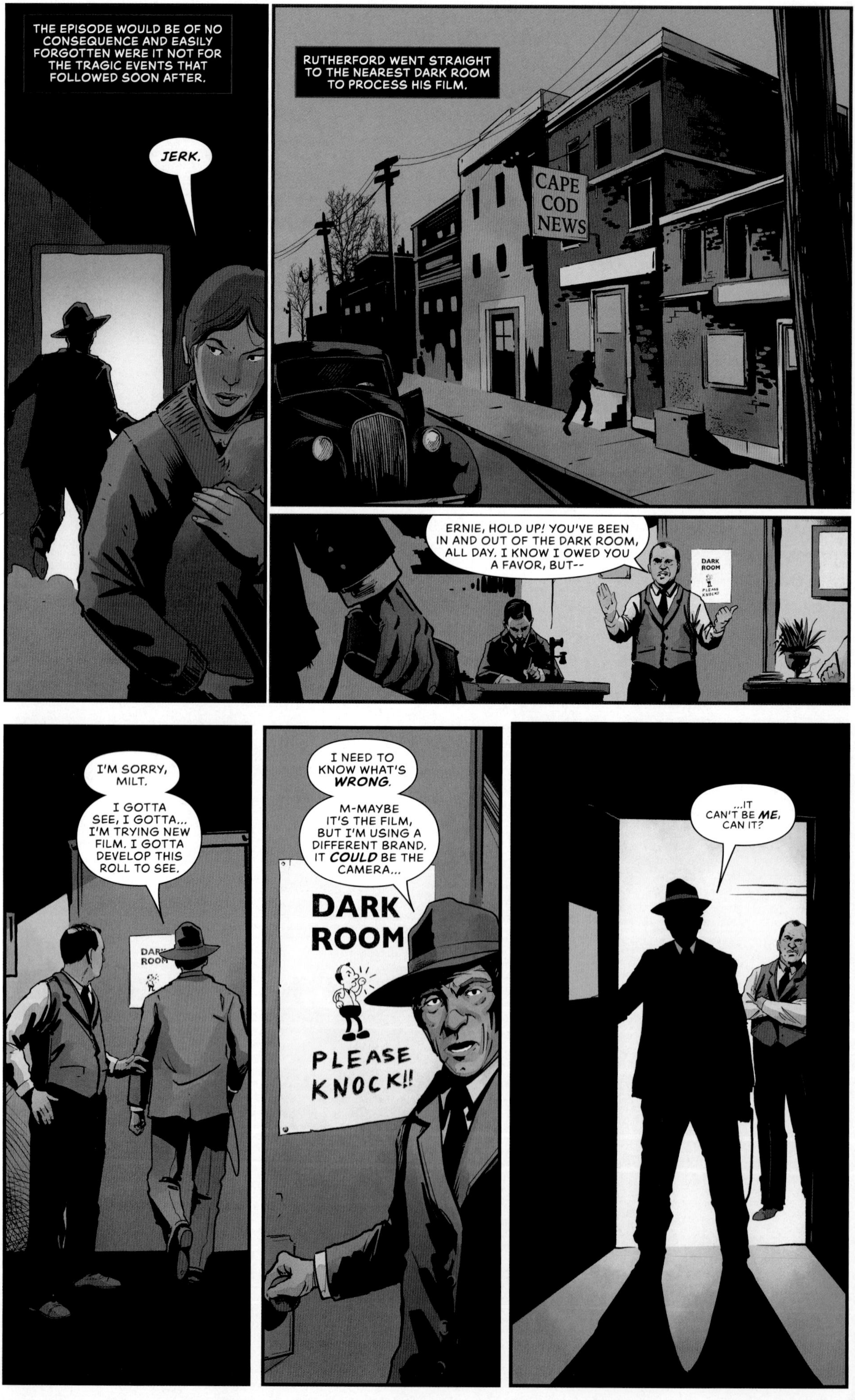
THE EPISODE WOULD BE OF NO CONSEQUENCE AND EASILY FORGOTTEN WERE IT NOT FOR THE TRAGIC EVENTS THAT FOLLOWED SOON AFTER.
JERK.
RUTHERFORD WENT STRAIGHT TO THE NEAREST DARK ROOM TO PROCESS HIS FILM.
CAPE COD NEWS
ERNIE, HOLD UP! YOU'VE BEEN IN AND OUT OF THE DARK ROOM, ALL DAY. I KNOW I OWED YOU A FAVOR, BUT--
DARK ROOM PLEASE KNOCK!!
I'M SORRY, MILT.
I GOTTA SEE, I GOTTA... I'M TRYING NEW FILM. I GOTTA DEVELOP THIS ROLL TO SEE.
I NEED TO KNOW WHAT'S WRONG.
M-MAYBE IT'S THE FILM, BUT I'M USING A DIFFERENT BRAND. IT COULD BE THE CAMERA...
DARK ROOM
PLEASE KNOCK!!
...IT CAN'T BE ME, CAN IT?

RUTHERFORD ENTERED THE DARK ROOM HOPING TO PRINT THE IMAGE HE SAW THROUGH THE LENS.

HE WAS A DESPERATE MAN BY THIS POINT.

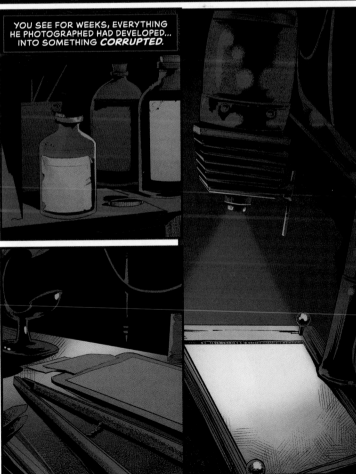

YOU SEE FOR WEEKS, EVERYTHING HE PHOTOGRAPHED HAD DEVELOPED... INTO SOMETHING *CORRUPTED.*

THE PHOTOCHEMICAL PROCESS OF TURNING DELICATE FILM INTO NEGATIVES AND THEN PRINTS IS AN ART UNTO ITSELF...AND IT'S *TIME CONSUMING.*

HE WAS A RELIGIOUS MAN, AND I SUSPECT HE WAS QUITE TORTURED THAT AFTERNOON.

WAITING IN THE DARK TO SEE WHAT HE'D CAPTURED IN THE LIGHT...PRAYING THIS PORTRAIT DIDN'T DEVELOP LIKE THE OTHERS.

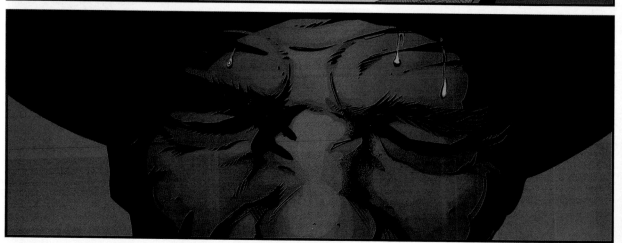

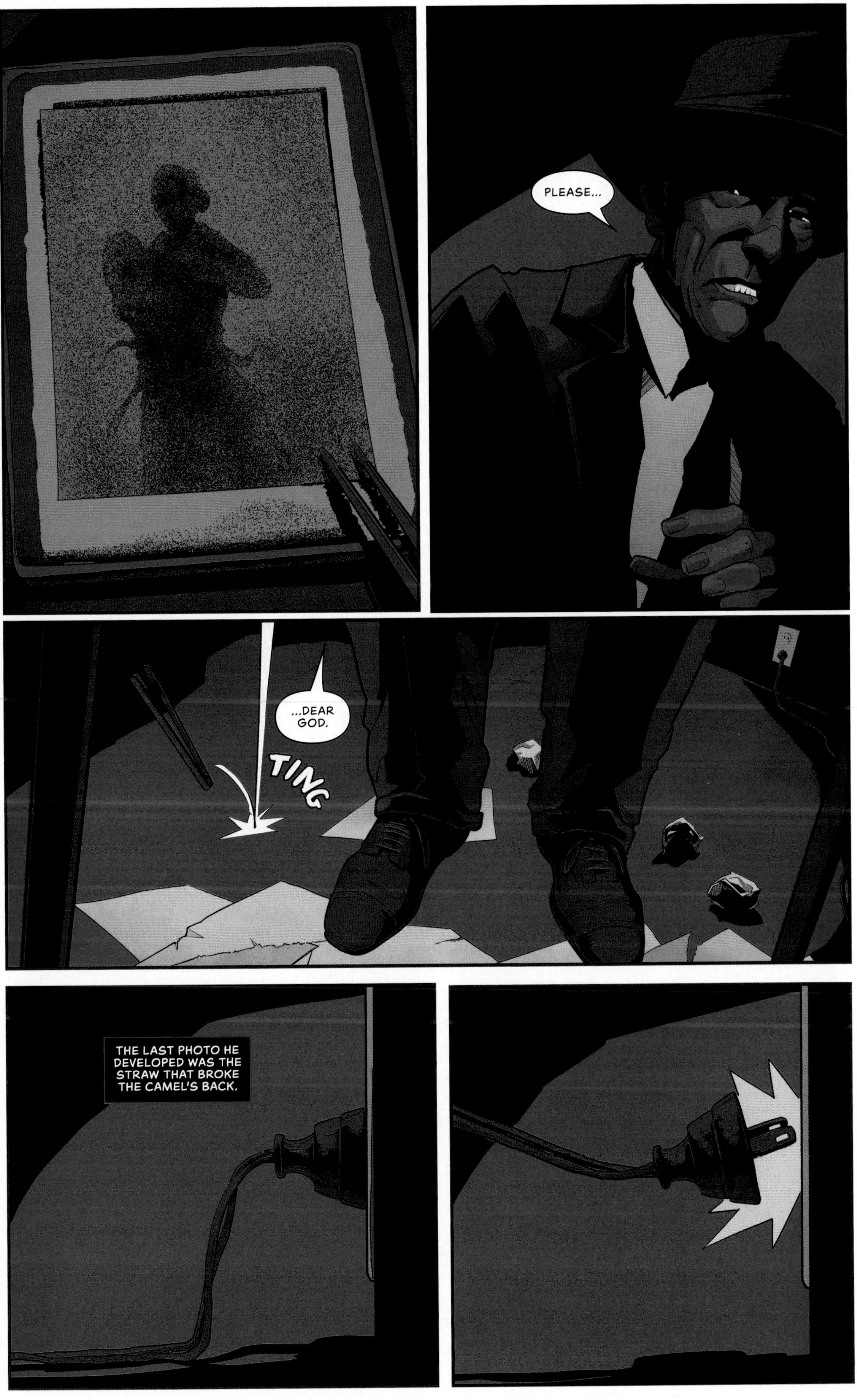
PLEASE...
...DEAR GOD.
TING
THE LAST PHOTO HE DEVELOPED WAS THE STRAW THAT BROKE THE CAMEL'S BACK.

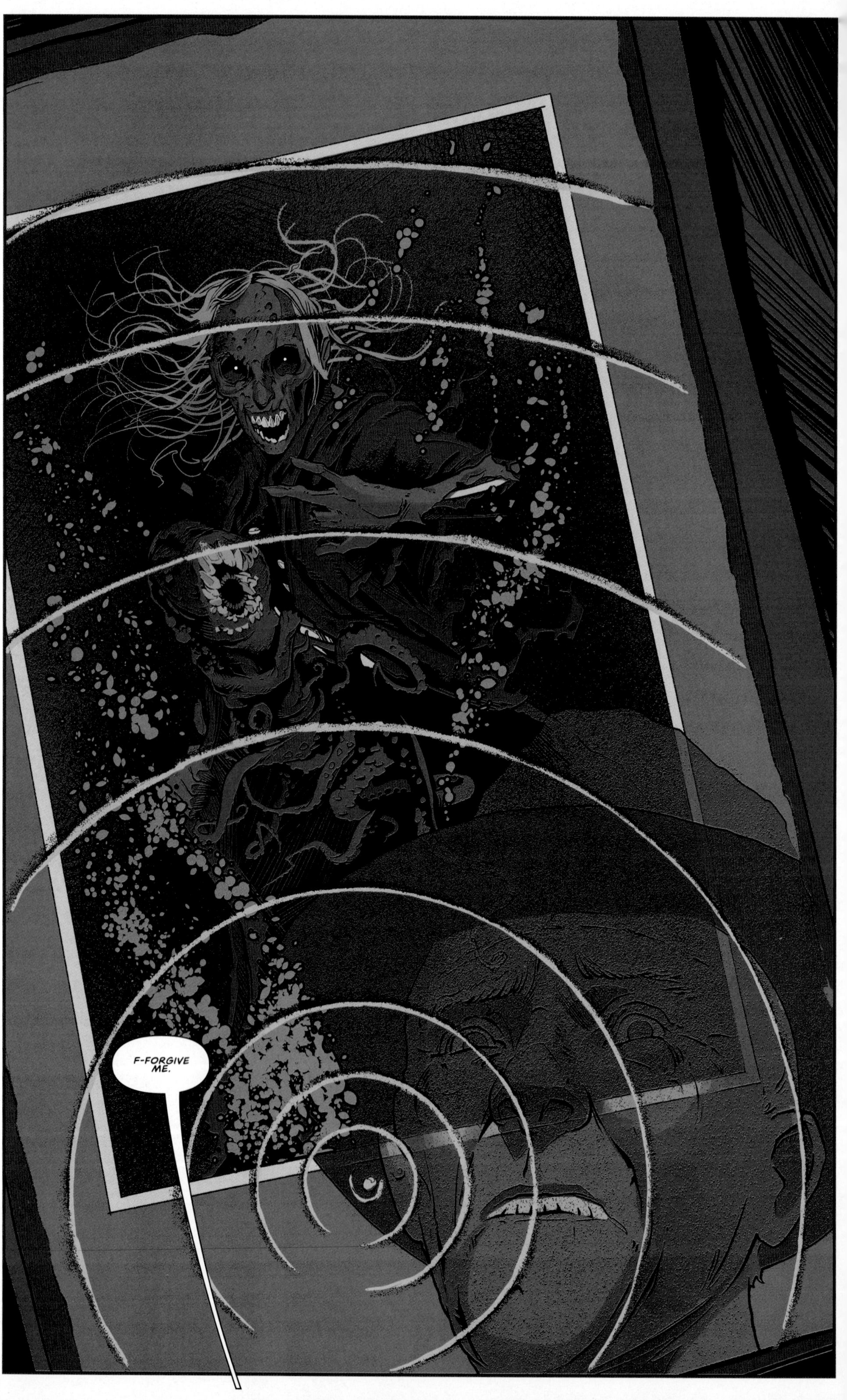
F-FORGIVE ME.

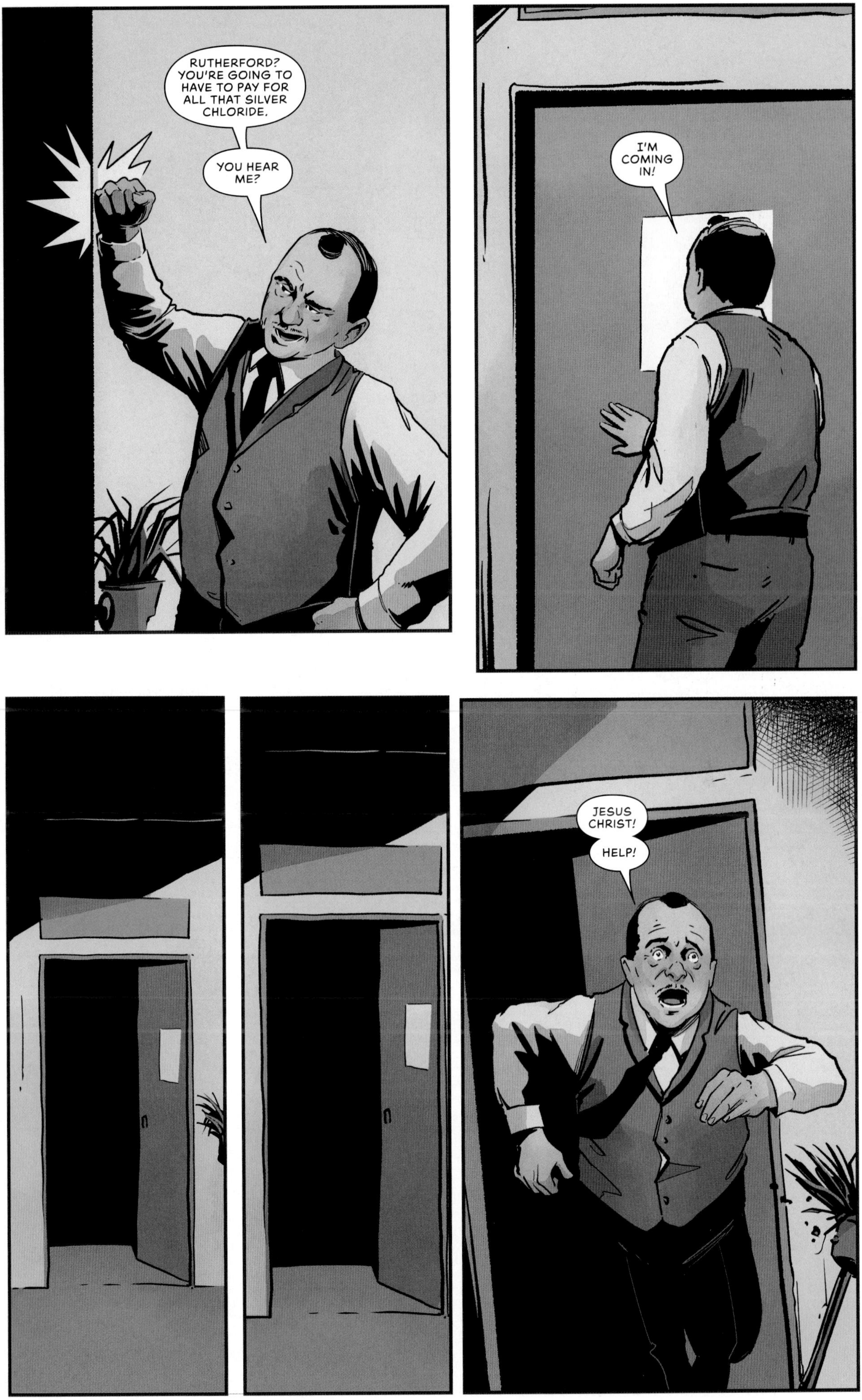
RUTHERFORD? YOU'RE GOING TO HAVE TO PAY FOR ALL THAT SILVER CHLORIDE.
YOU HEAR ME?
I'M COMING IN!
JESUS CHRIST!
HELP!

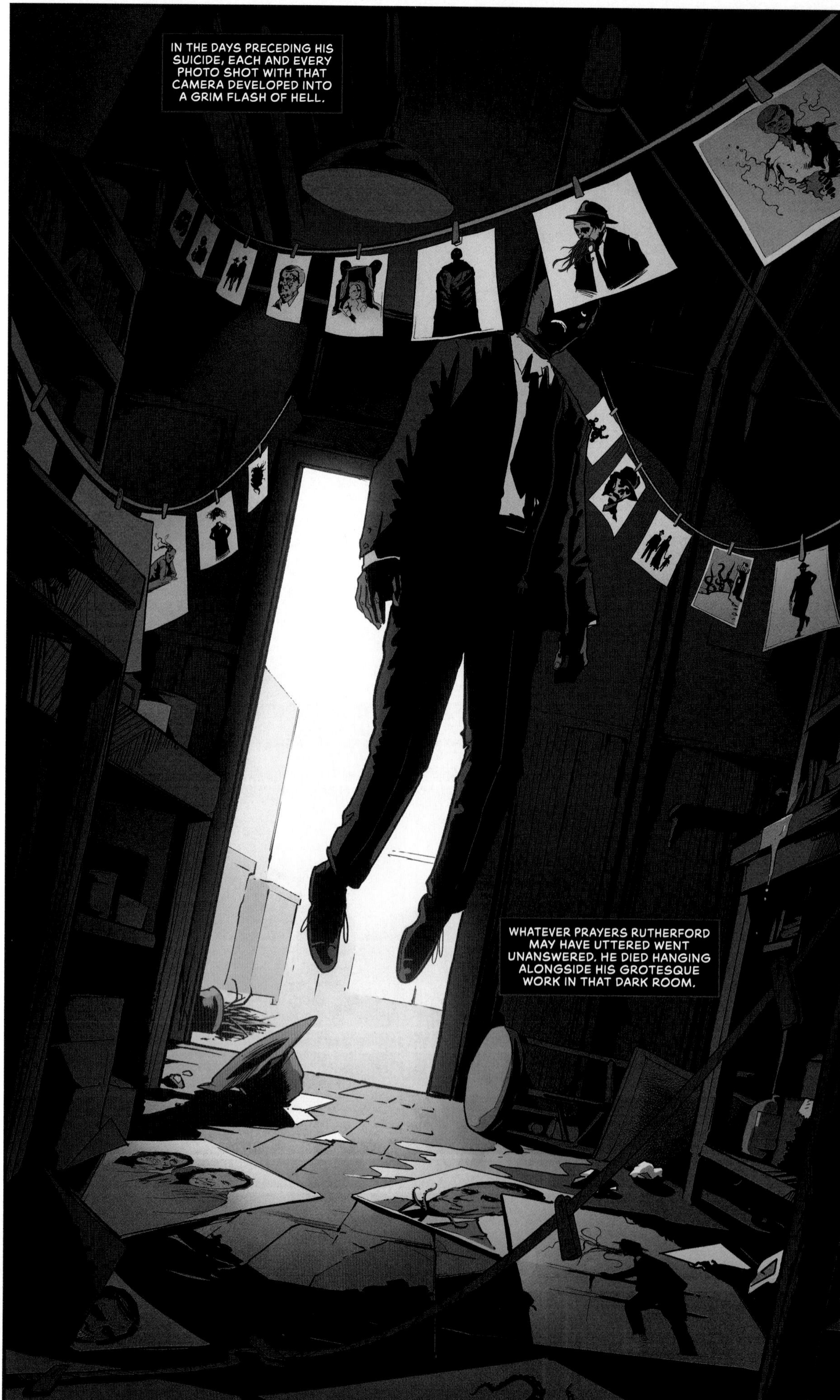
IN THE DAYS PRECEDING HIS SUICIDE, EACH AND EVERY PHOTO SHOT WITH THAT CAMERA DEVELOPED INTO A GRIM FLASH OF HELL.
WHATEVER PRAYERS RUTHERFORD MAY HAVE UTTERED WENT UNANSWERED. HE DIED HANGING ALONGSIDE HIS GROTESQUE WORK IN THAT DARK ROOM.

CHAPTER ONE

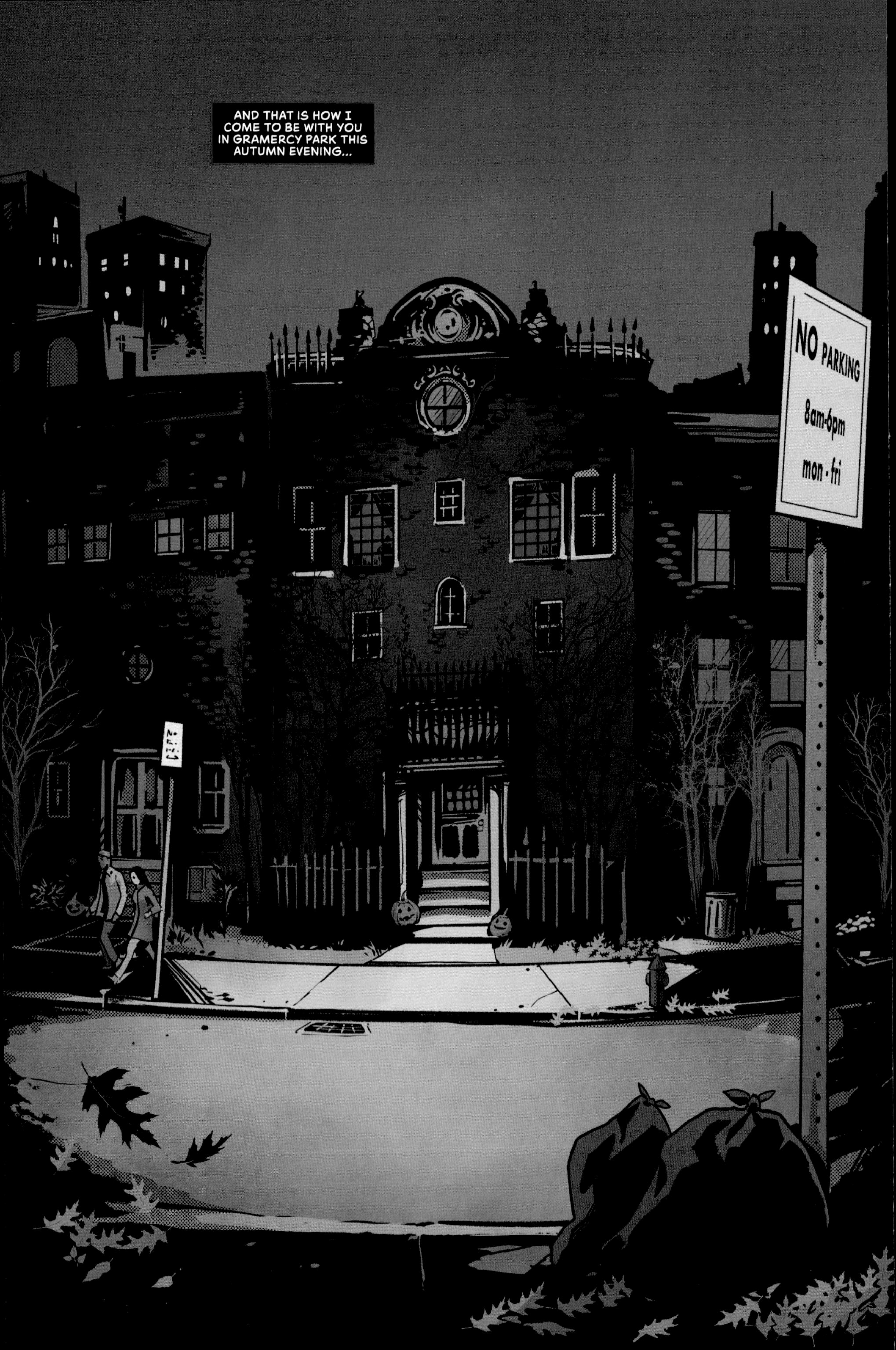
AND THAT IS HOW I COME TO BE WITH YOU IN GRAMERCY PARK THIS AUTUMN EVENING...
NO PARKING
8am-6pm
mon - fri

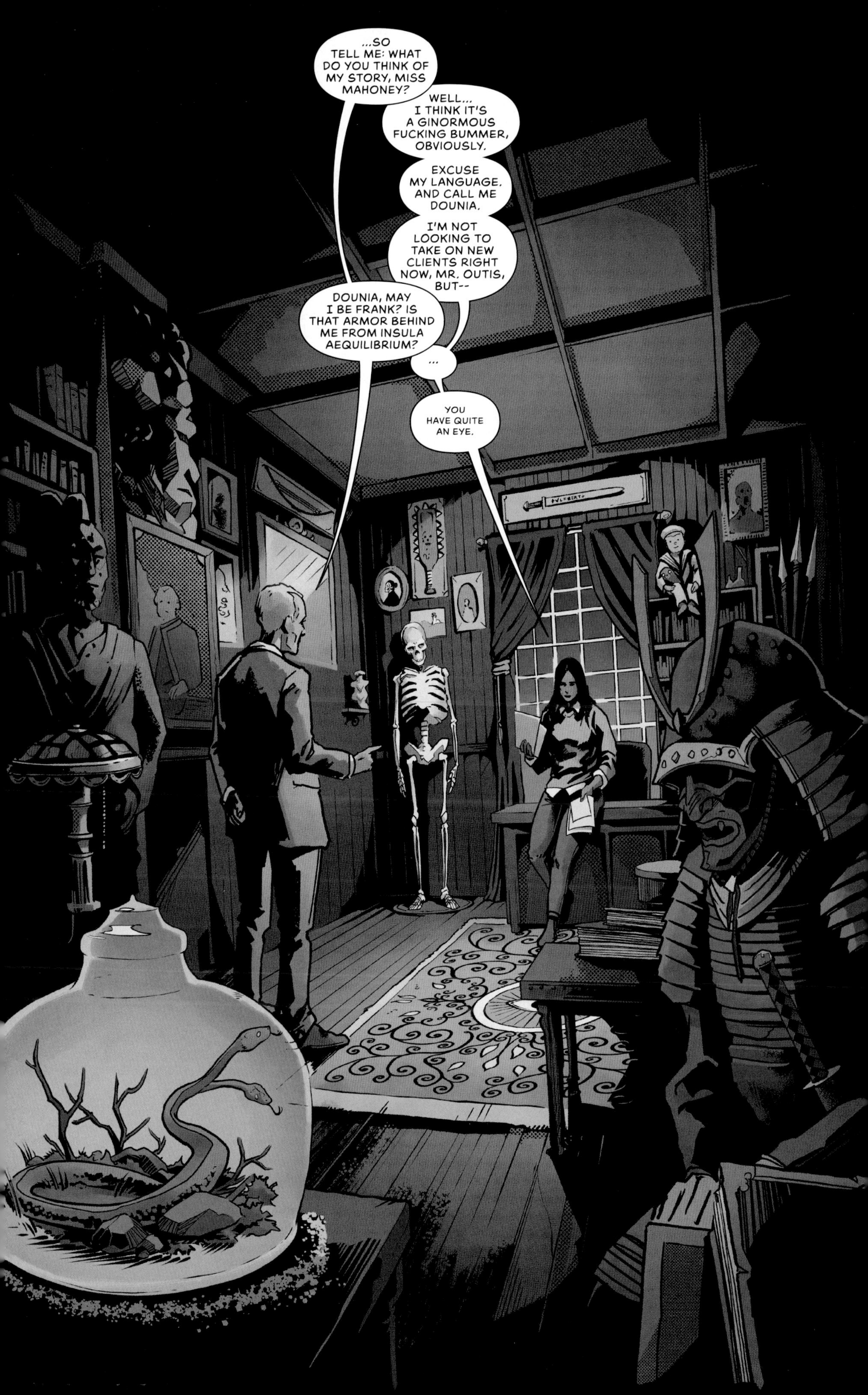
...SO TELL ME: WHAT DO YOU THINK OF MY STORY, MISS MAHONEY?
WELL... I THINK IT'S A GINORMOUS FUCKING BUMMER, OBVIOUSLY.
EXCUSE MY LANGUAGE, AND CALL ME DOUNIA.
I'M NOT LOOKING TO TAKE ON NEW CLIENTS RIGHT NOW, MR. OUTIS, BUT--
DOUNIA, MAY I BE FRANK? IS THAT ARMOR BEHIND ME FROM INSULA AEQUILIBRIUM?
...
YOU HAVE QUITE AN EYE.

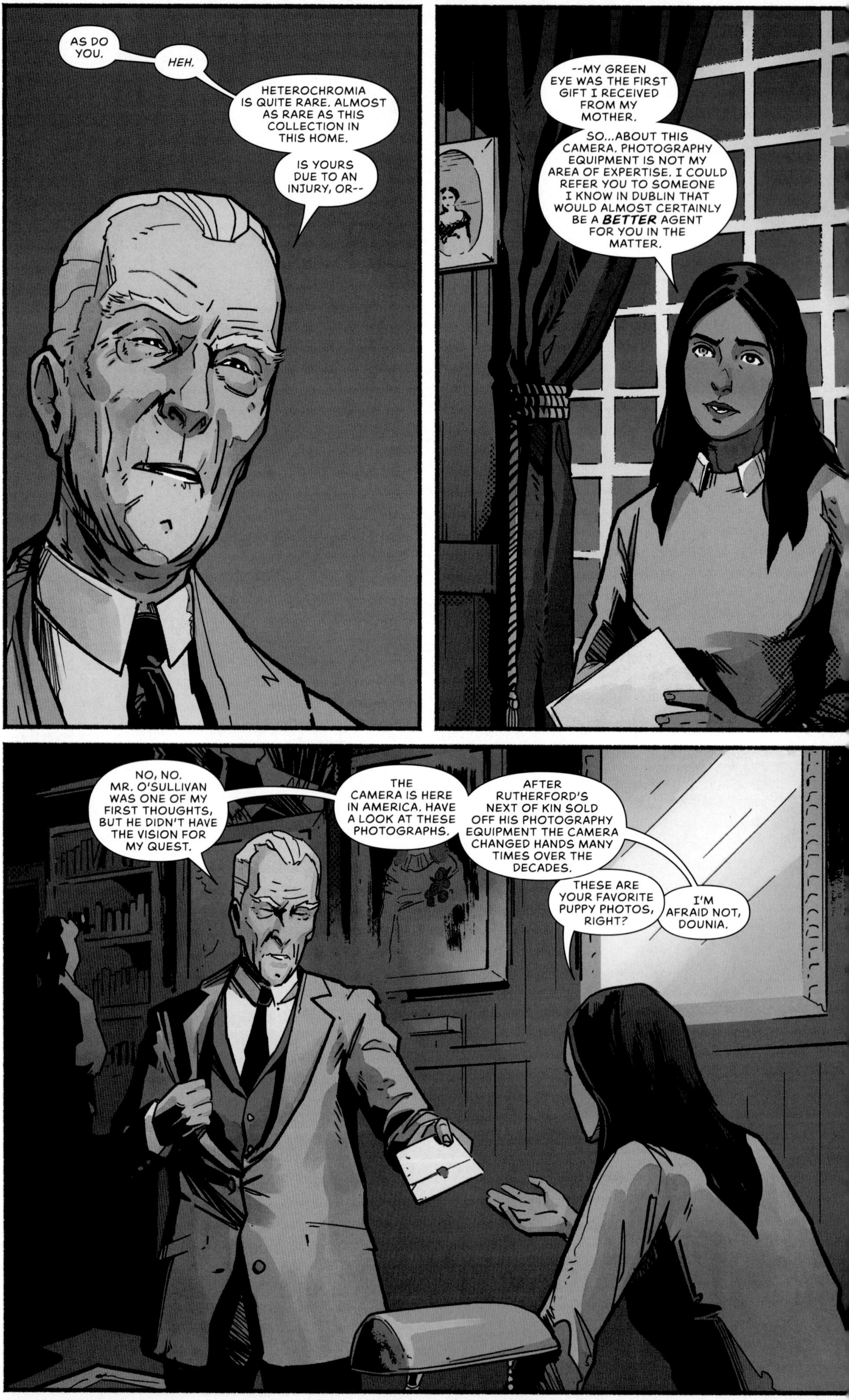
AS DO YOU.
HEH.
HETEROCHROMIA IS QUITE RARE. ALMOST AS RARE AS THIS COLLECTION IN THIS HOME.
IS YOURS DUE TO AN INJURY, OR--
--MY GREEN EYE WAS THE FIRST GIFT I RECEIVED FROM MY MOTHER.
SO...ABOUT THIS CAMERA. PHOTOGRAPHY EQUIPMENT IS NOT MY AREA OF EXPERTISE. I COULD REFER YOU TO SOMEONE I KNOW IN DUBLIN THAT WOULD ALMOST CERTAINLY BE A **BETTER** AGENT FOR YOU IN THE MATTER.
NO, NO. MR. O'SULLIVAN WAS ONE OF MY FIRST THOUGHTS, BUT HE DIDN'T HAVE THE VISION FOR MY QUEST.
THE CAMERA IS HERE IN AMERICA. HAVE A LOOK AT THESE PHOTOGRAPHS.
AFTER RUTHERFORD'S NEXT OF KIN SOLD OFF HIS PHOTOGRAPHY EQUIPMENT THE CAMERA CHANGED HANDS MANY TIMES OVER THE DECADES.
THESE ARE YOUR FAVORITE PUPPY PHOTOS, RIGHT?
I'M AFRAID NOT, DOUNIA.

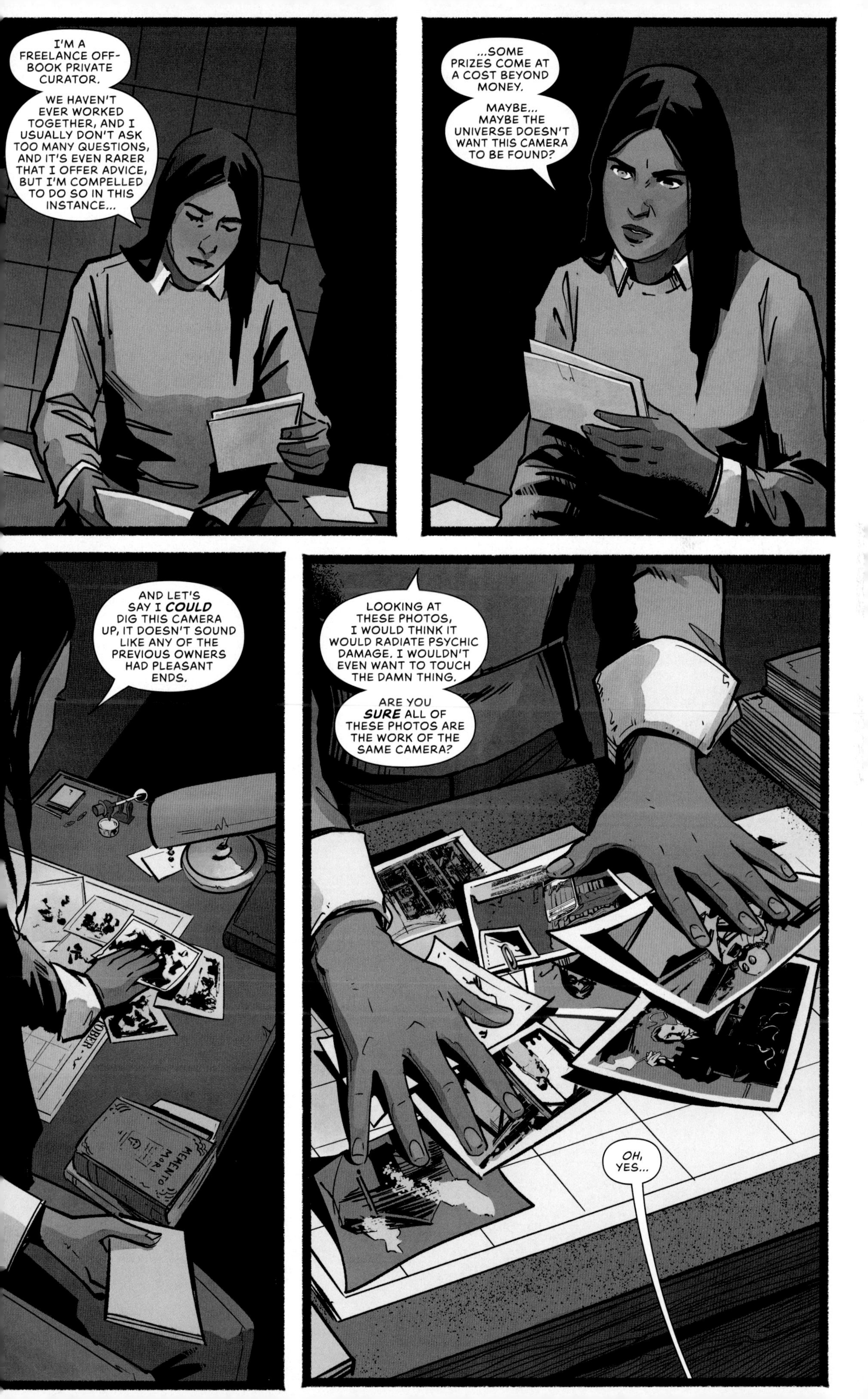
I'M A FREELANCE OFF-BOOK PRIVATE CURATOR.
WE HAVEN'T EVER WORKED TOGETHER, AND I USUALLY DON'T ASK TOO MANY QUESTIONS, AND IT'S EVEN RARER THAT I OFFER ADVICE, BUT I'M COMPELLED TO DO SO IN THIS INSTANCE...
...SOME PRIZES COME AT A COST BEYOND MONEY.
MAYBE... MAYBE THE UNIVERSE DOESN'T WANT THIS CAMERA TO BE FOUND?
AND LET'S SAY I **COULD** DIG THIS CAMERA UP, IT DOESN'T SOUND LIKE ANY OF THE PREVIOUS OWNERS HAD PLEASANT ENDS.
MEMENTO MORI
LOOKING AT THESE PHOTOS, I WOULD THINK IT WOULD RADIATE PSYCHIC DAMAGE. I WOULDN'T EVEN WANT TO TOUCH THE DAMN THING.
ARE YOU **SURE** ALL OF THESE PHOTOS ARE THE WORK OF THE SAME CAMERA?
OH, YES...

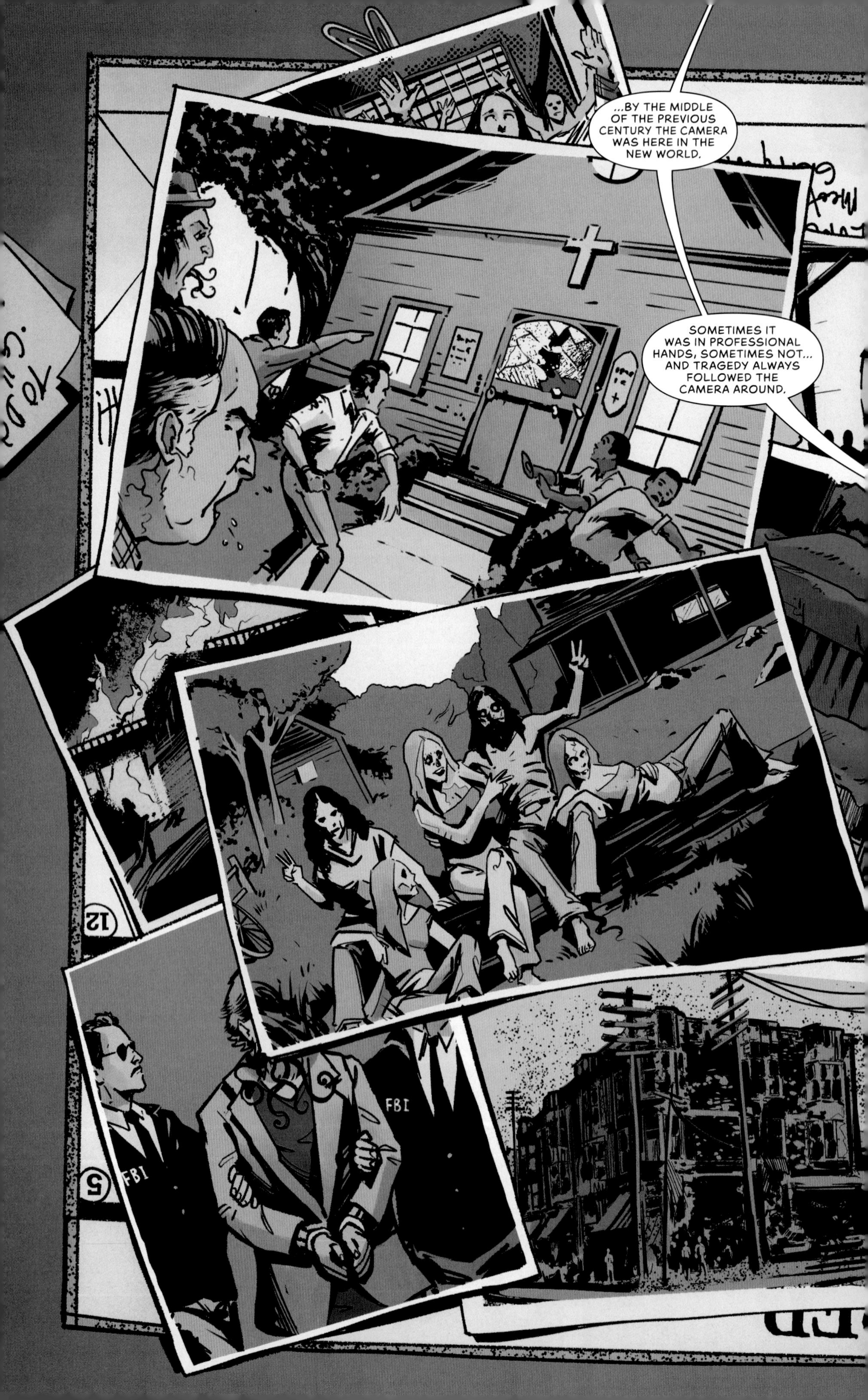
...BY THE MIDDLE OF THE PREVIOUS CENTURY THE CAMERA WAS HERE IN THE NEW WORLD.
SOMETIMES IT WAS IN PROFESSIONAL HANDS, SOMETIMES NOT... AND TRAGEDY ALWAYS FOLLOWED THE CAMERA AROUND.
FBI
FBI

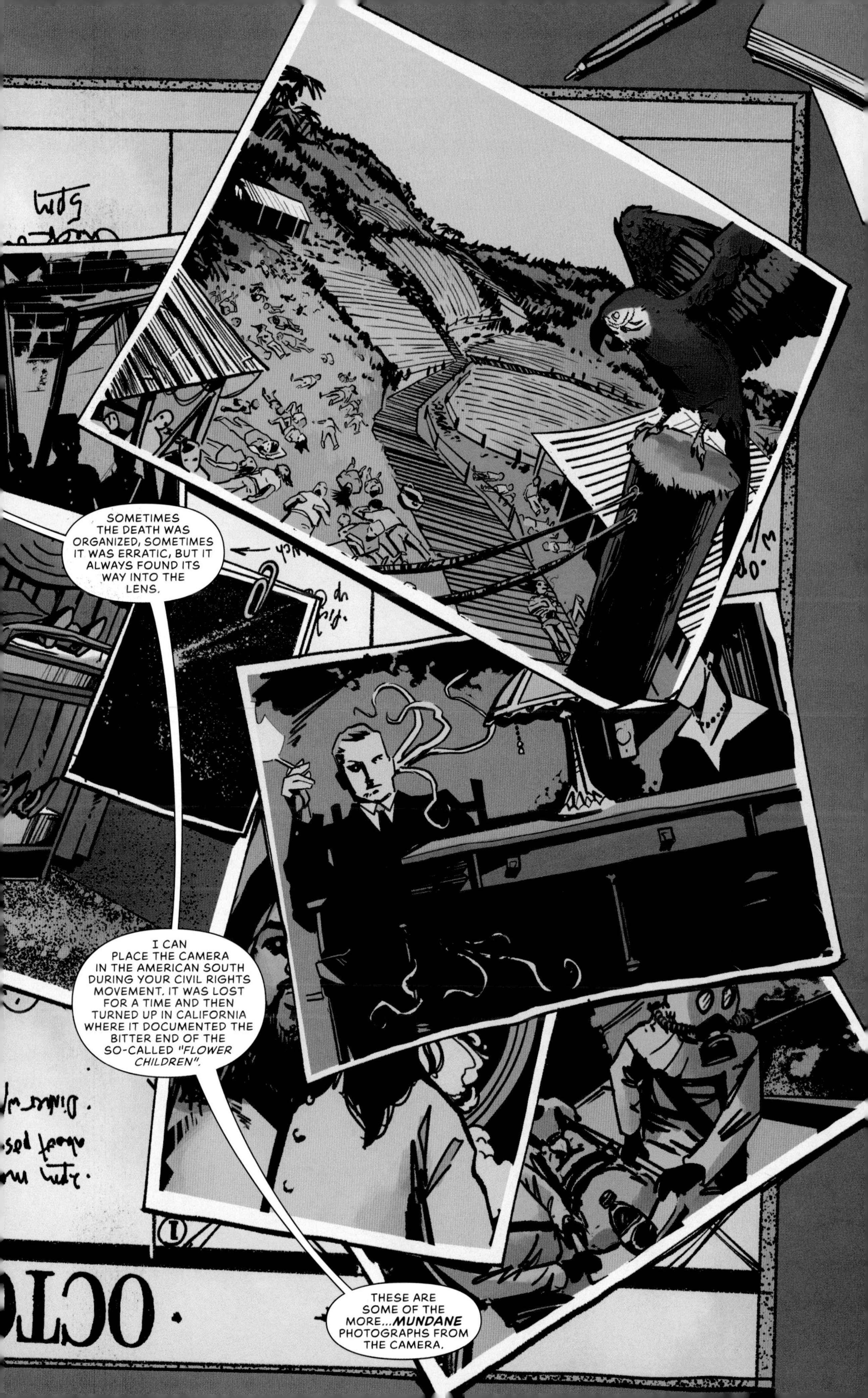
SOMETIMES THE DEATH WAS ORGANIZED, SOMETIMES IT WAS ERRATIC, BUT IT ALWAYS FOUND ITS WAY INTO THE LENS.
I CAN PLACE THE CAMERA IN THE AMERICAN SOUTH DURING YOUR CIVIL RIGHTS MOVEMENT. IT WAS LOST FOR A TIME AND THEN TURNED UP IN CALIFORNIA WHERE IT DOCUMENTED THE BITTER END OF THE SO-CALLED *"FLOWER CHILDREN"*.
THESE ARE SOME OF THE MORE... ***MUNDANE*** PHOTOGRAPHS FROM THE CAMERA.

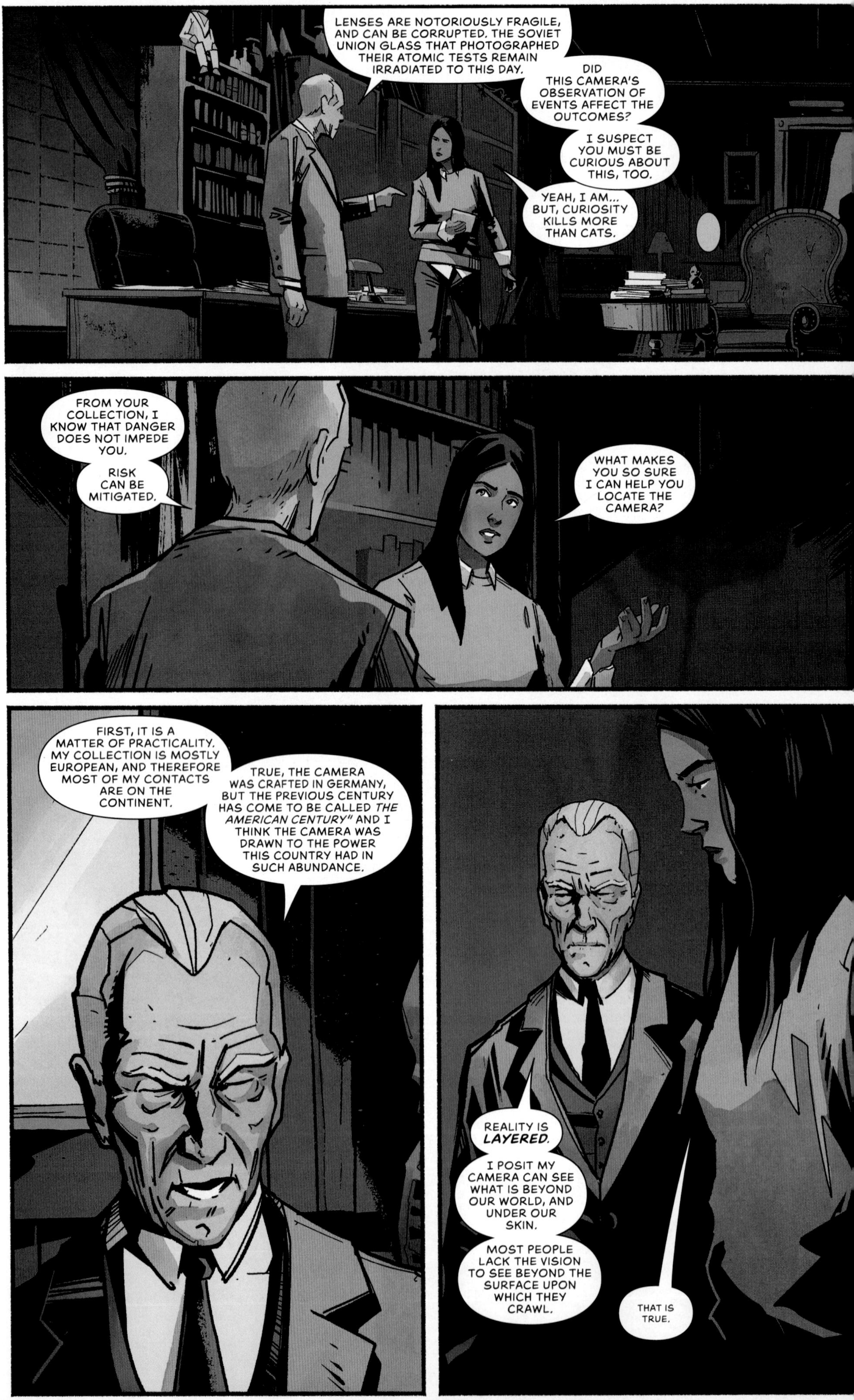
LENSES ARE NOTORIOUSLY FRAGILE, AND CAN BE CORRUPTED. THE SOVIET UNION GLASS THAT PHOTOGRAPHED THEIR ATOMIC TESTS REMAIN IRRADIATED TO THIS DAY.
DID THIS CAMERA'S OBSERVATION OF EVENTS AFFECT THE OUTCOMES?
I SUSPECT YOU MUST BE CURIOUS ABOUT THIS, TOO.
YEAH, I AM... BUT, CURIOSITY KILLS MORE THAN CATS.
FROM YOUR COLLECTION, I KNOW THAT DANGER DOES NOT IMPEDE YOU.
RISK CAN BE MITIGATED.
WHAT MAKES YOU SO SURE I CAN HELP YOU LOCATE THE CAMERA?
FIRST, IT IS A MATTER OF PRACTICALITY. MY COLLECTION IS MOSTLY EUROPEAN, AND THEREFORE MOST OF MY CONTACTS ARE ON THE CONTINENT.
TRUE, THE CAMERA WAS CRAFTED IN GERMANY, BUT THE PREVIOUS CENTURY HAS COME TO BE CALLED *THE AMERICAN CENTURY"* AND I THINK THE CAMERA WAS DRAWN TO THE POWER THIS COUNTRY HAD IN SUCH ABUNDANCE.
REALITY IS ***LAYERED***.
I POSIT MY CAMERA CAN SEE WHAT IS BEYOND OUR WORLD, AND UNDER OUR SKIN.
MOST PEOPLE LACK THE VISION TO SEE BEYOND THE SURFACE UPON WHICH THEY CRAWL.
THAT IS TRUE.

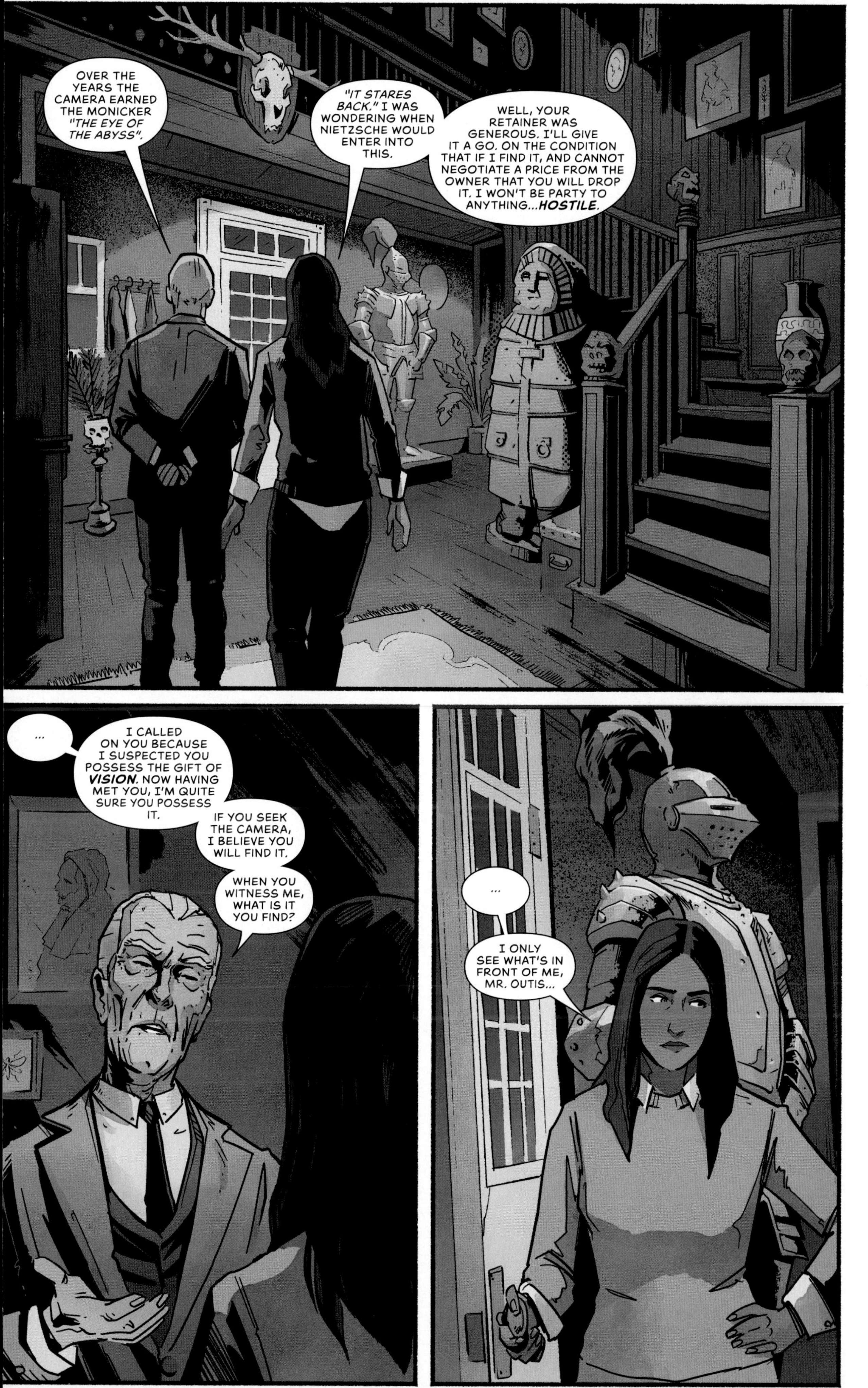
OVER THE YEARS THE CAMERA EARNED THE MONICKER *"THE EYE OF THE ABYSS"*.
"IT STARES BACK." I WAS WONDERING WHEN NIETZSCHE WOULD ENTER INTO THIS.
WELL, YOUR RETAINER WAS GENEROUS. I'LL GIVE IT A GO. ON THE CONDITION THAT IF I FIND IT, AND CANNOT NEGOTIATE A PRICE FROM THE OWNER THAT YOU WILL DROP IT. I WON'T BE PARTY TO ANYTHING...***HOSTILE***.
...
I CALLED ON YOU BECAUSE I SUSPECTED YOU POSSESS THE GIFT OF ***VISION***. NOW HAVING MET YOU, I'M QUITE SURE YOU POSSESS IT.
IF YOU SEEK THE CAMERA, I BELIEVE YOU WILL FIND IT.
WHEN YOU WITNESS ME, WHAT IS IT YOU FIND?
...
I ONLY SEE WHAT'S IN FRONT OF ME, MR. OUTIS...

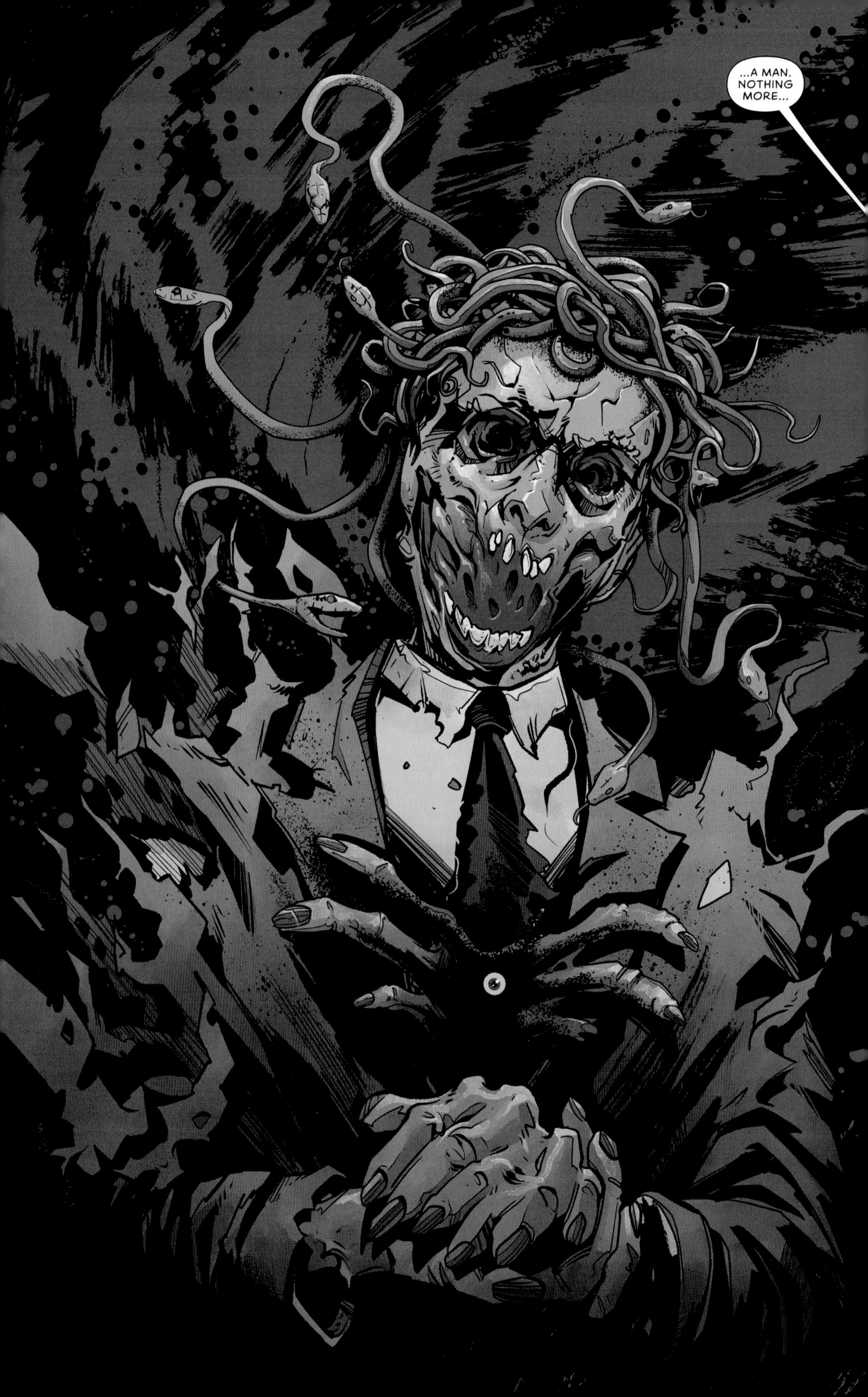
...A MAN, NOTHING MORE...

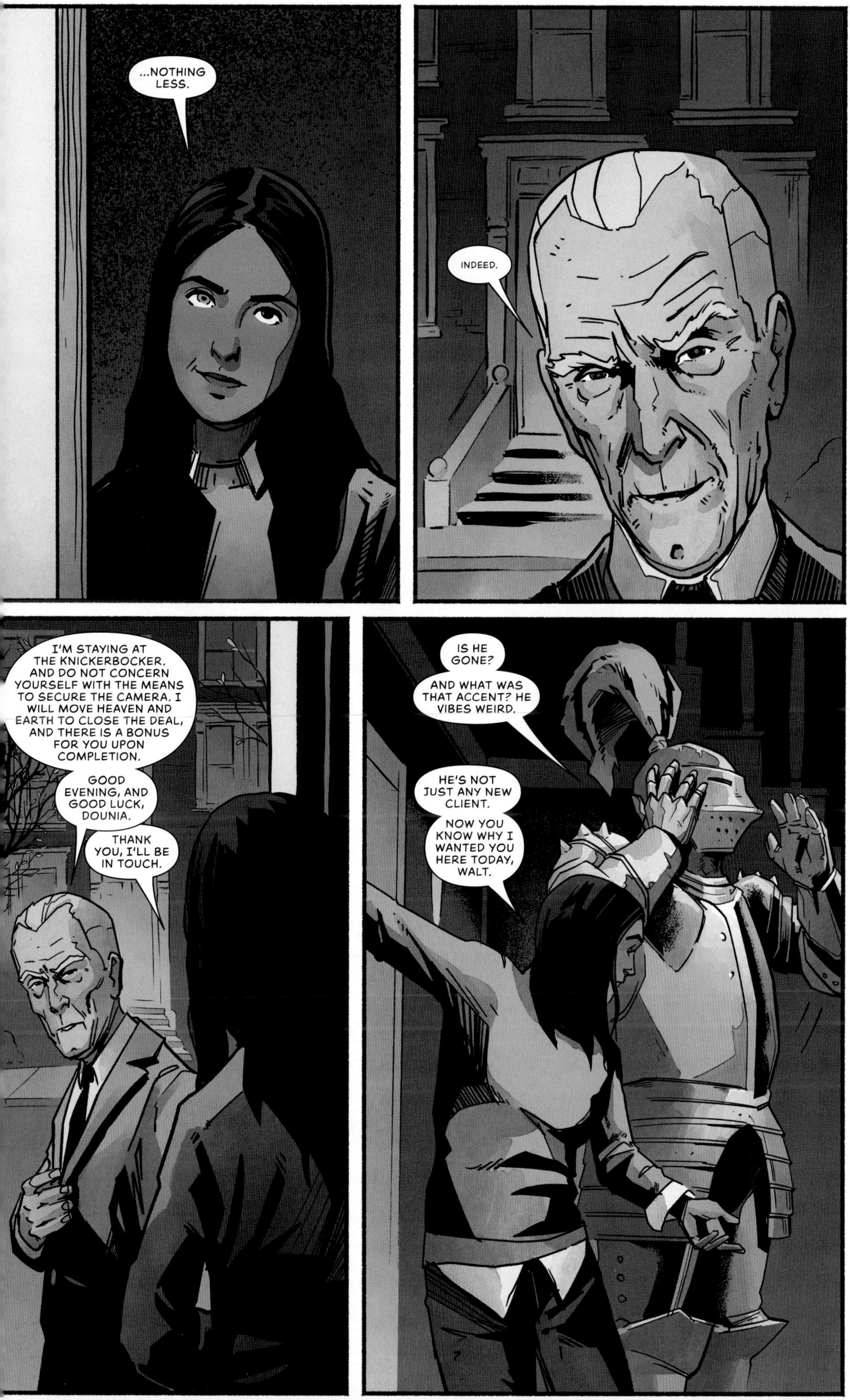
...NOTHING LESS.
INDEED.
I'M STAYING AT THE KNICKERBOCKER, AND DO NOT CONCERN YOURSELF WITH THE MEANS TO SECURE THE CAMERA. I WILL MOVE HEAVEN AND EARTH TO CLOSE THE DEAL, AND THERE IS A BONUS FOR YOU UPON COMPLETION.
GOOD EVENING, AND GOOD LUCK, DOUNIA.
THANK YOU, I'LL BE IN TOUCH.
IS HE GONE?
AND WHAT WAS THAT ACCENT? HE VIBES WEIRD.
HE'S NOT JUST ANY NEW CLIENT.
NOW YOU KNOW WHY I WANTED YOU HERE TODAY, WALT.

THAT'S ME, A LITERAL KNIGHT IN SHINING ARMOR.

WE'RE NOT GOING TO HELP HIM ARE WE?

I CAN THINK OF EIGHT FIGURES WHY WE WOULD.

YOU'RE ALWAYS TALKING ABOUT *"MONEY NOT BEING YOUR MOTIVATOR"*, BUT THEN YOU GET A WHIFF OF A BAG, AND OFF WE GO.

FIRST OF ALL...THIS GUY'S... *NOT A GUY*, SECOND: I'M PLAYING BALL UNTIL I GET THE WHOLE STORY, HE WASN'T WORKING VERY HARD TO HIDE MUCH.

GO PUT ON SOME CIVILIAN CLOTHES. WE GOTTA GO TO THE PUB, AND LET THE DOGS OUT OF THEIR KENNEL.

COOL.

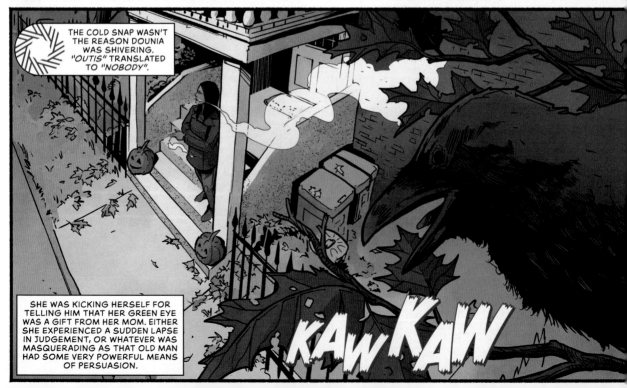

THE COLD SNAP WASN'T THE REASON DOUNIA WAS SHIVERING. *"OUTIS"* TRANSLATED TO *"NOBODY"*.

SHE WAS KICKING HERSELF FOR TELLING HIM THAT HER GREEN EYE WAS A GIFT FROM HER MOM. EITHER SHE EXPERIENCED A SUDDEN LAPSE IN JUDGEMENT, OR WHATEVER WAS MASQUERADING AS THAT OLD MAN HAD SOME VERY POWERFUL MEANS OF PERSUASION.

KAW KAW

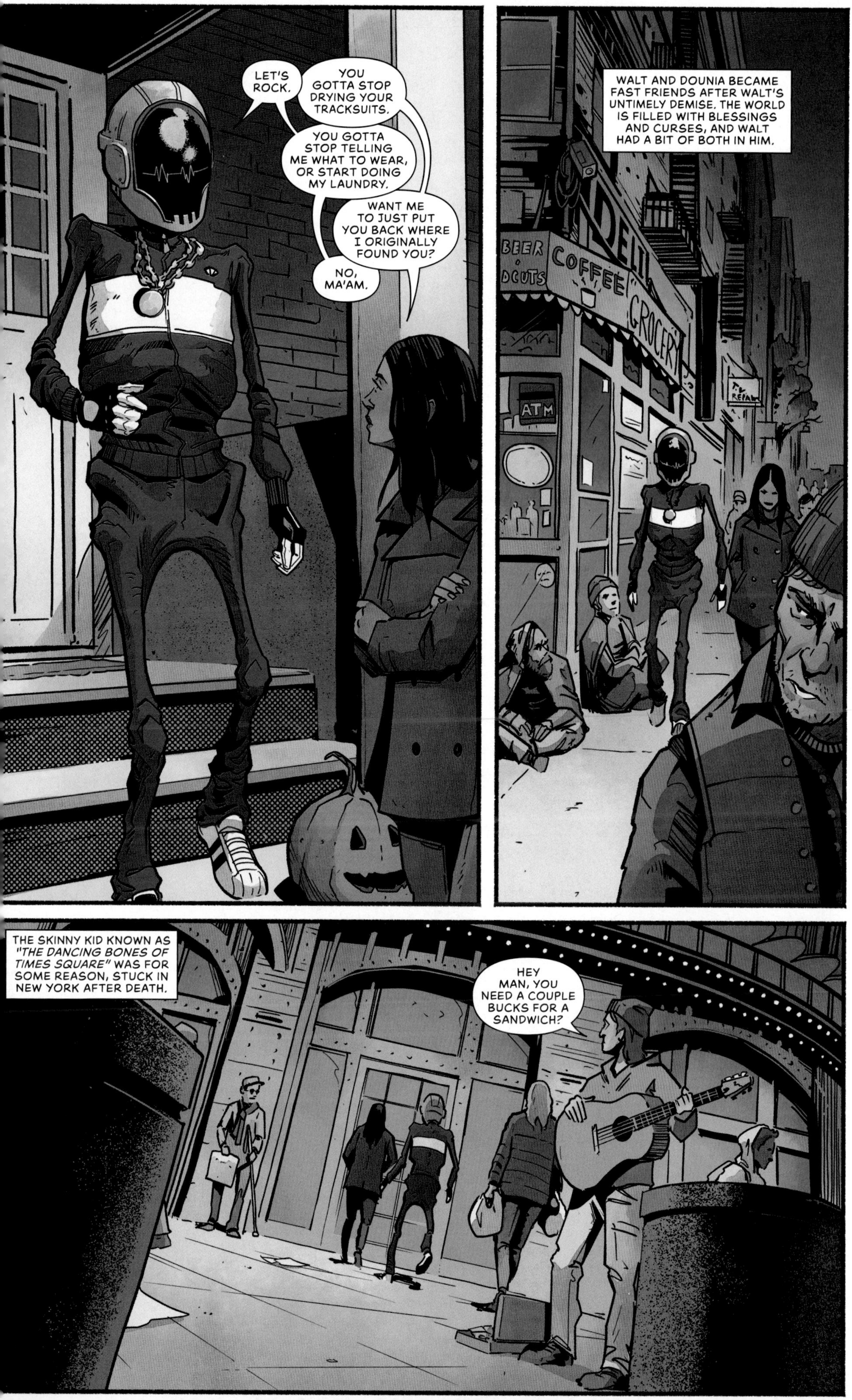
LET'S ROCK.
YOU GOTTA STOP DRYING YOUR TRACKSUITS.
YOU GOTTA STOP TELLING ME WHAT TO WEAR, OR START DOING MY LAUNDRY.
WANT ME TO JUST PUT YOU BACK WHERE I ORIGINALLY FOUND YOU?
NO, MA'AM.
WALT AND DOUNIA BECAME FAST FRIENDS AFTER WALT'S UNTIMELY DEMISE. THE WORLD IS FILLED WITH BLESSINGS AND CURSES, AND WALT HAD A BIT OF BOTH IN HIM.
BEER
COFFEE
DELI
GROCERY
ATM
THE SKINNY KID KNOWN AS *"THE DANCING BONES OF TIMES SQUARE"* WAS FOR SOME REASON, STUCK IN NEW YORK AFTER DEATH.
HEY MAN, YOU NEED A COUPLE BUCKS FOR A SANDWICH?

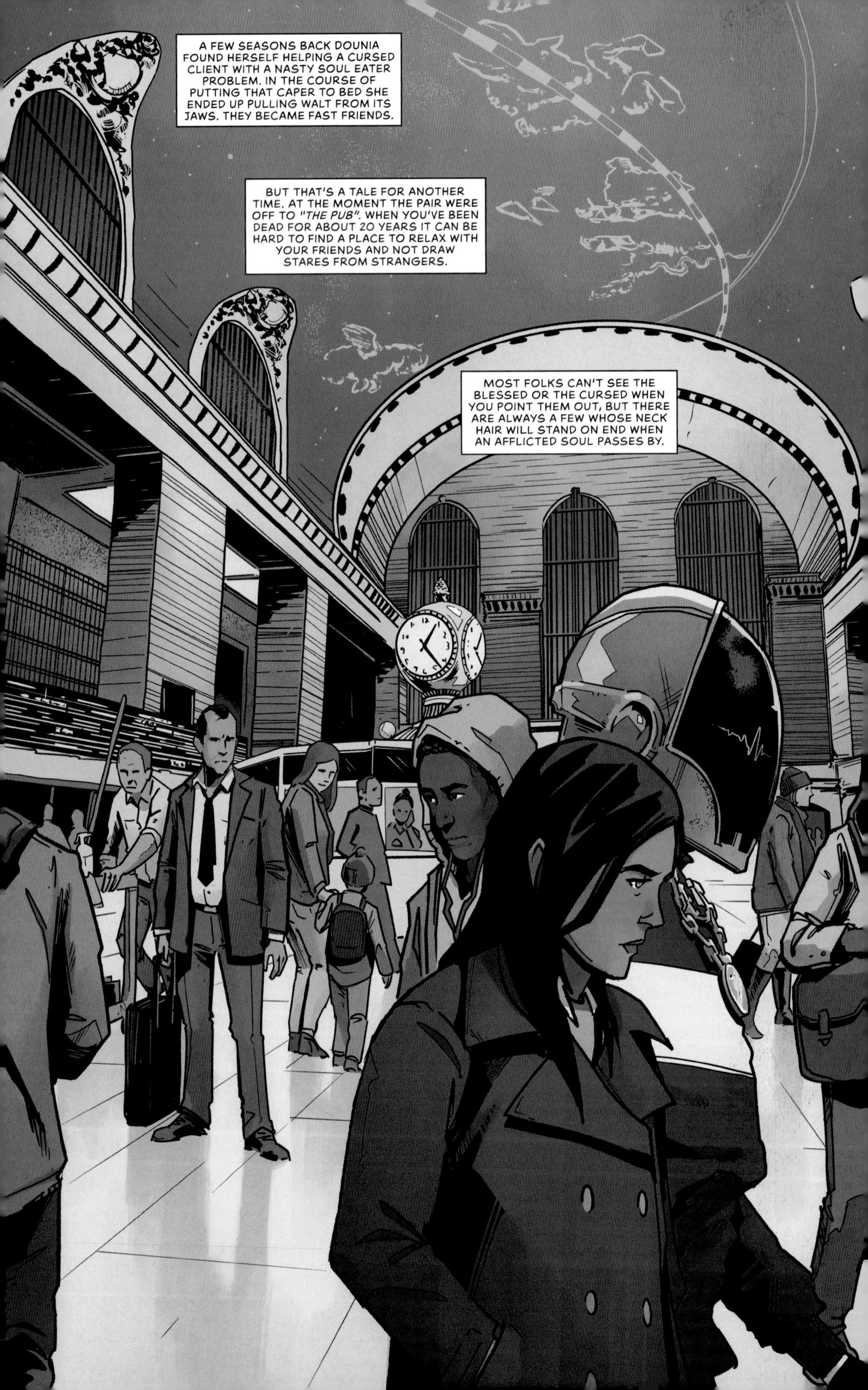
A FEW SEASONS BACK DOUNIA FOUND HERSELF HELPING A CURSED CLIENT WITH A NASTY SOUL EATER PROBLEM. IN THE COURSE OF PUTTING THAT CAPER TO BED SHE ENDED UP PULLING WALT FROM ITS JAWS. THEY BECAME FAST FRIENDS.
BUT THAT'S A TALE FOR ANOTHER TIME. AT THE MOMENT THE PAIR WERE OFF TO *"THE PUB"*. WHEN YOU'VE BEEN DEAD FOR ABOUT 20 YEARS IT CAN BE HARD TO FIND A PLACE TO RELAX WITH YOUR FRIENDS AND NOT DRAW STARES FROM STRANGERS.
MOST FOLKS CAN'T SEE THE BLESSED OR THE CURSED WHEN YOU POINT THEM OUT, BUT THERE ARE ALWAYS A FEW WHOSE NECK HAIR WILL STAND ON END WHEN AN AFFLICTED SOUL PASSES BY.

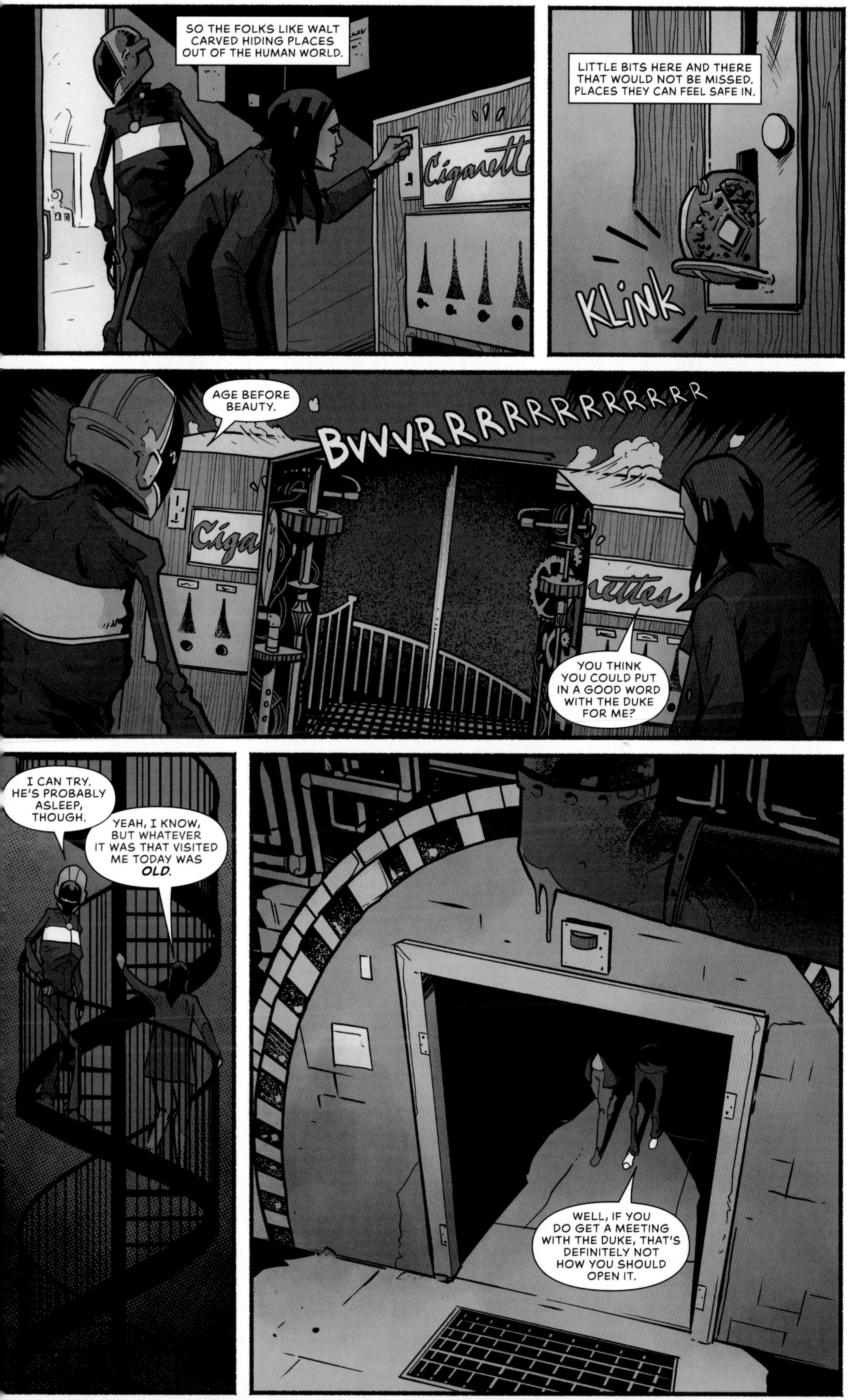
SO THE FOLKS LIKE WALT CARVED HIDING PLACES OUT OF THE HUMAN WORLD.
Cigarette
LITTLE BITS HERE AND THERE THAT WOULD NOT BE MISSED. PLACES THEY CAN FEEL SAFE IN.
KLINK
AGE BEFORE BEAUTY.
BVVVRRRRRRRRRRRRR
Ciga
ettes
YOU THINK YOU COULD PUT IN A GOOD WORD WITH THE DUKE FOR ME?
I CAN TRY. HE'S PROBABLY ASLEEP, THOUGH.
YEAH, I KNOW, BUT WHATEVER IT WAS THAT VISITED ME TODAY WAS *OLD*.
WELL, IF YOU DO GET A MEETING WITH THE DUKE, THAT'S DEFINITELY NOT HOW YOU SHOULD OPEN IT.

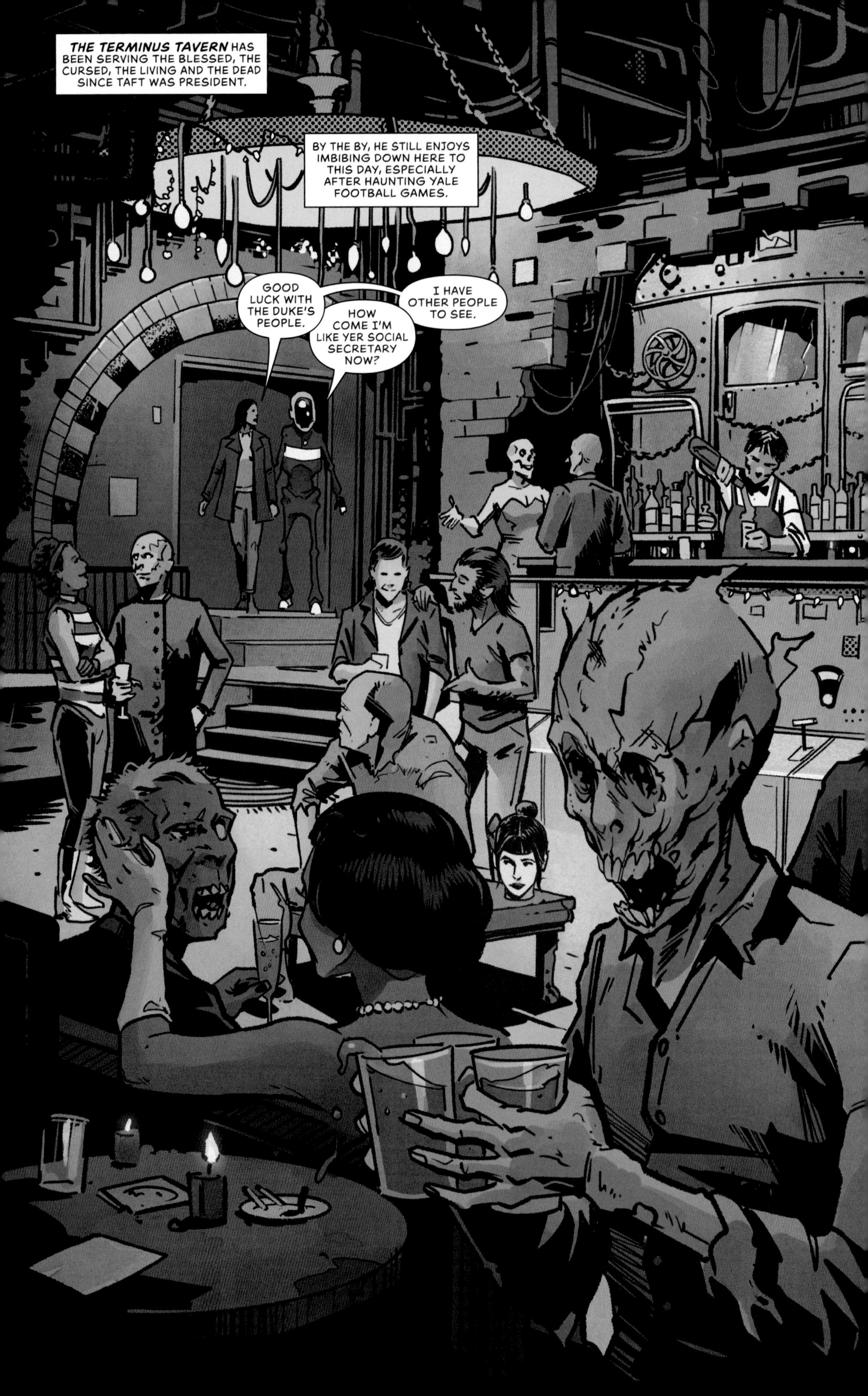

THE TERMINUS TAVERN HAS BEEN SERVING THE BLESSED, THE CURSED, THE LIVING AND THE DEAD SINCE TAFT WAS PRESIDENT.
BY THE BY, HE STILL ENJOYS IMBIBING DOWN HERE TO THIS DAY, ESPECIALLY AFTER HAUNTING YALE FOOTBALL GAMES.
GOOD LUCK WITH THE DUKE'S PEOPLE.
I HAVE OTHER PEOPLE TO SEE.
HOW COME I'M LIKE YER SOCIAL SECRETARY NOW?

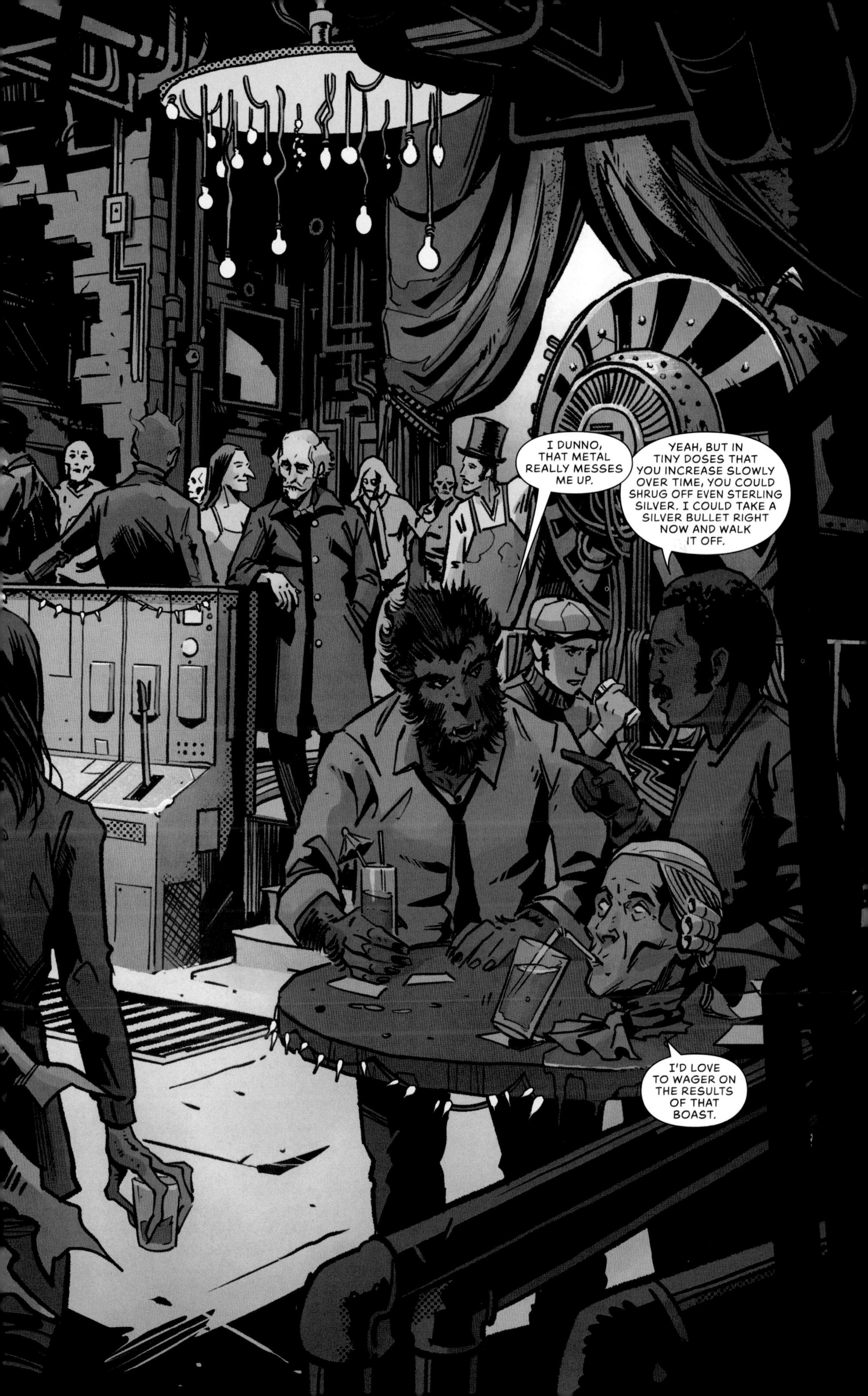
I DUNNO, THAT METAL REALLY MESSES ME UP.
YEAH, BUT IN TINY DOSES THAT YOU INCREASE SLOWLY OVER TIME, YOU COULD SHRUG OFF EVEN STERLING SILVER. I COULD TAKE A SILVER BULLET RIGHT NOW AND WALK IT OFF.
I'D LOVE TO WAGER ON THE RESULTS OF THAT BOAST.

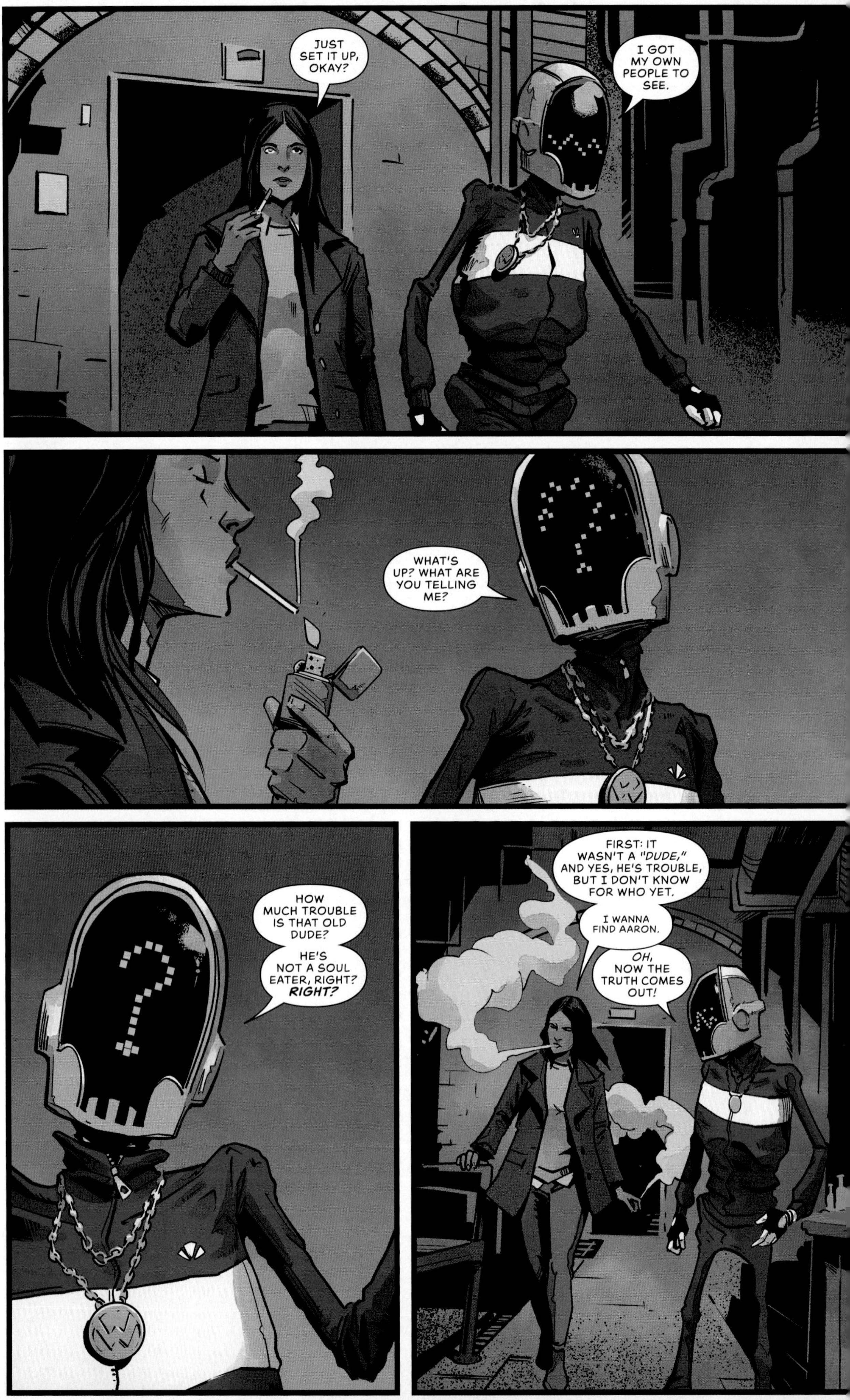
JUST SET IT UP, OKAY?
I GOT MY OWN PEOPLE TO SEE.
WHAT'S UP? WHAT ARE YOU TELLING ME?
HOW MUCH TROUBLE IS THAT OLD DUDE?
HE'S NOT A SOUL EATER, RIGHT? RIGHT?
FIRST: IT WASN'T A "DUDE," AND YES, HE'S TROUBLE, BUT I DON'T KNOW FOR WHO YET.
I WANNA FIND AARON.
OH, NOW THE TRUTH COMES OUT!

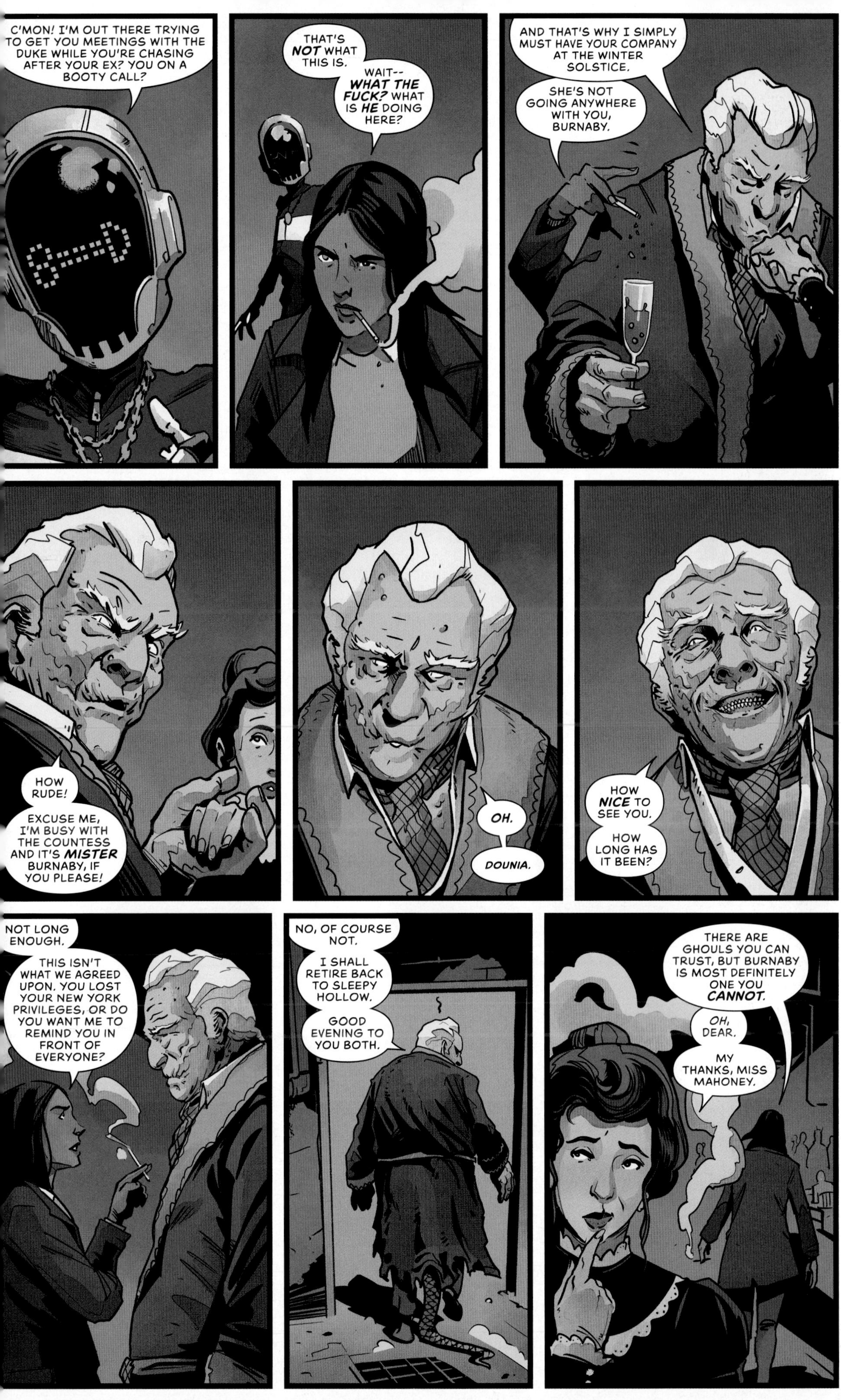
C'MON! I'M OUT THERE TRYING TO GET YOU MEETINGS WITH THE DUKE WHILE YOU'RE CHASING AFTER YOUR EX? YOU ON A BOOTY CALL?
THAT'S **NOT** WHAT THIS IS.
WAIT-- **WHAT THE FUCK?** WHAT IS **HE** DOING HERE?
AND THAT'S WHY I SIMPLY MUST HAVE YOUR COMPANY AT THE WINTER SOLSTICE.
SHE'S NOT GOING ANYWHERE WITH YOU, BURNABY.
HOW RUDE!
EXCUSE ME, I'M BUSY WITH THE COUNTESS AND IT'S **MISTER** BURNABY, IF YOU PLEASE!
OH.
DOUNIA.
HOW **NICE** TO SEE YOU.
HOW LONG HAS IT BEEN?
NOT LONG ENOUGH.
THIS ISN'T WHAT WE AGREED UPON. YOU LOST YOUR NEW YORK PRIVILEGES, OR DO YOU WANT ME TO REMIND YOU IN FRONT OF EVERYONE?
NO, OF COURSE NOT.
I SHALL RETIRE BACK TO SLEEPY HOLLOW.
GOOD EVENING TO YOU BOTH.
THERE ARE GHOULS YOU CAN TRUST, BUT BURNABY IS MOST DEFINITELY ONE YOU **CANNOT**.
OH, DEAR.
MY THANKS, MISS MAHONEY.

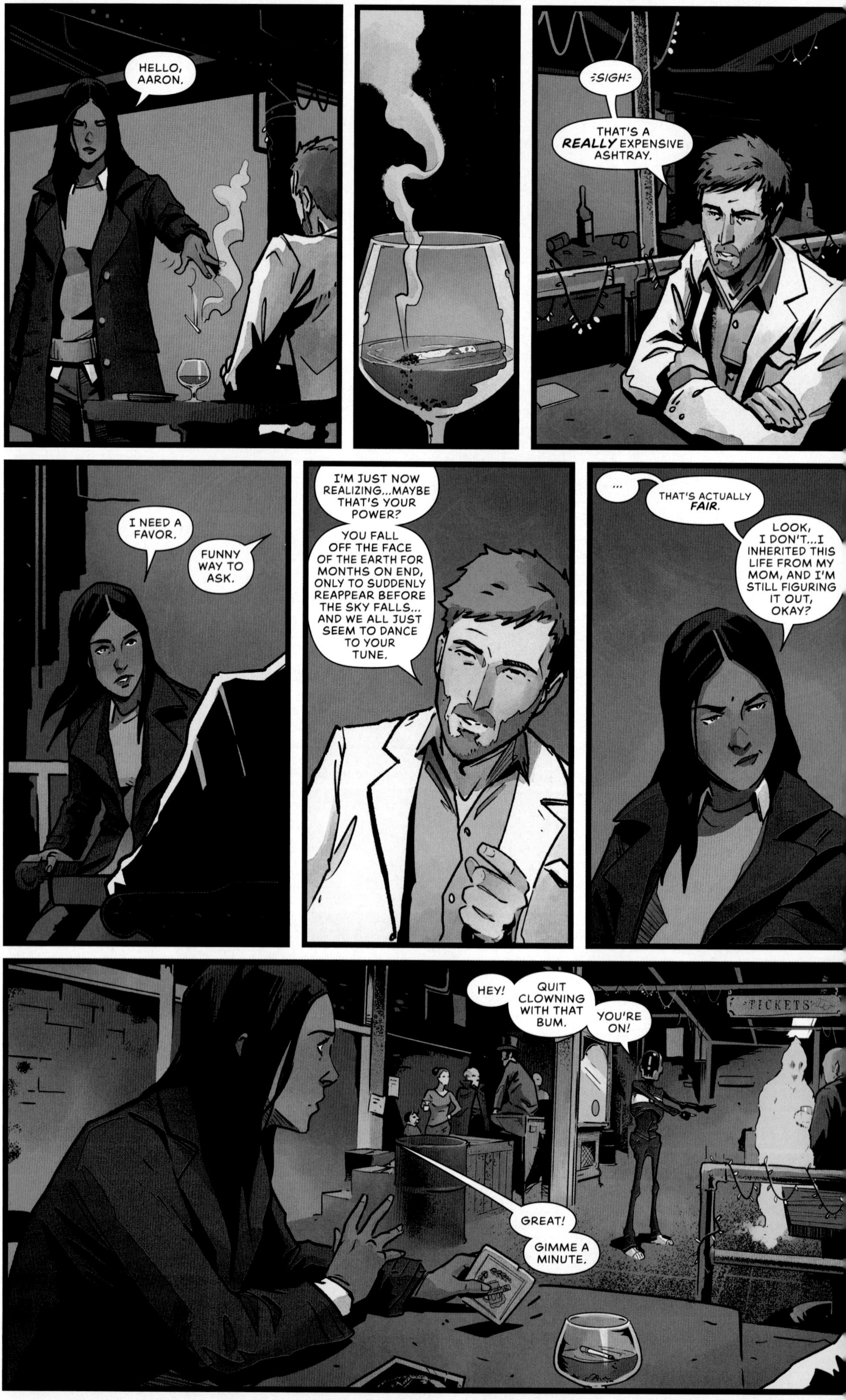
HELLO, AARON.
SIGH
THAT'S A REALLY EXPENSIVE ASHTRAY.
I NEED A FAVOR.
FUNNY WAY TO ASK.
I'M JUST NOW REALIZING...MAYBE THAT'S YOUR POWER?
YOU FALL OFF THE FACE OF THE EARTH FOR MONTHS ON END, ONLY TO SUDDENLY REAPPEAR BEFORE THE SKY FALLS... AND WE ALL JUST SEEM TO DANCE TO YOUR TUNE.
...
THAT'S ACTUALLY FAIR.
LOOK, I DON'T...I INHERITED THIS LIFE FROM MY MOM, AND I'M STILL FIGURING IT OUT, OKAY?
HEY!
QUIT CLOWNING WITH THAT BUM.
YOU'RE ON!
TICKETS
GREAT!
GIMME A MINUTE.

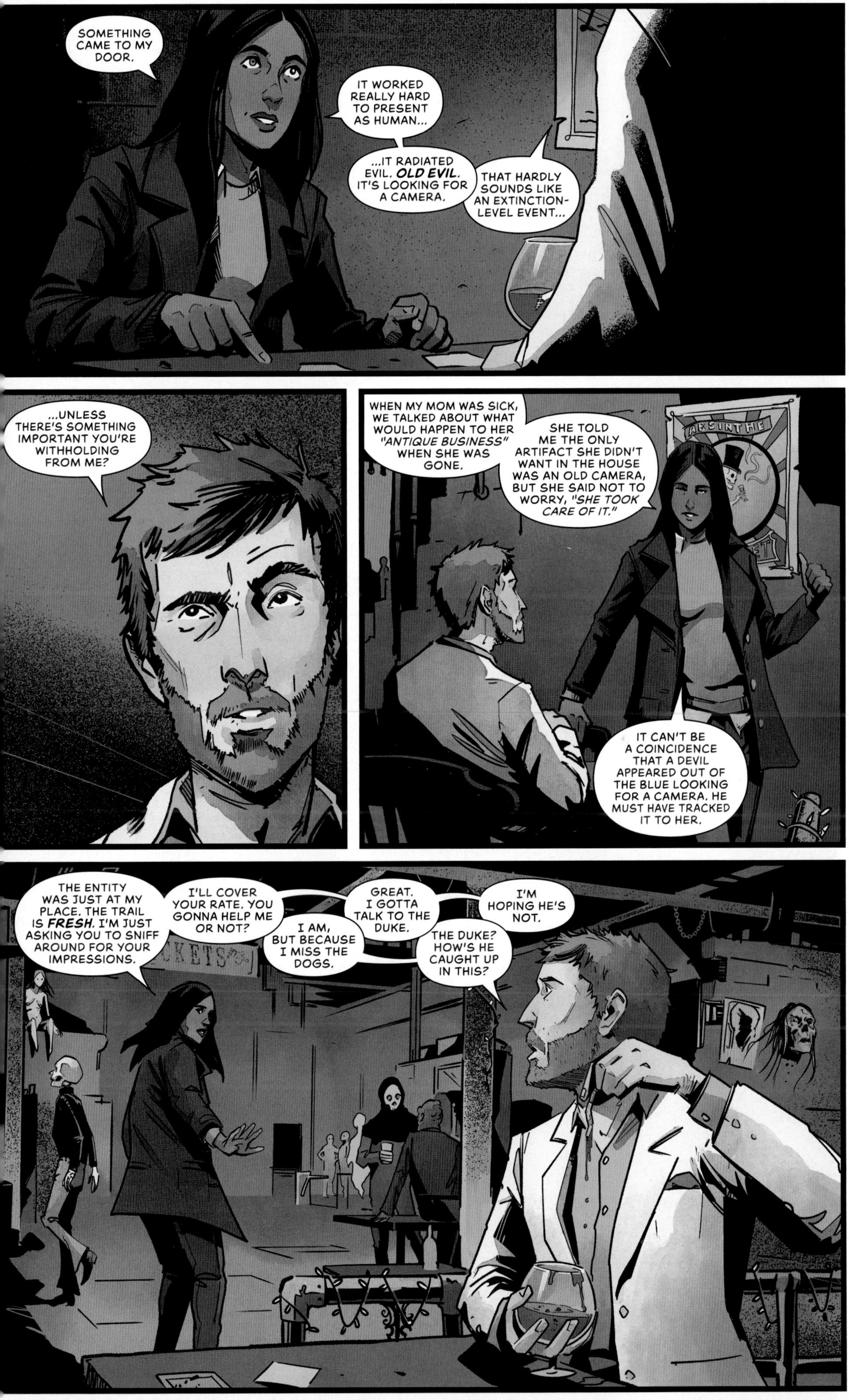
SOMETHING CAME TO MY DOOR.
IT WORKED REALLY HARD TO PRESENT AS HUMAN...
...IT RADIATED EVIL. ***OLD EVIL.*** IT'S LOOKING FOR A CAMERA.
THAT HARDLY SOUNDS LIKE AN EXTINCTION-LEVEL EVENT...
...UNLESS THERE'S SOMETHING IMPORTANT YOU'RE WITHHOLDING FROM ME?
WHEN MY MOM WAS SICK, WE TALKED ABOUT WHAT WOULD HAPPEN TO HER *"ANTIQUE BUSINESS"* WHEN SHE WAS GONE.
SHE TOLD ME THE ONLY ARTIFACT SHE DIDN'T WANT IN THE HOUSE WAS AN OLD CAMERA, BUT SHE SAID NOT TO WORRY, *"SHE TOOK CARE OF IT."*
ABSINTHE
IT CAN'T BE A COINCIDENCE THAT A DEVIL APPEARED OUT OF THE BLUE LOOKING FOR A CAMERA. HE MUST HAVE TRACKED IT TO HER.
THE ENTITY WAS JUST AT MY PLACE. THE TRAIL IS ***FRESH***. I'M JUST ASKING YOU TO SNIFF AROUND FOR YOUR IMPRESSIONS.
I'LL COVER YOUR RATE. YOU GONNA HELP ME OR NOT?
I AM, BUT BECAUSE I MISS THE DOGS.
GREAT. I GOTTA TALK TO THE DUKE.
THE DUKE? HOW'S HE CAUGHT UP IN THIS?
I'M HOPING HE'S NOT.

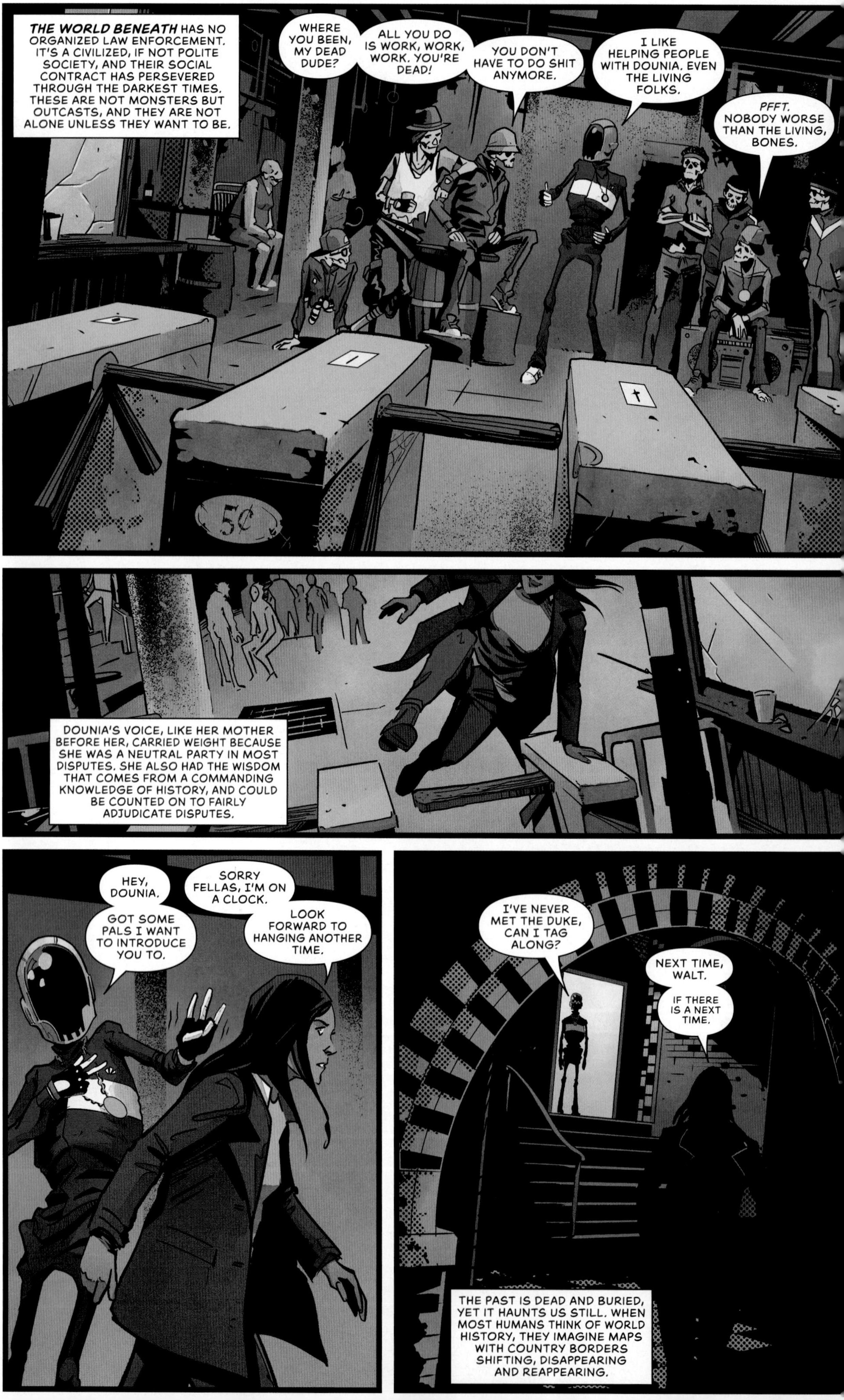
THE WORLD BENEATH HAS NO ORGANIZED LAW ENFORCEMENT. IT'S A CIVILIZED, IF NOT POLITE SOCIETY, AND THEIR SOCIAL CONTRACT HAS PERSEVERED THROUGH THE DARKEST TIMES. THESE ARE NOT MONSTERS BUT OUTCASTS, AND THEY ARE NOT ALONE UNLESS THEY WANT TO BE.
WHERE YOU BEEN, MY DEAD DUDE?
ALL YOU DO IS WORK, WORK, WORK. YOU'RE DEAD!
YOU DON'T HAVE TO DO SHIT ANYMORE.
I LIKE HELPING PEOPLE WITH DOUNIA. EVEN THE LIVING FOLKS.
PFFT. NOBODY WORSE THAN THE LIVING, BONES.
5¢
DOUNIA'S VOICE, LIKE HER MOTHER BEFORE HER, CARRIED WEIGHT BECAUSE SHE WAS A NEUTRAL PARTY IN MOST DISPUTES. SHE ALSO HAD THE WISDOM THAT COMES FROM A COMMANDING KNOWLEDGE OF HISTORY, AND COULD BE COUNTED ON TO FAIRLY ADJUDICATE DISPUTES.
HEY, DOUNIA.
GOT SOME PALS I WANT TO INTRODUCE YOU TO.
SORRY FELLAS, I'M ON A CLOCK.
LOOK FORWARD TO HANGING ANOTHER TIME.
I'VE NEVER MET THE DUKE, CAN I TAG ALONG?
NEXT TIME, WALT.
IF THERE IS A NEXT TIME.
THE PAST IS DEAD AND BURIED, YET IT HAUNTS US STILL. WHEN MOST HUMANS THINK OF WORLD HISTORY, THEY IMAGINE MAPS WITH COUNTRY BORDERS SHIFTING, DISAPPEARING AND REAPPEARING.

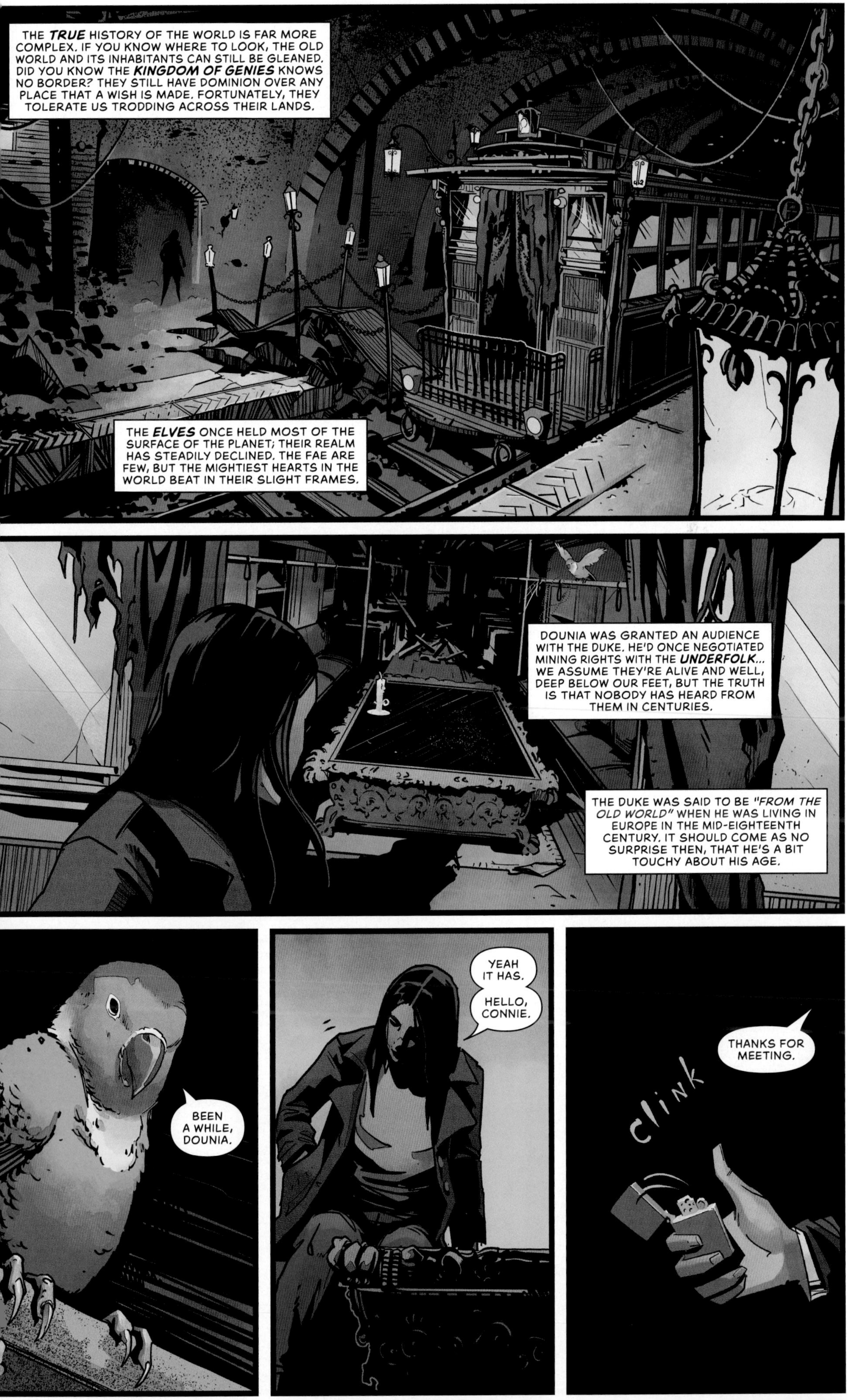
THE TRUE HISTORY OF THE WORLD IS FAR MORE COMPLEX. IF YOU KNOW WHERE TO LOOK, THE OLD WORLD AND ITS INHABITANTS CAN STILL BE GLEANED. DID YOU KNOW THE KINGDOM OF GENIES KNOWS NO BORDER? THEY STILL HAVE DOMINION OVER ANY PLACE THAT A WISH IS MADE. FORTUNATELY, THEY TOLERATE US TRODDING ACROSS THEIR LANDS.
THE ELVES ONCE HELD MOST OF THE SURFACE OF THE PLANET; THEIR REALM HAS STEADILY DECLINED. THE FAE ARE FEW, BUT THE MIGHTIEST HEARTS IN THE WORLD BEAT IN THEIR SLIGHT FRAMES.
DOUNIA WAS GRANTED AN AUDIENCE WITH THE DUKE. HE'D ONCE NEGOTIATED MINING RIGHTS WITH THE UNDERFOLK... WE ASSUME THEY'RE ALIVE AND WELL, DEEP BELOW OUR FEET, BUT THE TRUTH IS THAT NOBODY HAS HEARD FROM THEM IN CENTURIES.
THE DUKE WAS SAID TO BE "FROM THE OLD WORLD" WHEN HE WAS LIVING IN EUROPE IN THE MID-EIGHTEENTH CENTURY. IT SHOULD COME AS NO SURPRISE THEN, THAT HE'S A BIT TOUCHY ABOUT HIS AGE.
BEEN A WHILE, DOUNIA.
YEAH IT HAS.
HELLO, CONNIE.
THANKS FOR MEETING.
clink

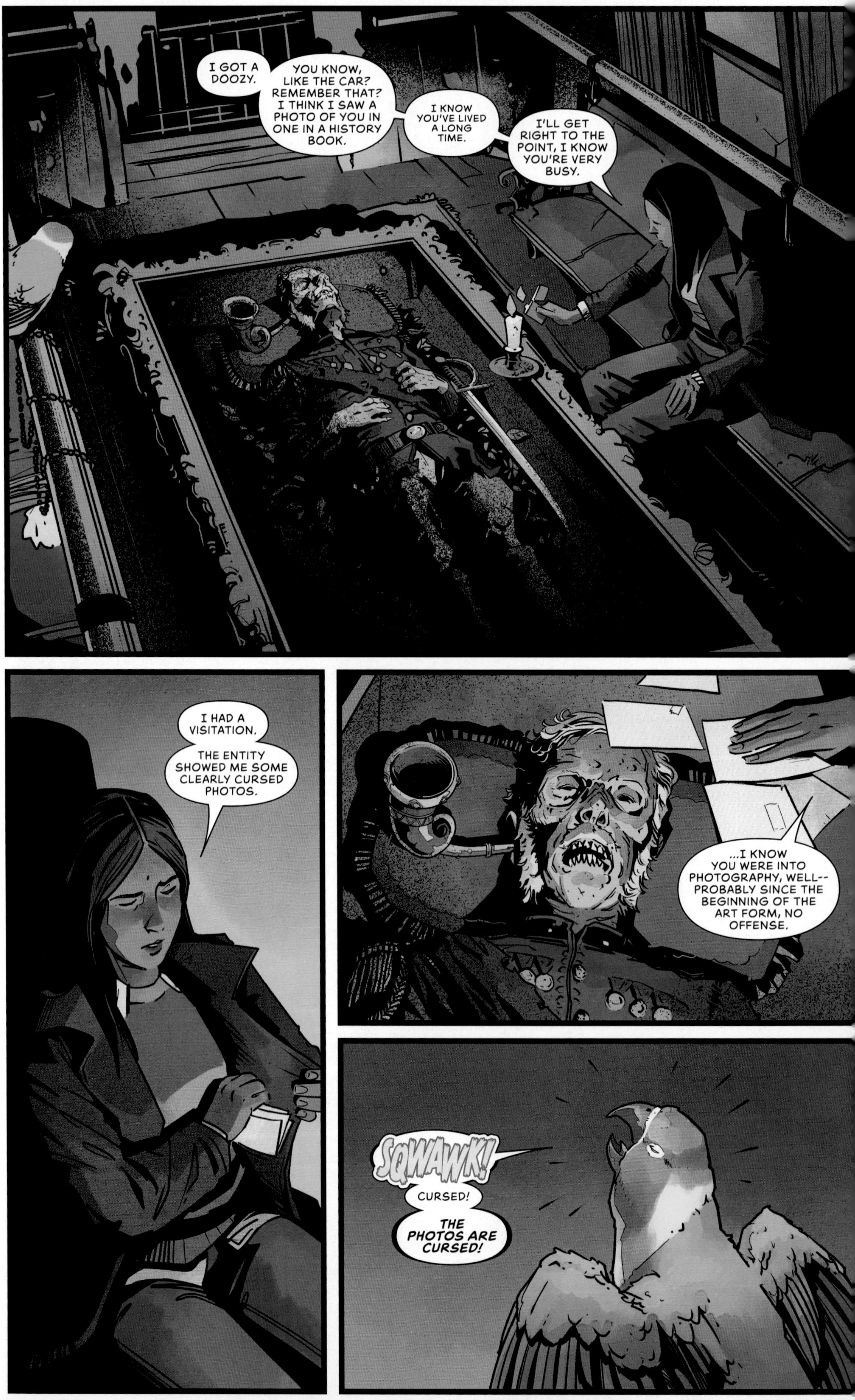
I GOT A DOOZY.
YOU KNOW, LIKE THE CAR? REMEMBER THAT? I THINK I SAW A PHOTO OF YOU IN ONE IN A HISTORY BOOK.
I KNOW YOU'VE LIVED A LONG TIME.
I'LL GET RIGHT TO THE POINT, I KNOW YOU'RE VERY BUSY.
I HAD A VISITATION.
THE ENTITY SHOWED ME SOME CLEARLY CURSED PHOTOS.
...I KNOW YOU WERE INTO PHOTOGRAPHY, WELL-- PROBABLY SINCE THE BEGINNING OF THE ART FORM, NO OFFENSE.
SQWAWK!
CURSED!
THE PHOTOS ARE CURSED!

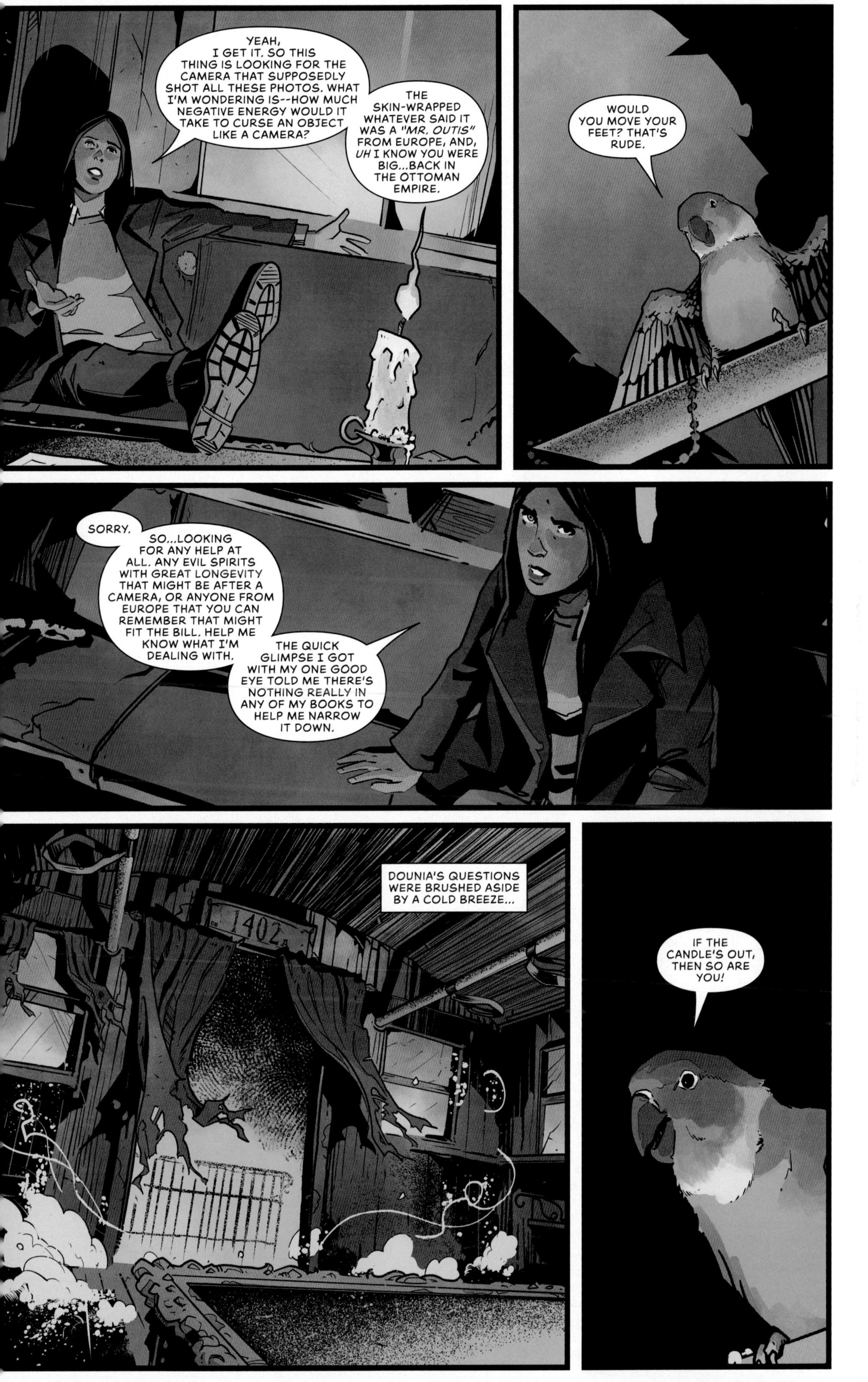
YEAH, I GET IT. SO THIS THING IS LOOKING FOR THE CAMERA THAT SUPPOSEDLY SHOT ALL THESE PHOTOS. WHAT I'M WONDERING IS--HOW MUCH NEGATIVE ENERGY WOULD IT TAKE TO CURSE AN OBJECT LIKE A CAMERA?
THE SKIN-WRAPPED WHATEVER SAID IT WAS A *"MR. OUTIS"* FROM EUROPE, AND, *UH* I KNOW YOU WERE BIG...BACK IN THE OTTOMAN EMPIRE.
WOULD YOU MOVE YOUR FEET? THAT'S RUDE.
SORRY.
SO...LOOKING FOR ANY HELP AT ALL. ANY EVIL SPIRITS WITH GREAT LONGEVITY THAT MIGHT BE AFTER A CAMERA, OR ANYONE FROM EUROPE THAT YOU CAN REMEMBER THAT MIGHT FIT THE BILL. HELP ME KNOW WHAT I'M DEALING WITH.
THE QUICK GLIMPSE I GOT WITH MY ONE GOOD EYE TOLD ME THERE'S NOTHING REALLY IN ANY OF MY BOOKS TO HELP ME NARROW IT DOWN.
DOUNIA'S QUESTIONS WERE BRUSHED ASIDE BY A COLD BREEZE...
1402
IF THE CANDLE'S OUT, THEN SO ARE YOU!

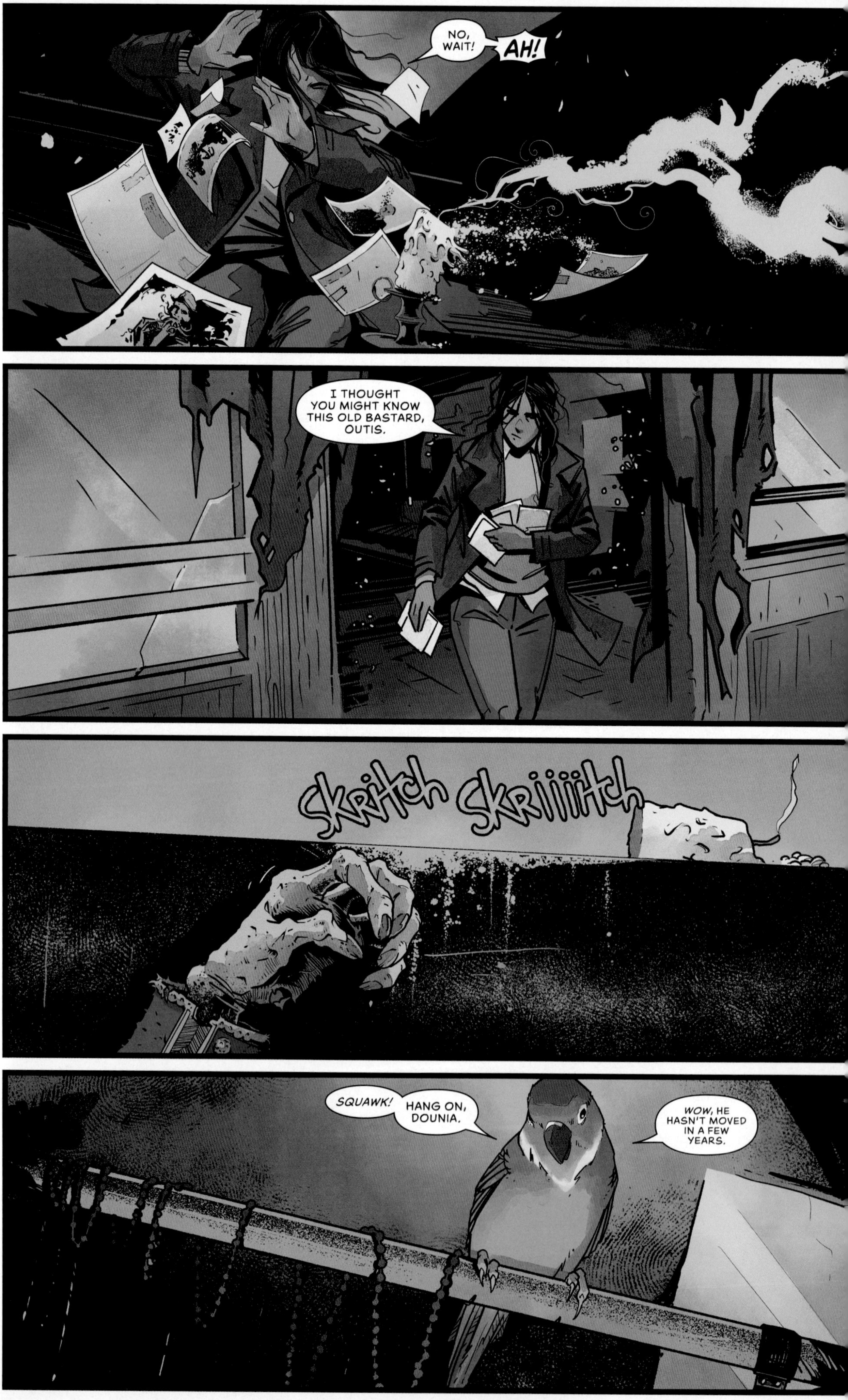
NO, WAIT!
AH!
I THOUGHT YOU MIGHT KNOW THIS OLD BASTARD, OUTIS.
Skritch Skriiiitch
SQUAWK!
HANG ON, DOUNIA.
WOW, HE HASN'T MOVED IN A FEW YEARS.

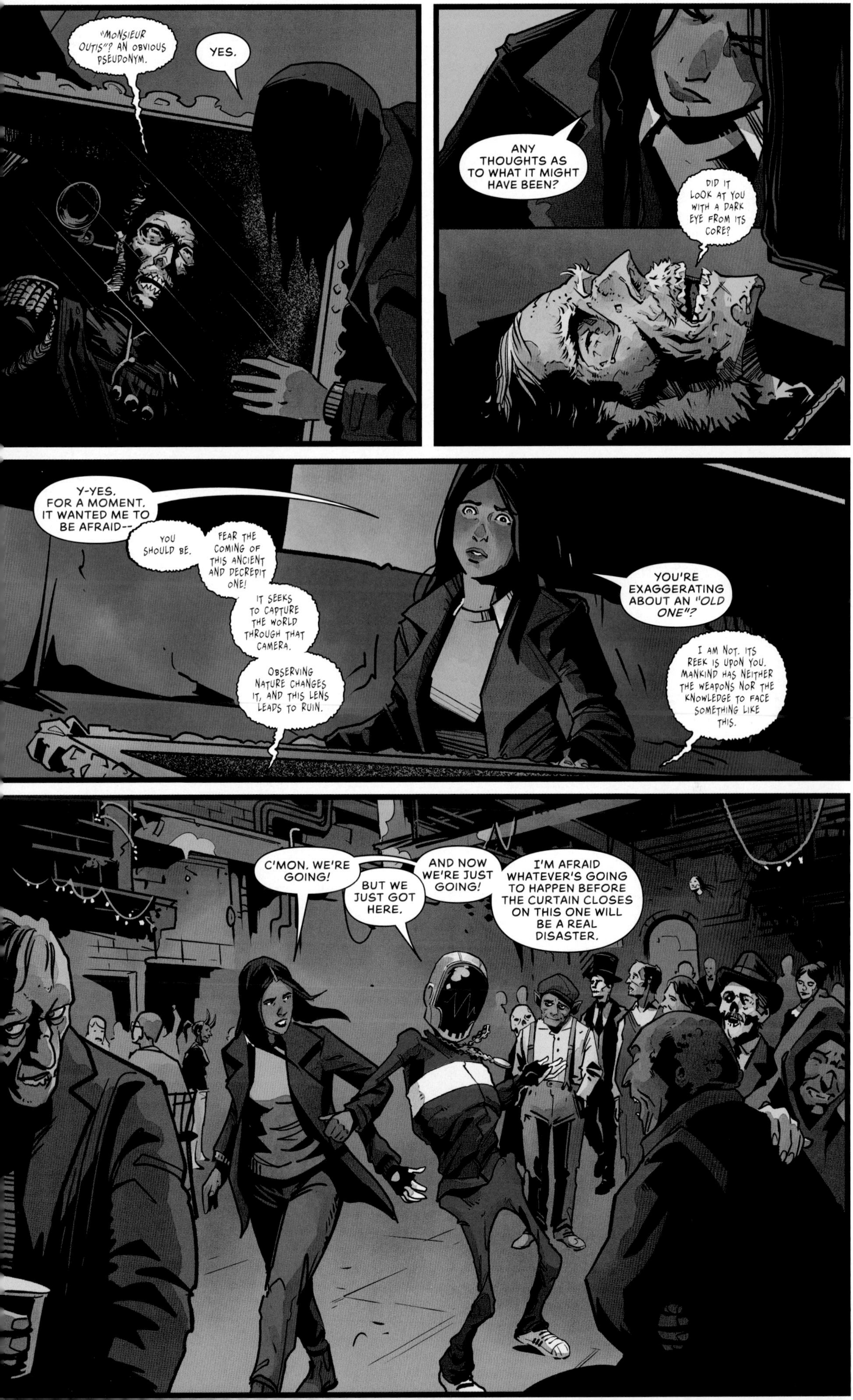
"MONSIEUR OUTIS"? AN OBVIOUS PSEUDONYM.
YES.
ANY THOUGHTS AS TO WHAT IT MIGHT HAVE BEEN?
DID IT LOOK AT YOU WITH A DARK EYE FROM ITS CORE?
Y-YES. FOR A MOMENT. IT WANTED ME TO BE AFRAID--
YOU SHOULD BE.
FEAR THE COMING OF THIS ANCIENT AND DECREPIT ONE!
IT SEEKS TO CAPTURE THE WORLD THROUGH THAT CAMERA.
OBSERVING NATURE CHANGES IT, AND THIS LENS LEADS TO RUIN.
YOU'RE EXAGGERATING ABOUT AN "OLD ONE"?
I AM NOT. ITS REEK IS UPON YOU. MANKIND HAS NEITHER THE WEAPONS NOR THE KNOWLEDGE TO FACE SOMETHING LIKE THIS.
C'MON. WE'RE GOING!
BUT WE JUST GOT HERE.
AND NOW WE'RE JUST GOING!
I'M AFRAID WHATEVER'S GOING TO HAPPEN BEFORE THE CURTAIN CLOSES ON THIS ONE WILL BE A REAL DISASTER.

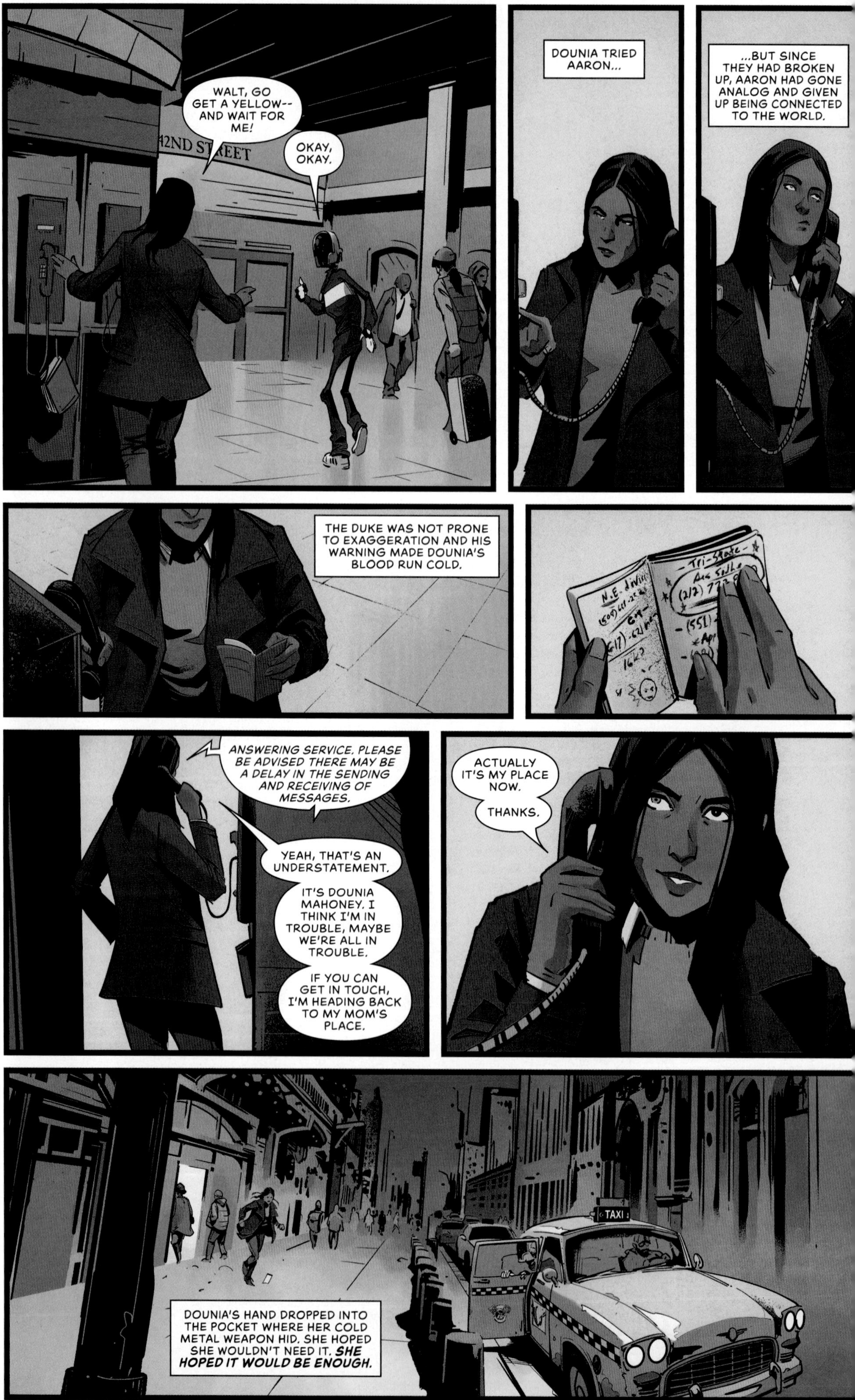

WALT, GO GET A YELLOW-- AND WAIT FOR ME!
42ND STREET
OKAY, OKAY.
DOUNIA TRIED AARON...
...BUT SINCE THEY HAD BROKEN UP, AARON HAD GONE ANALOG AND GIVEN UP BEING CONNECTED TO THE WORLD.
THE DUKE WAS NOT PRONE TO EXAGGERATION AND HIS WARNING MADE DOUNIA'S BLOOD RUN COLD.
ANSWERING SERVICE. PLEASE BE ADVISED THERE MAY BE A DELAY IN THE SENDING AND RECEIVING OF MESSAGES.
YEAH, THAT'S AN UNDERSTATEMENT.
IT'S DOUNIA MAHONEY. I THINK I'M IN TROUBLE, MAYBE WE'RE ALL IN TROUBLE.
IF YOU CAN GET IN TOUCH, I'M HEADING BACK TO MY MOM'S PLACE.
ACTUALLY IT'S MY PLACE NOW.
THANKS.
TAXI
DOUNIA'S HAND DROPPED INTO THE POCKET WHERE HER COLD METAL WEAPON HID. SHE HOPED SHE WOULDN'T NEED IT. ***SHE HOPED IT WOULD BE ENOUGH.***

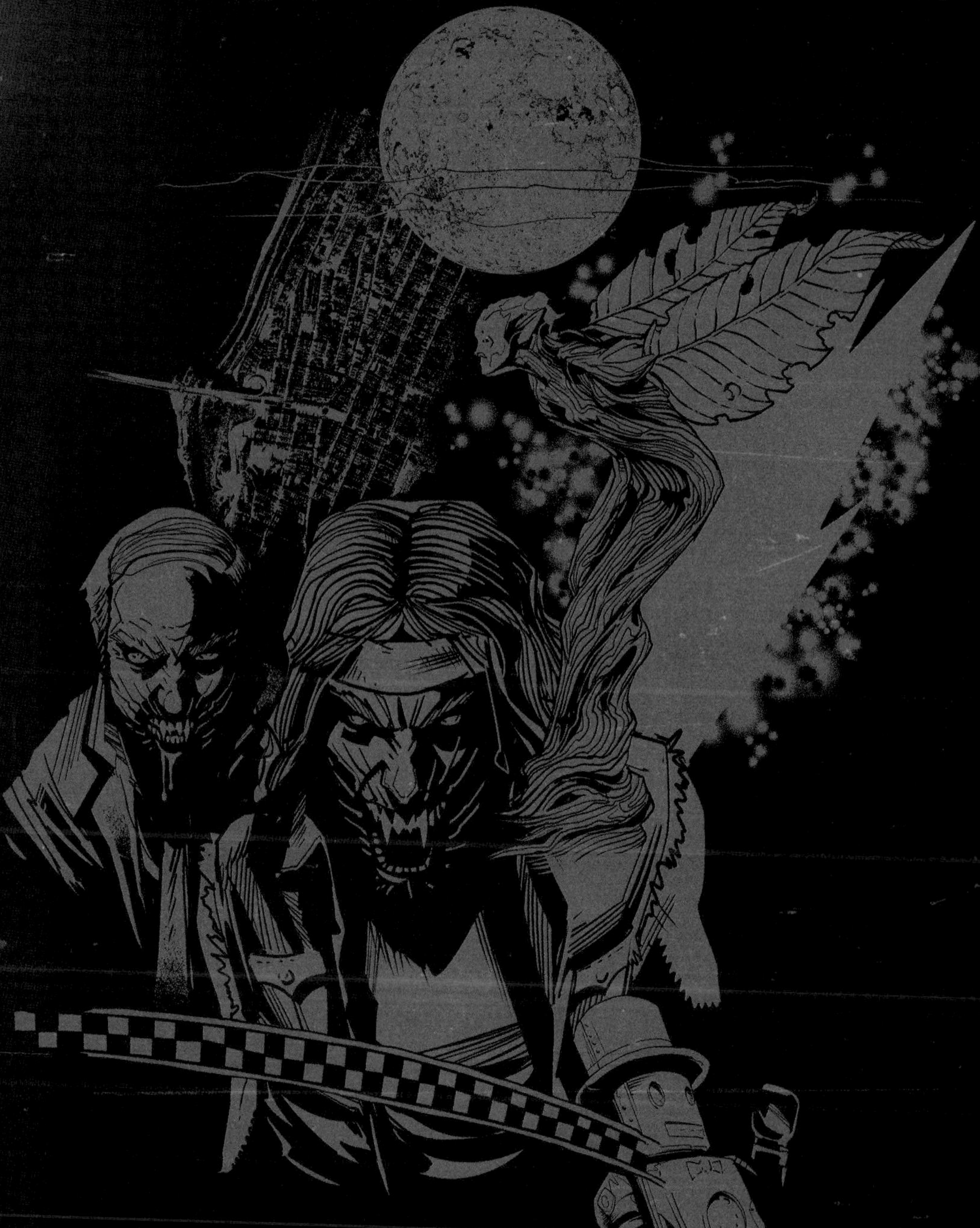

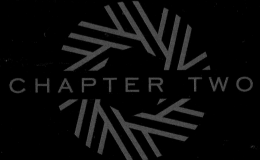

CHAPTER TWO

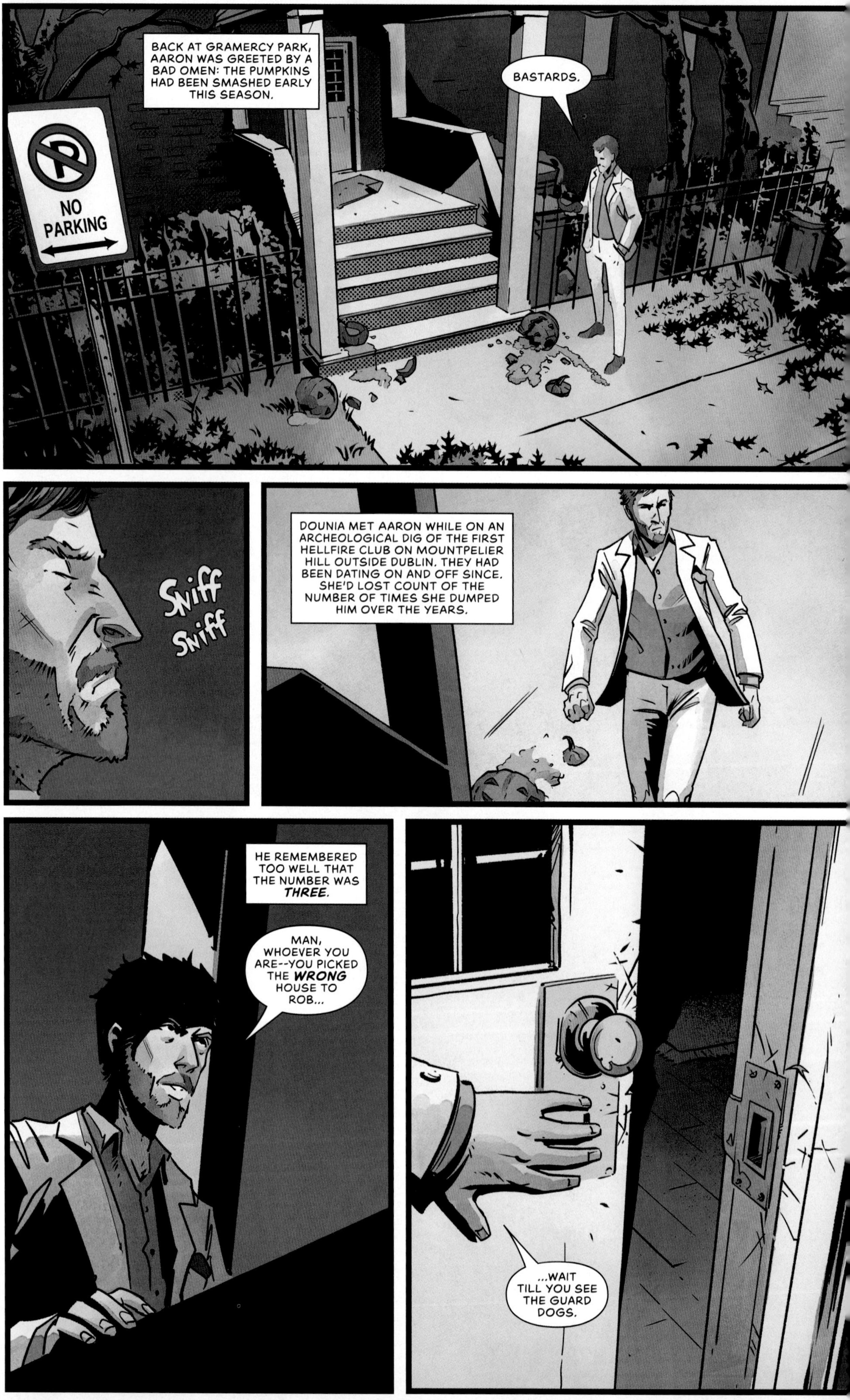
BACK AT GRAMERCY PARK, AARON WAS GREETED BY A BAD OMEN: THE PUMPKINS HAD BEEN SMASHED EARLY THIS SEASON.
BASTARDS.
NO PARKING
SNIFF SNIFF
DOUNIA MET AARON WHILE ON AN ARCHEOLOGICAL DIG OF THE FIRST HELLFIRE CLUB ON MOUNTPELIER HILL OUTSIDE DUBLIN. THEY HAD BEEN DATING ON AND OFF SINCE. SHE'D LOST COUNT OF THE NUMBER OF TIMES SHE DUMPED HIM OVER THE YEARS.
HE REMEMBERED TOO WELL THAT THE NUMBER WAS ***THREE.***
MAN, WHOEVER YOU ARE--YOU PICKED THE ***WRONG*** HOUSE TO ROB...
...WAIT TILL YOU SEE THE GUARD DOGS.

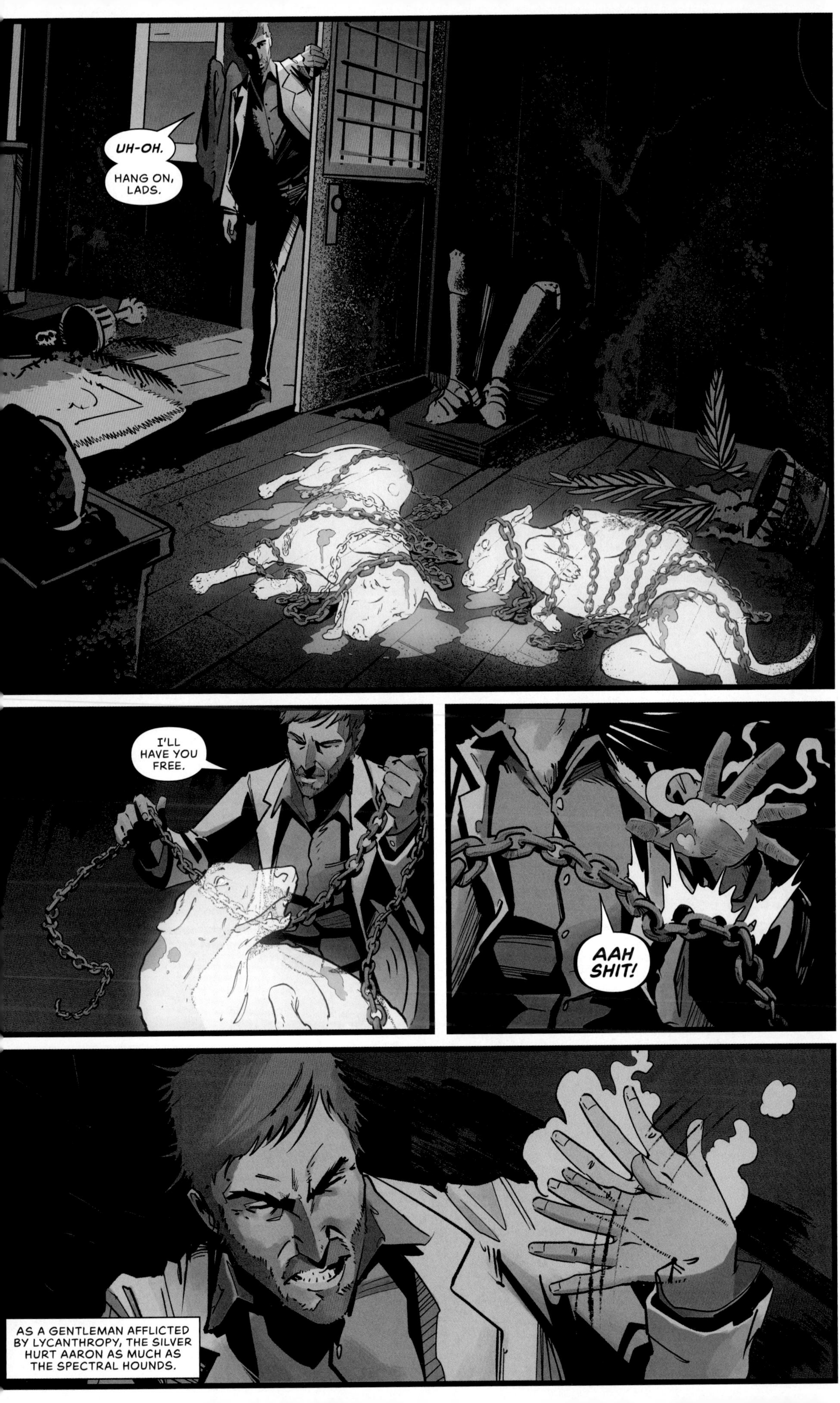
UH-OH.
HANG ON, LADS.
I'LL HAVE YOU FREE.
AAH SHIT!
AS A GENTLEMAN AFFLICTED BY LYCANTHROPY, THE SILVER HURT AARON AS MUCH AS THE SPECTRAL HOUNDS.

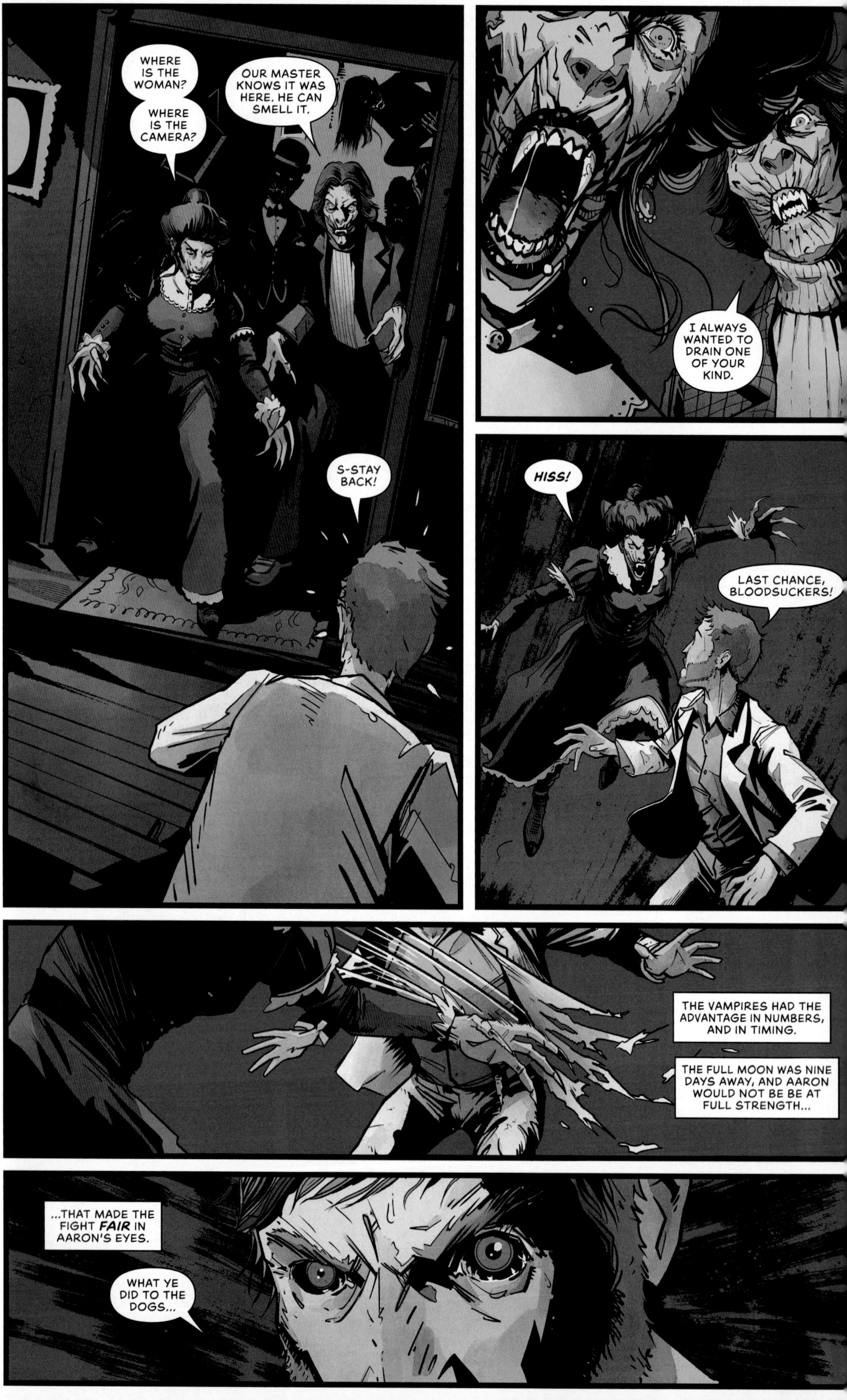
WHERE IS THE WOMAN?
WHERE IS THE CAMERA?
OUR MASTER KNOWS IT WAS HERE. HE CAN SMELL IT.
S-STAY BACK!
I ALWAYS WANTED TO DRAIN ONE OF YOUR KIND.
HISS!
LAST CHANCE, BLOODSUCKERS!
THE VAMPIRES HAD THE ADVANTAGE IN NUMBERS, AND IN TIMING.
THE FULL MOON WAS NINE DAYS AWAY, AND AARON WOULD NOT BE BE AT FULL STRENGTH...
...THAT MADE THE FIGHT FAIR IN AARON'S EYES.
WHAT YE DID TO THE DOGS...

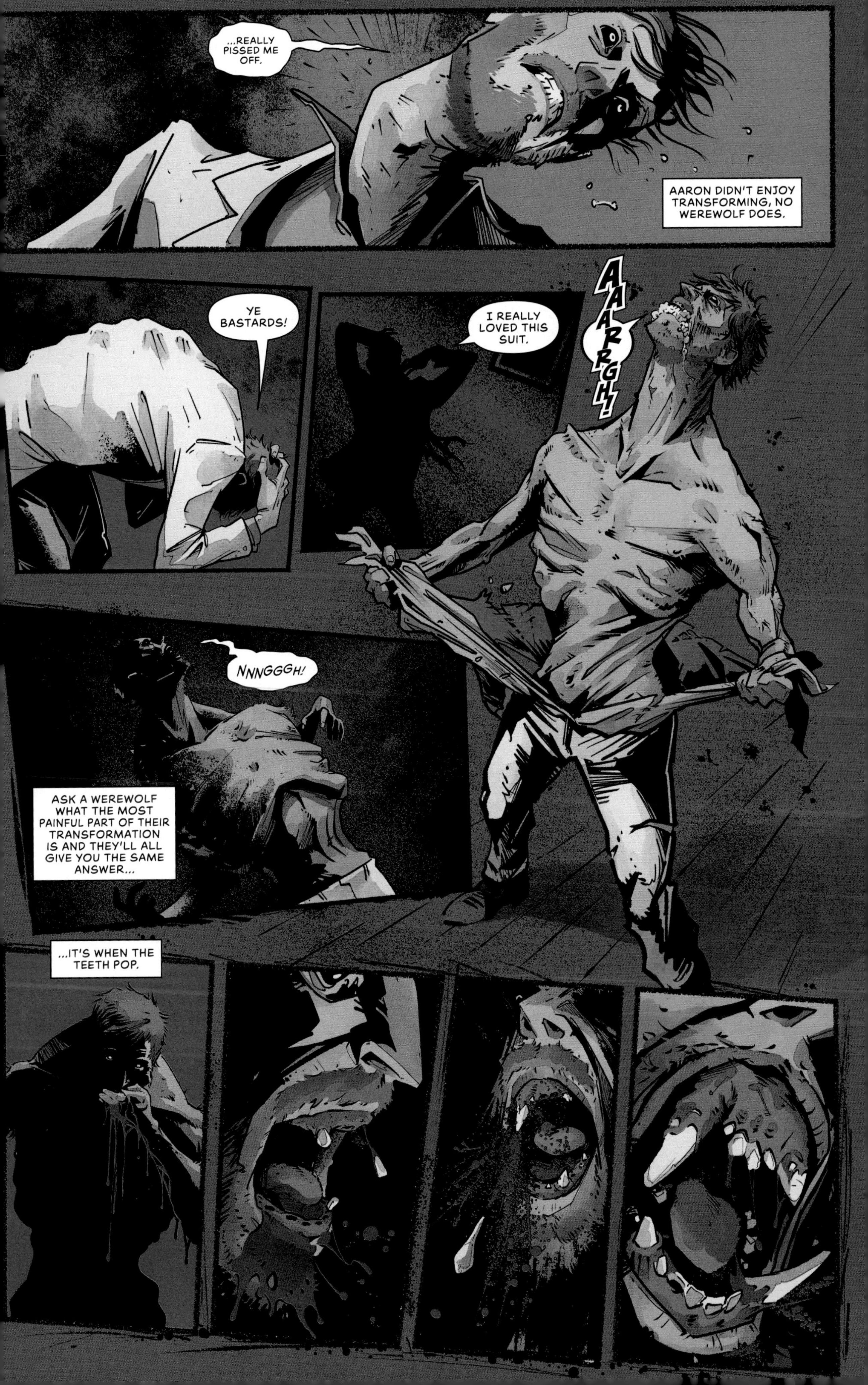
...REALLY PISSED ME OFF.
AARON DIDN'T ENJOY TRANSFORMING, NO WEREWOLF DOES.
YE BASTARDS!
I REALLY LOVED THIS SUIT.
AAARRGH!
NNNGGGH!
ASK A WEREWOLF WHAT THE MOST PAINFUL PART OF THEIR TRANSFORMATION IS AND THEY'LL ALL GIVE YOU THE SAME ANSWER...
...IT'S WHEN THE TEETH POP.

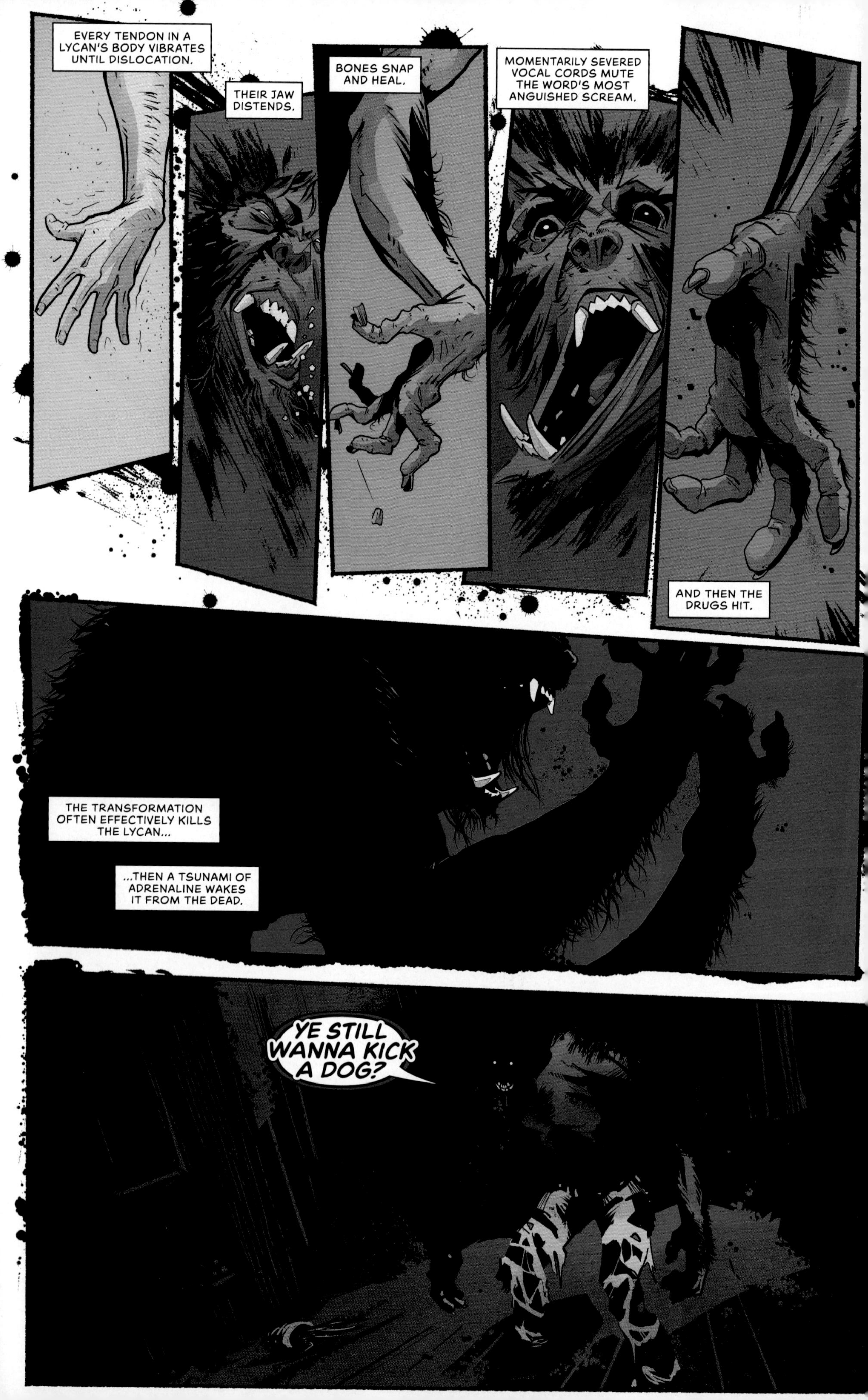
EVERY TENDON IN A LYCAN'S BODY VIBRATES UNTIL DISLOCATION.
THEIR JAW DISTENDS.
BONES SNAP AND HEAL.
MOMENTARILY SEVERED VOCAL CORDS MUTE THE WORD'S MOST ANGUISHED SCREAM.
AND THEN THE DRUGS HIT.
THE TRANSFORMATION OFTEN EFFECTIVELY KILLS THE LYCAN...
...THEN A TSUNAMI OF ADRENALINE WAKES IT FROM THE DEAD.
YE STILL WANNA KICK A DOG?

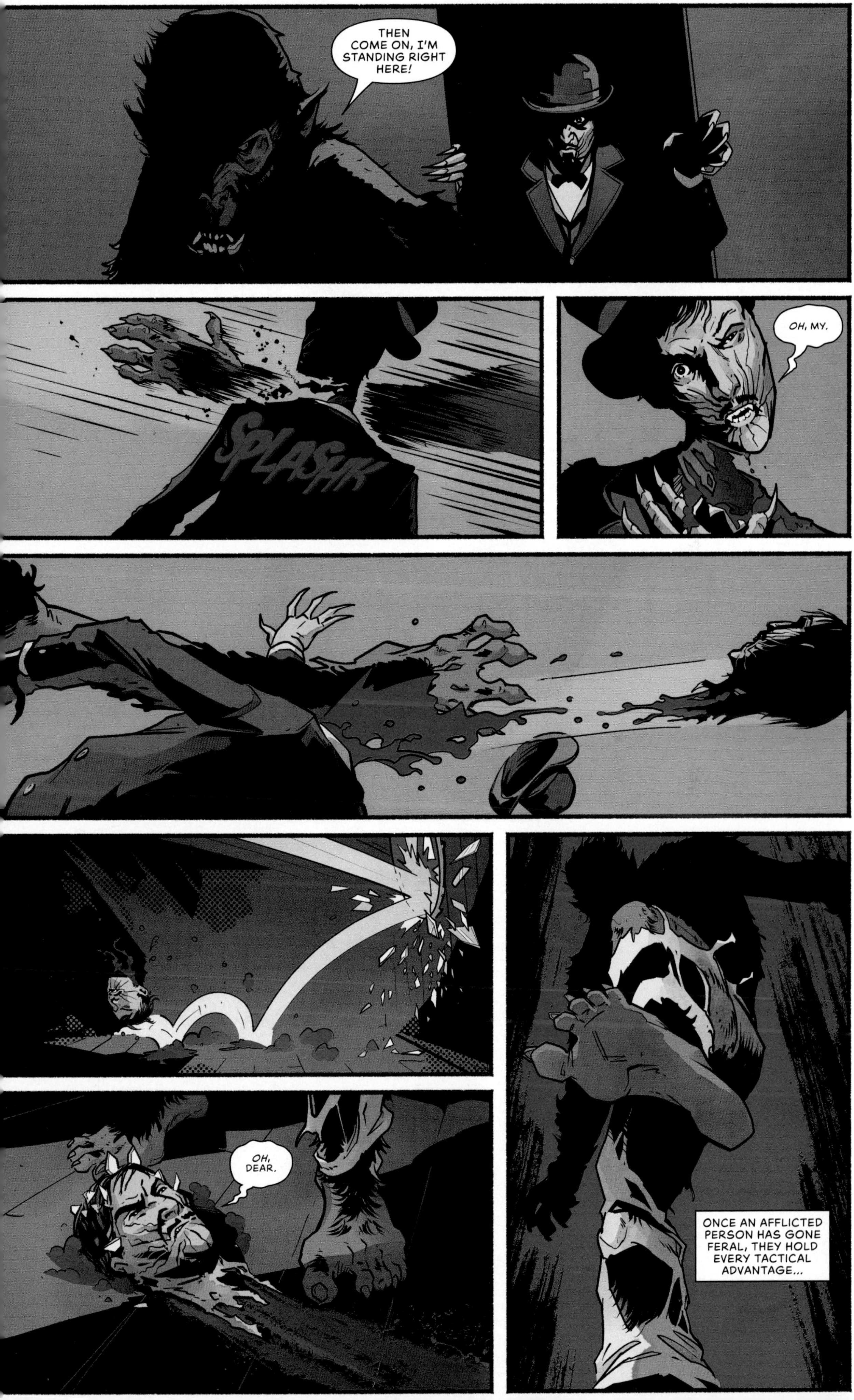
THEN COME ON, I'M STANDING RIGHT HERE!
SPLASHK
OH, MY.
OH, DEAR.
ONCE AN AFFLICTED PERSON HAS GONE FERAL, THEY HOLD EVERY TACTICAL ADVANTAGE...

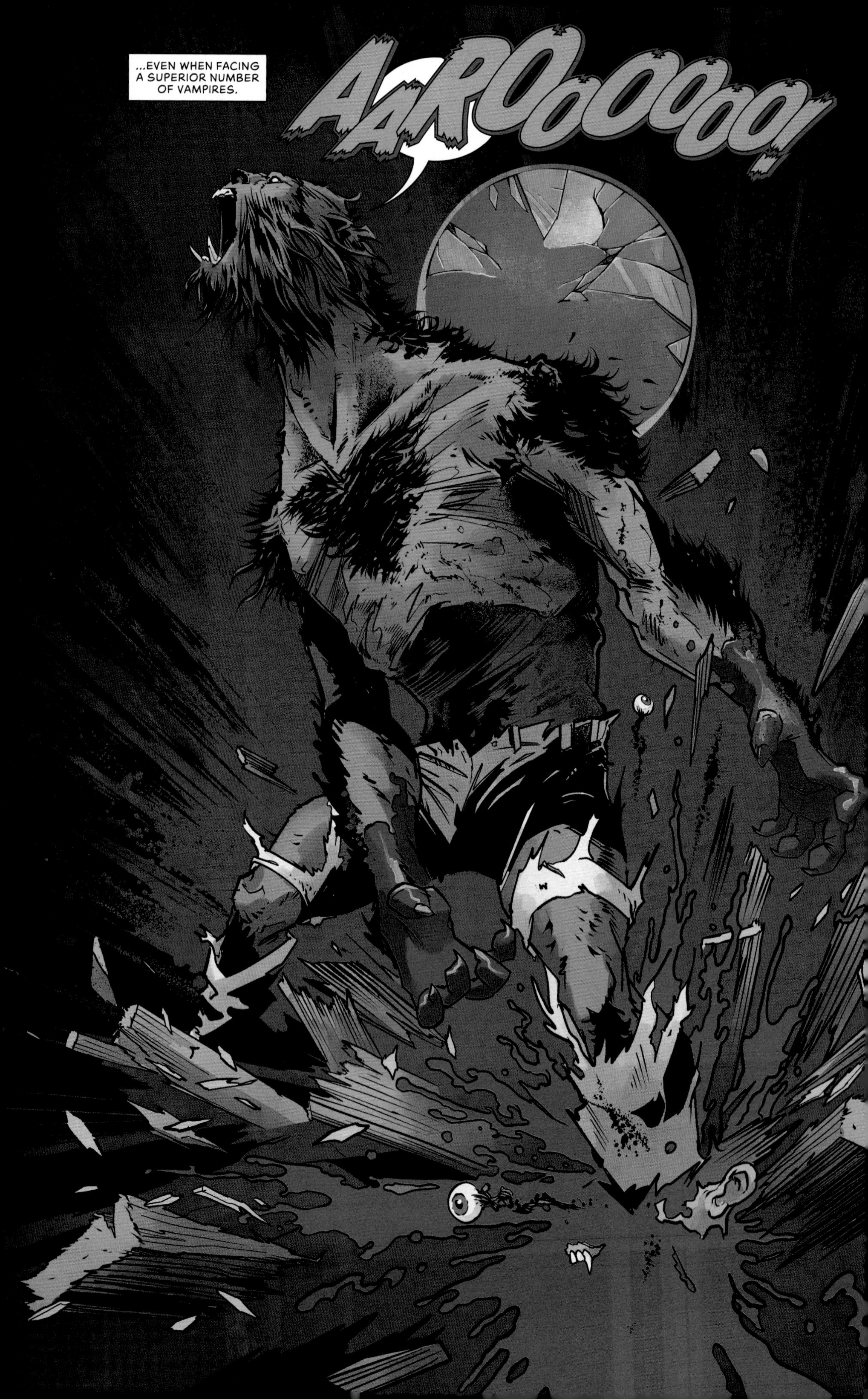
...EVEN WHEN FACING A SUPERIOR NUMBER OF VAMPIRES.
AAROOOOOO!

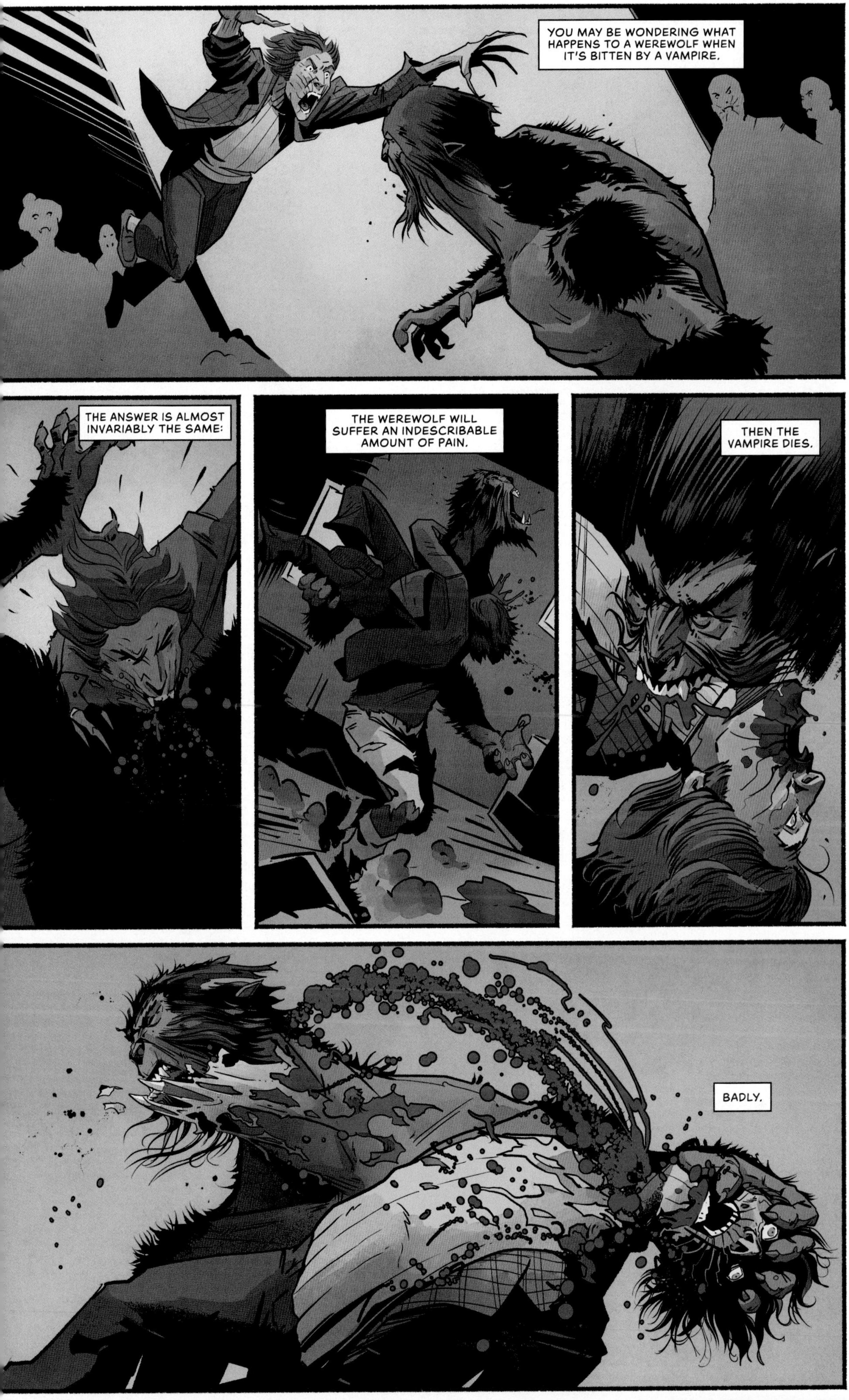
YOU MAY BE WONDERING WHAT HAPPENS TO A WEREWOLF WHEN IT'S BITTEN BY A VAMPIRE.
THE ANSWER IS ALMOST INVARIABLY THE SAME:
THE WEREWOLF WILL SUFFER AN INDESCRIBABLE AMOUNT OF PAIN.
THEN THE VAMPIRE DIES.
BADLY.

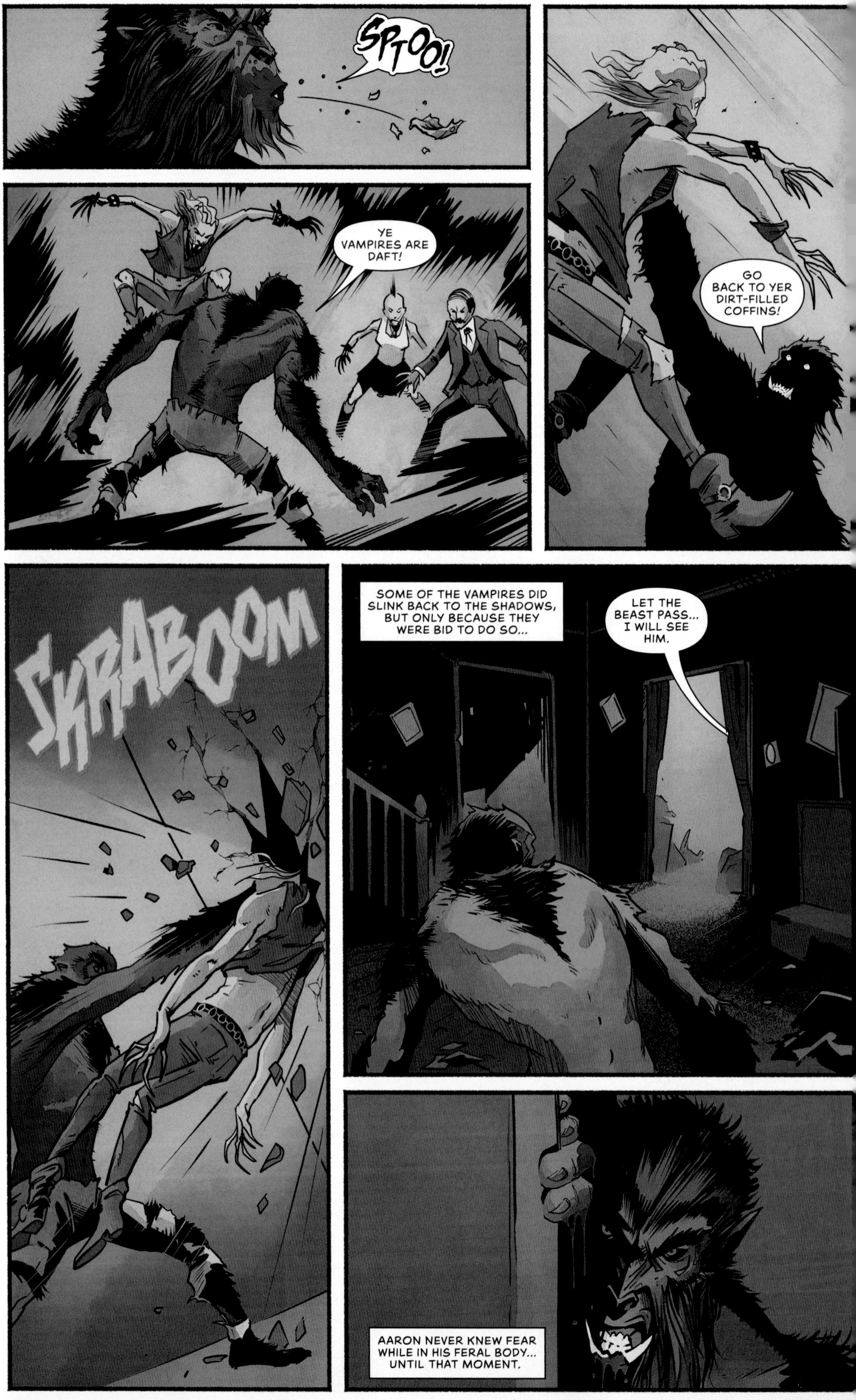
SPTOO!
YE VAMPIRES ARE DAFT!
GO BACK TO YER DIRT-FILLED COFFINS!
SKRABOOM
SOME OF THE VAMPIRES DID SLINK BACK TO THE SHADOWS, BUT ONLY BECAUSE THEY WERE BID TO DO SO...
LET THE BEAST PASS... I WILL SEE HIM.
AARON NEVER KNEW FEAR WHILE IN HIS FERAL BODY... UNTIL THAT MOMENT.

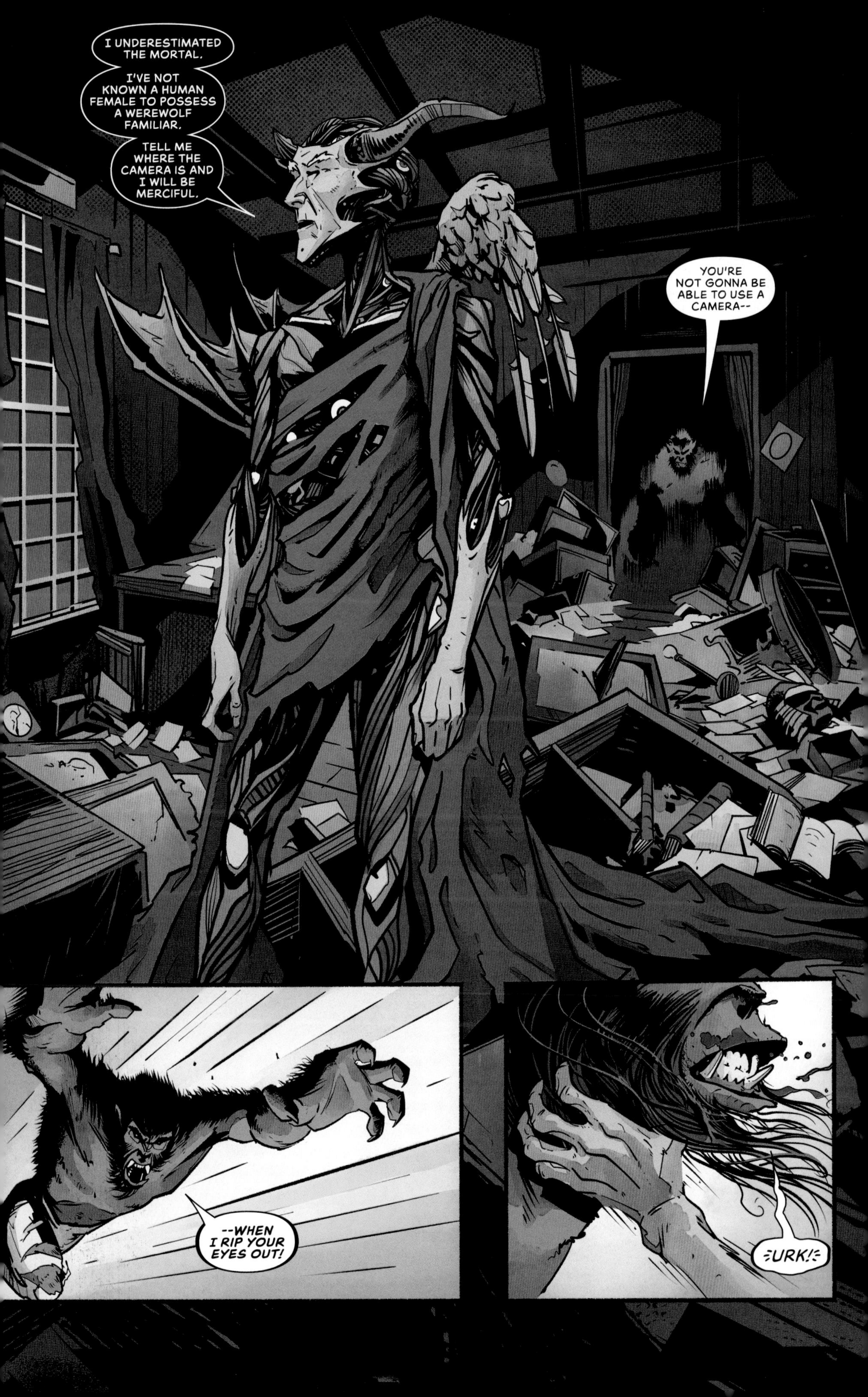
I UNDERESTIMATED THE MORTAL.
I'VE NOT KNOWN A HUMAN FEMALE TO POSSESS A WEREWOLF FAMILIAR.
TELL ME WHERE THE CAMERA IS AND I WILL BE MERCIFUL.
YOU'RE NOT GONNA BE ABLE TO USE A CAMERA--
--WHEN I RIP YOUR EYES OUT!
URK!

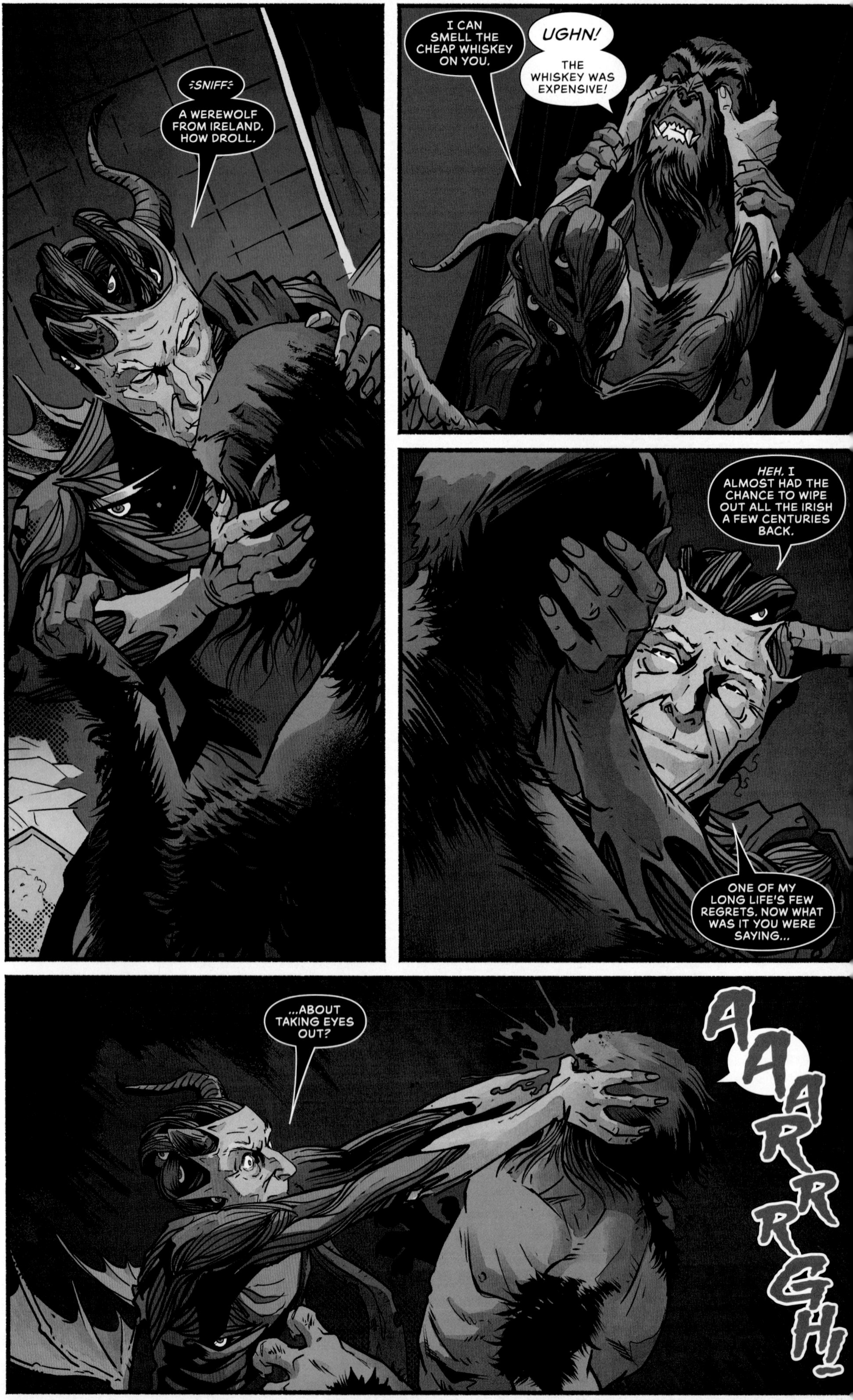
SNIFF
A WEREWOLF FROM IRELAND. HOW DROLL.
I CAN SMELL THE CHEAP WHISKEY ON YOU.
UGHN!
THE WHISKEY WAS EXPENSIVE!
HEH. I ALMOST HAD THE CHANCE TO WIPE OUT ALL THE IRISH A FEW CENTURIES BACK.
ONE OF MY LONG LIFE'S FEW REGRETS. NOW WHAT WAS IT YOU WERE SAYING...
...ABOUT TAKING EYES OUT?
AAARRRGH!

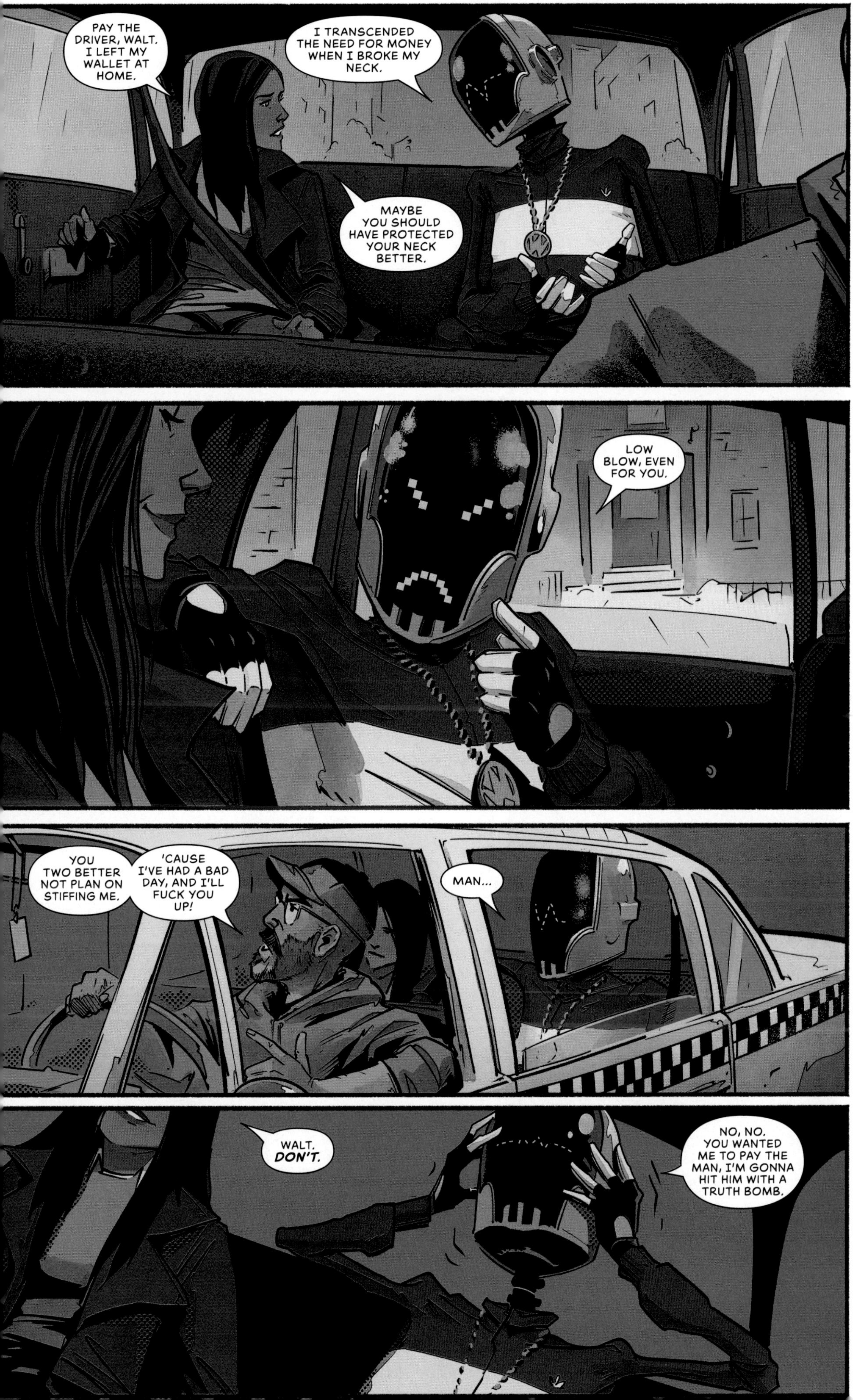
PAY THE DRIVER, WALT. I LEFT MY WALLET AT HOME.
I TRANSCENDED THE NEED FOR MONEY WHEN I BROKE MY NECK.
MAYBE YOU SHOULD HAVE PROTECTED YOUR NECK BETTER.
LOW BLOW, EVEN FOR YOU.
YOU TWO BETTER NOT PLAN ON STIFFING ME.
'CAUSE I'VE HAD A BAD DAY, AND I'LL FUCK YOU UP!
MAN...
WALT. ***DON'T.***
NO, NO. YOU WANTED ME TO PAY THE MAN, I'M GONNA HIT HIM WITH A TRUTH BOMB.

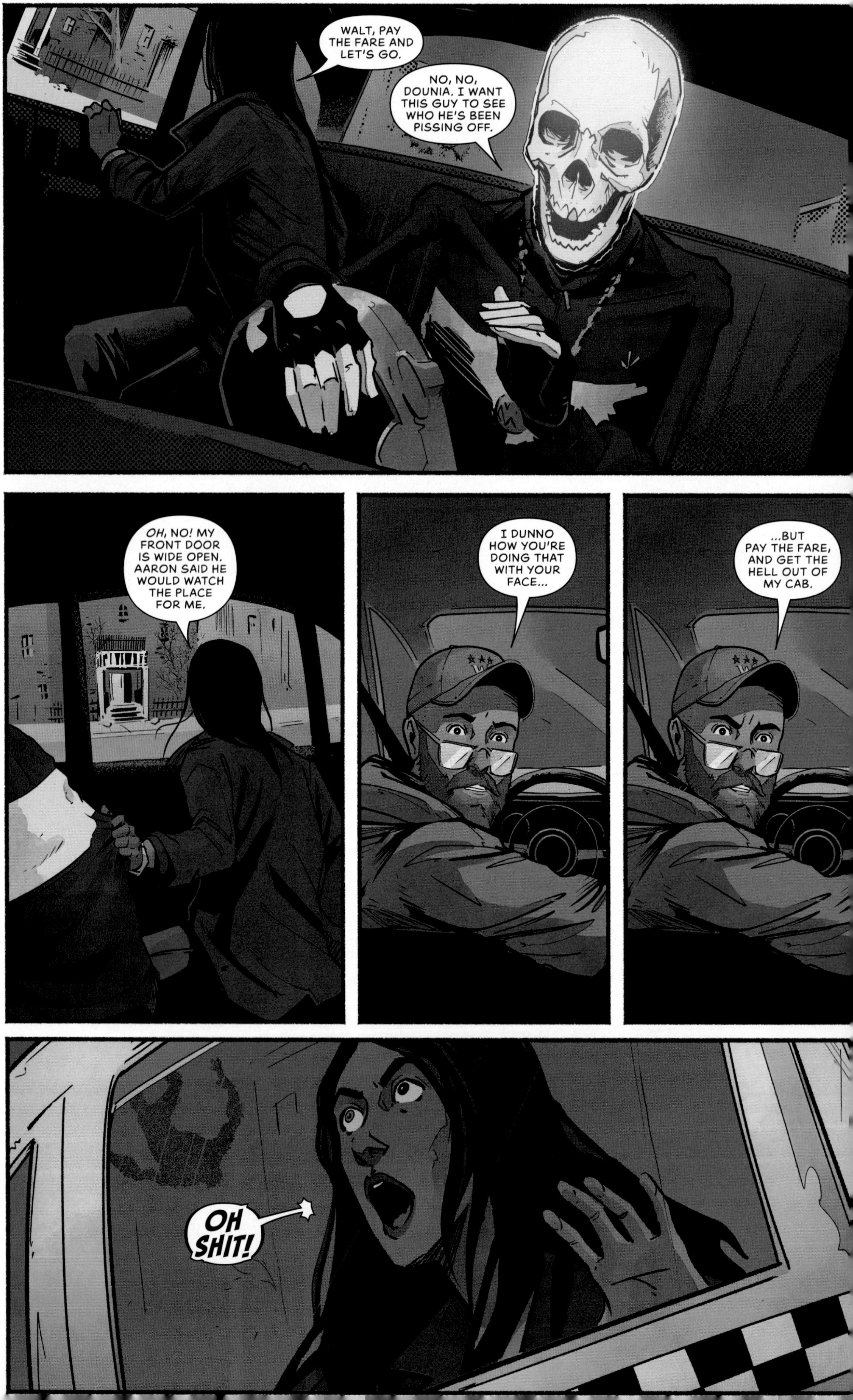
WALT, PAY THE FARE AND LET'S GO.
NO, NO, DOUNIA. I WANT THIS GUY TO SEE WHO HE'S BEEN PISSING OFF.
OH, NO! MY FRONT DOOR IS WIDE OPEN. AARON SAID HE WOULD WATCH THE PLACE FOR ME.
I DUNNO HOW YOU'RE DOING THAT WITH YOUR FACE...
...BUT PAY THE FARE, AND GET THE HELL OUT OF MY CAB.
OH SHIT!

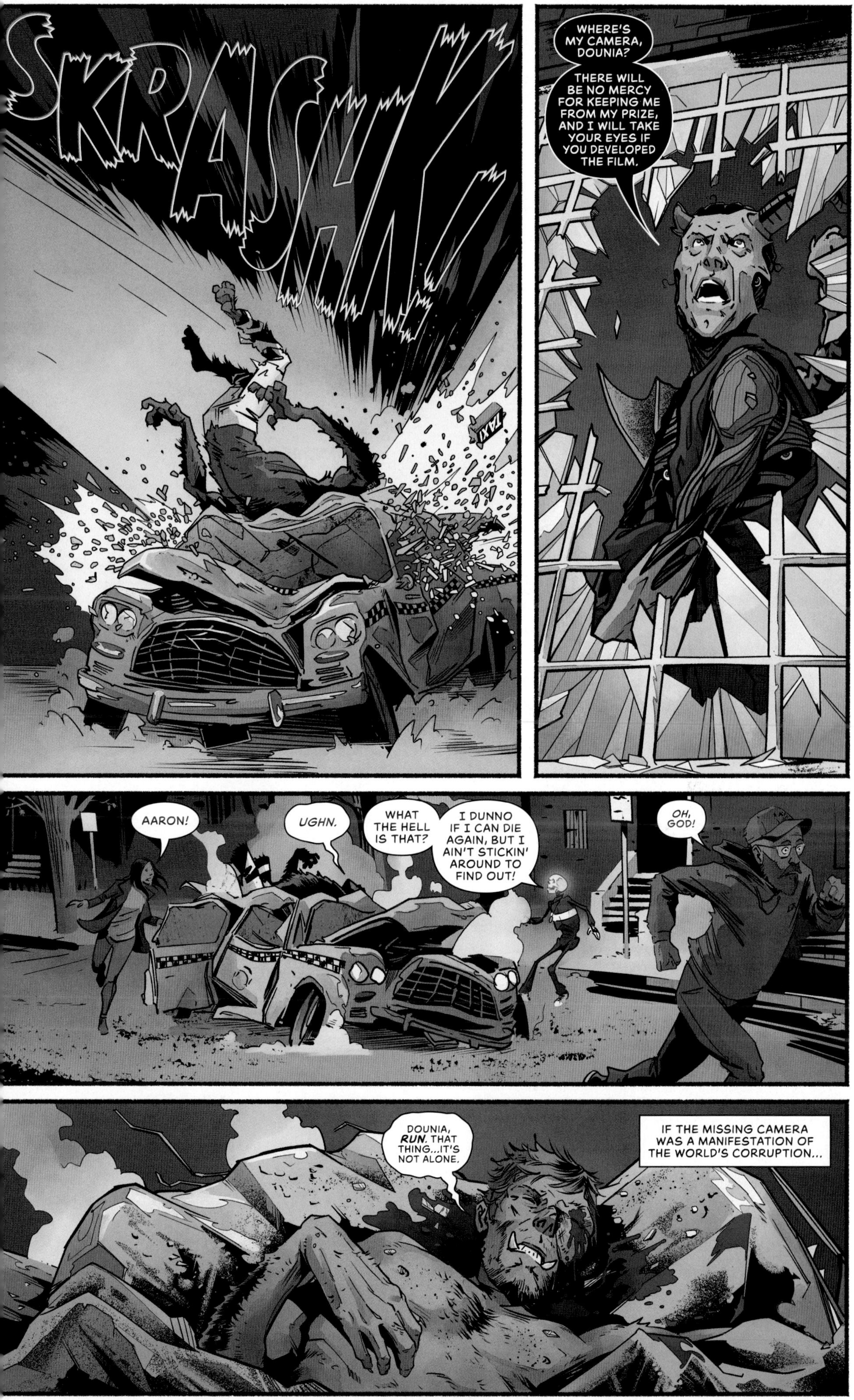
SKRASHK!
WHERE'S MY CAMERA, DOUNIA?
THERE WILL BE NO MERCY FOR KEEPING ME FROM MY PRIZE, AND I WILL TAKE YOUR EYES IF YOU DEVELOPED THE FILM.
AARON!
UGHN.
WHAT THE HELL IS THAT?
I DUNNO IF I CAN DIE AGAIN, BUT I AIN'T STICKIN' AROUND TO FIND OUT!
OH, GOD!
DOUNIA, **RUN**. THAT THING...IT'S NOT ALONE.
IF THE MISSING CAMERA WAS A MANIFESTATION OF THE WORLD'S CORRUPTION...

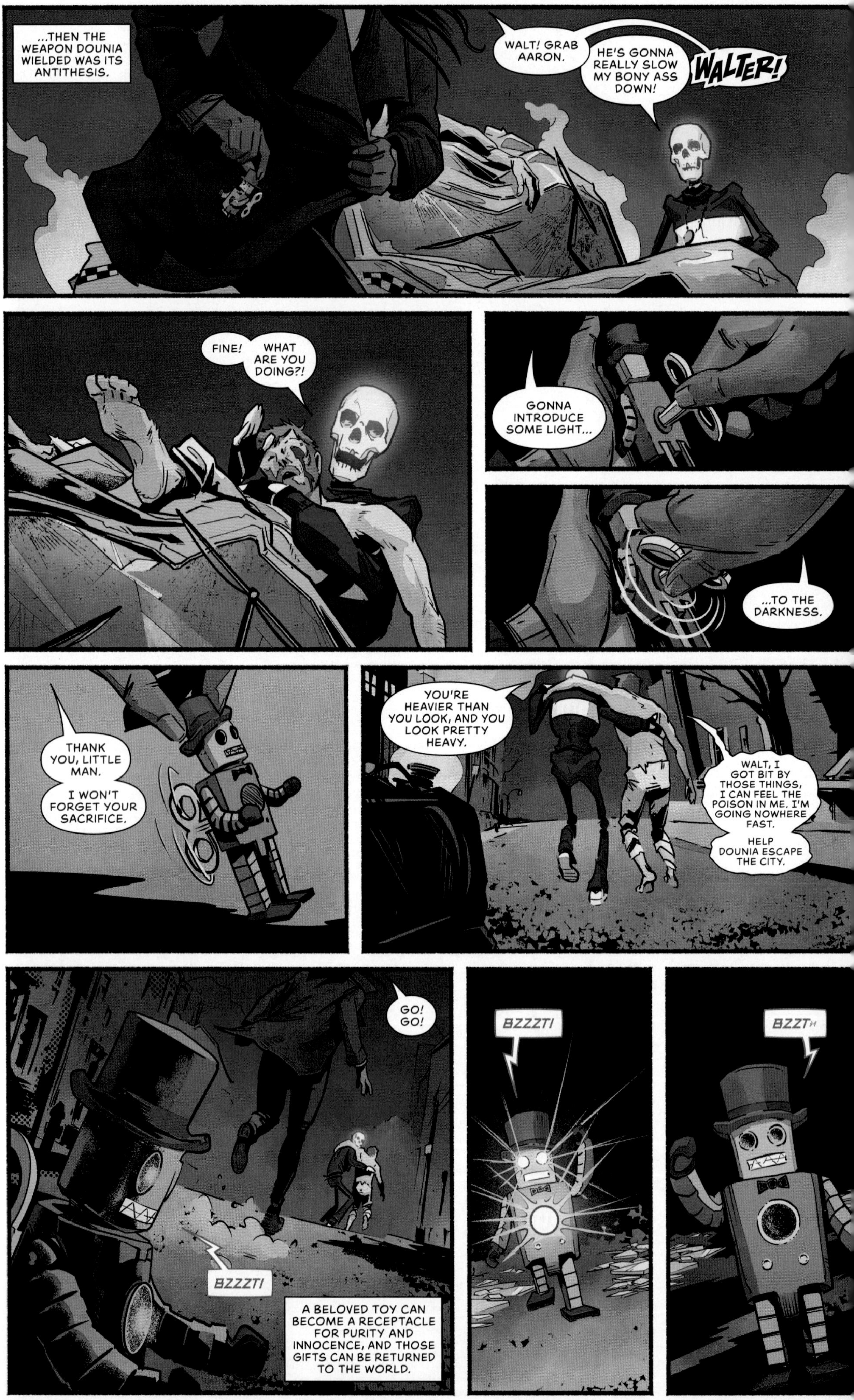
...THEN THE WEAPON DOUNIA WIELDED WAS ITS ANTITHESIS.
WALT! GRAB AARON.
HE'S GONNA REALLY SLOW MY BONY ASS DOWN!
WALTER!
FINE!
WHAT ARE YOU DOING?!
GONNA INTRODUCE SOME LIGHT...
...TO THE DARKNESS.
THANK YOU, LITTLE MAN.
I WON'T FORGET YOUR SACRIFICE.
YOU'RE HEAVIER THAN YOU LOOK, AND YOU LOOK PRETTY HEAVY.
WALT, I GOT BIT BY THOSE THINGS, I CAN FEEL THE POISON IN ME. I'M GOING NOWHERE FAST.
HELP DOUNIA ESCAPE THE CITY.
GO! GO!
BZZZT!
A BELOVED TOY CAN BECOME A RECEPTACLE FOR PURITY AND INNOCENCE, AND THOSE GIFTS CAN BE RETURNED TO THE WORLD.
BZZZT!
BZZT

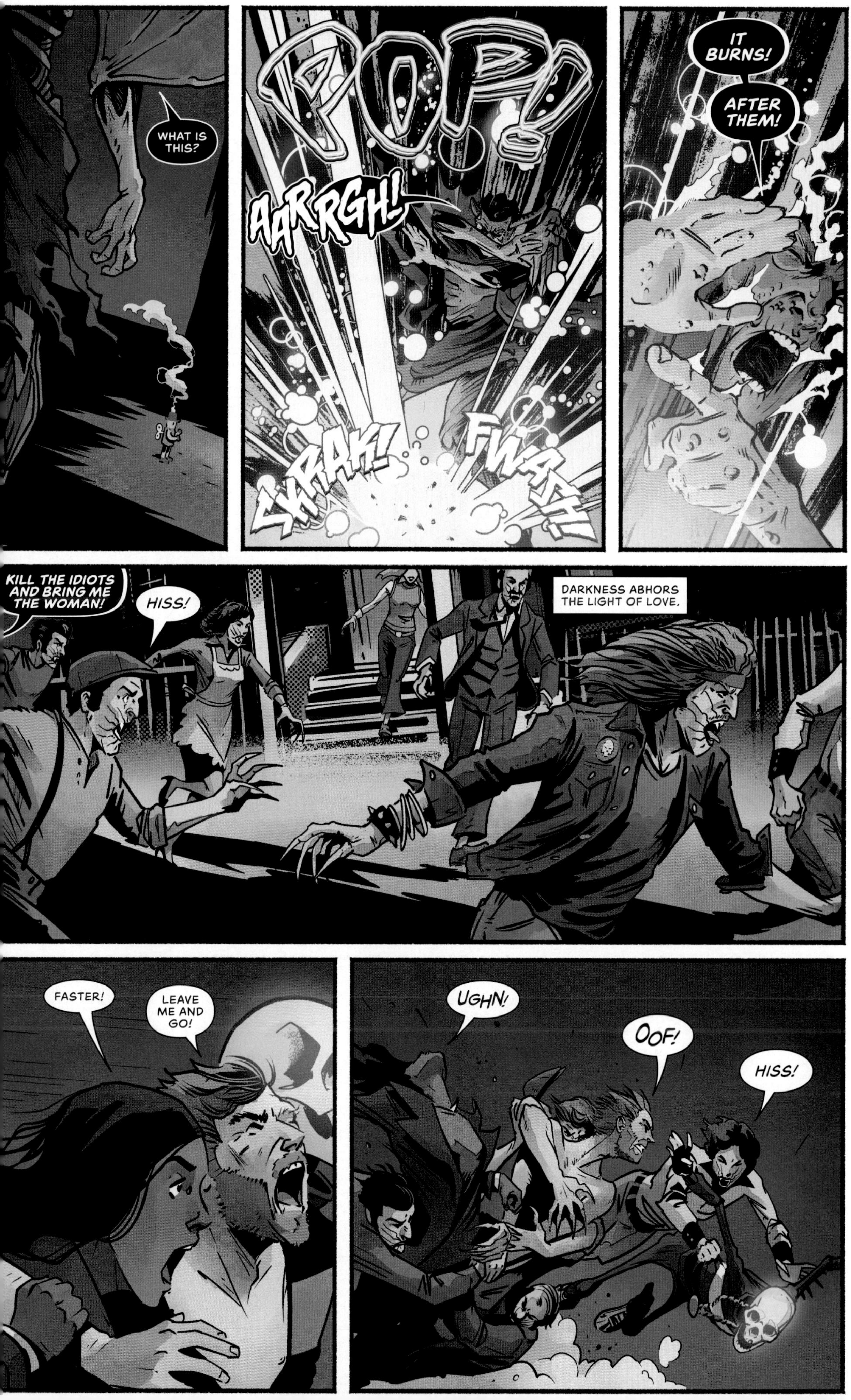
WHAT IS THIS?
POP!
AARRGH!
SKRAK!
FWASH!
IT BURNS!
AFTER THEM!
KILL THE IDIOTS AND BRING ME THE WOMAN!
HISS!
DARKNESS ABHORS THE LIGHT OF LOVE.
FASTER!
LEAVE ME AND GO!
UGHN!
OOF!
HISS!

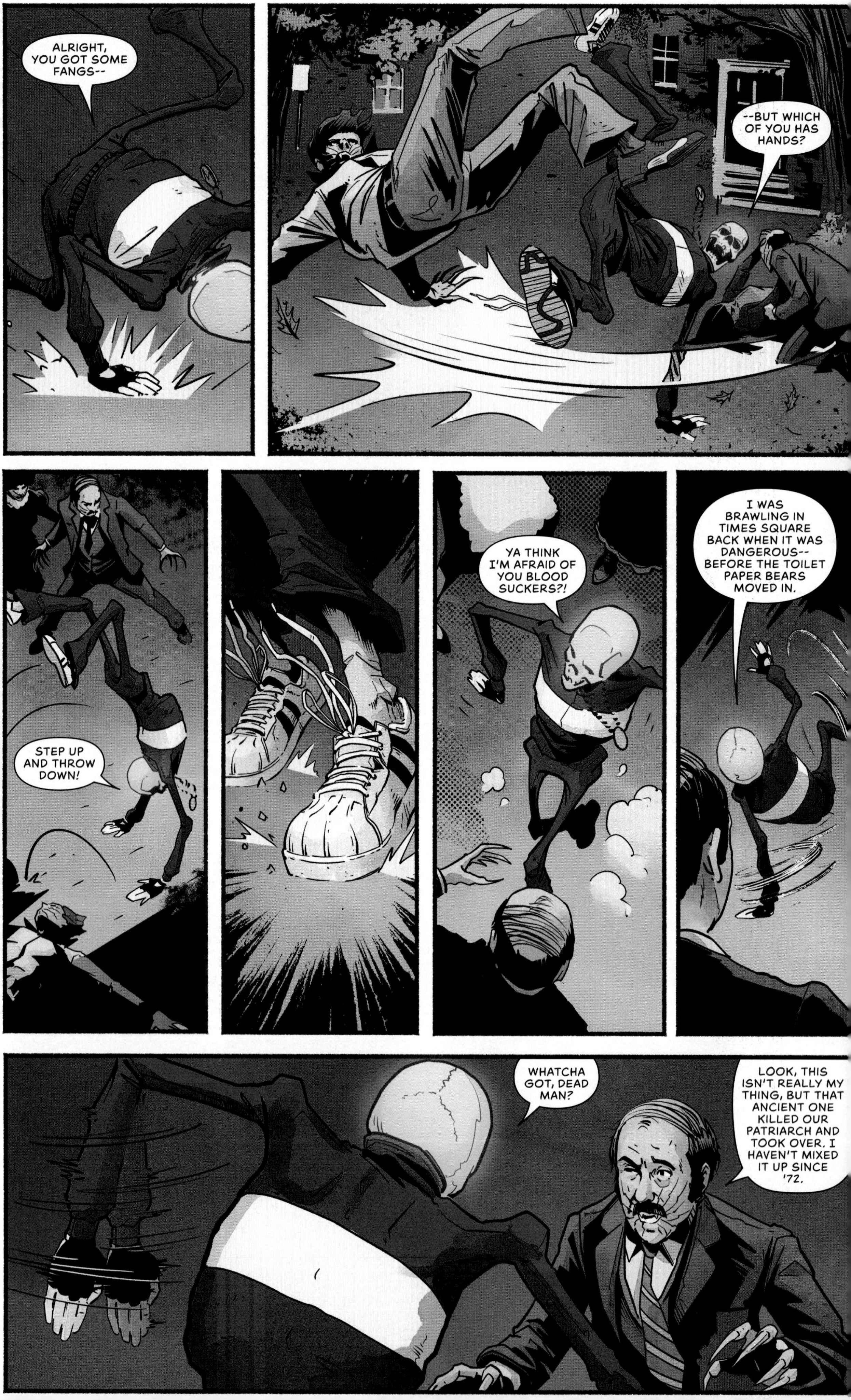
ALRIGHT, YOU GOT SOME FANGS--
--BUT WHICH OF YOU HAS HANDS?
STEP UP AND THROW DOWN!
YA THINK I'M AFRAID OF YOU BLOOD SUCKERS?!
I WAS BRAWLING IN TIMES SQUARE BACK WHEN IT WAS DANGEROUS-- BEFORE THE TOILET PAPER BEARS MOVED IN.
WHATCHA GOT, DEAD MAN?
LOOK, THIS ISN'T REALLY MY THING, BUT THAT ANCIENT ONE KILLED OUR PATRIARCH AND TOOK OVER. I HAVEN'T MIXED IT UP SINCE '72.

WRONG ANSWER, GRAMPIRE!

KRAK!!

AAH!

WANT MY FRIENDS? THEN YOU GOTTA GO THROUGH THE FIGHTING BONES OF TIMES SQUARE!

WOMP

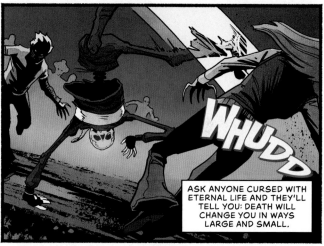

WHUDD

ASK ANYONE CURSED WITH ETERNAL LIFE AND THEY'LL TELL YOU: DEATH WILL CHANGE YOU IN WAYS LARGE AND SMALL.

THE ONE THING THAT WALT CARRIED WITH HIM FROM LIFE INTO DEATH WAS...

...OVERCONFIDENCE.

AW, SHIT.

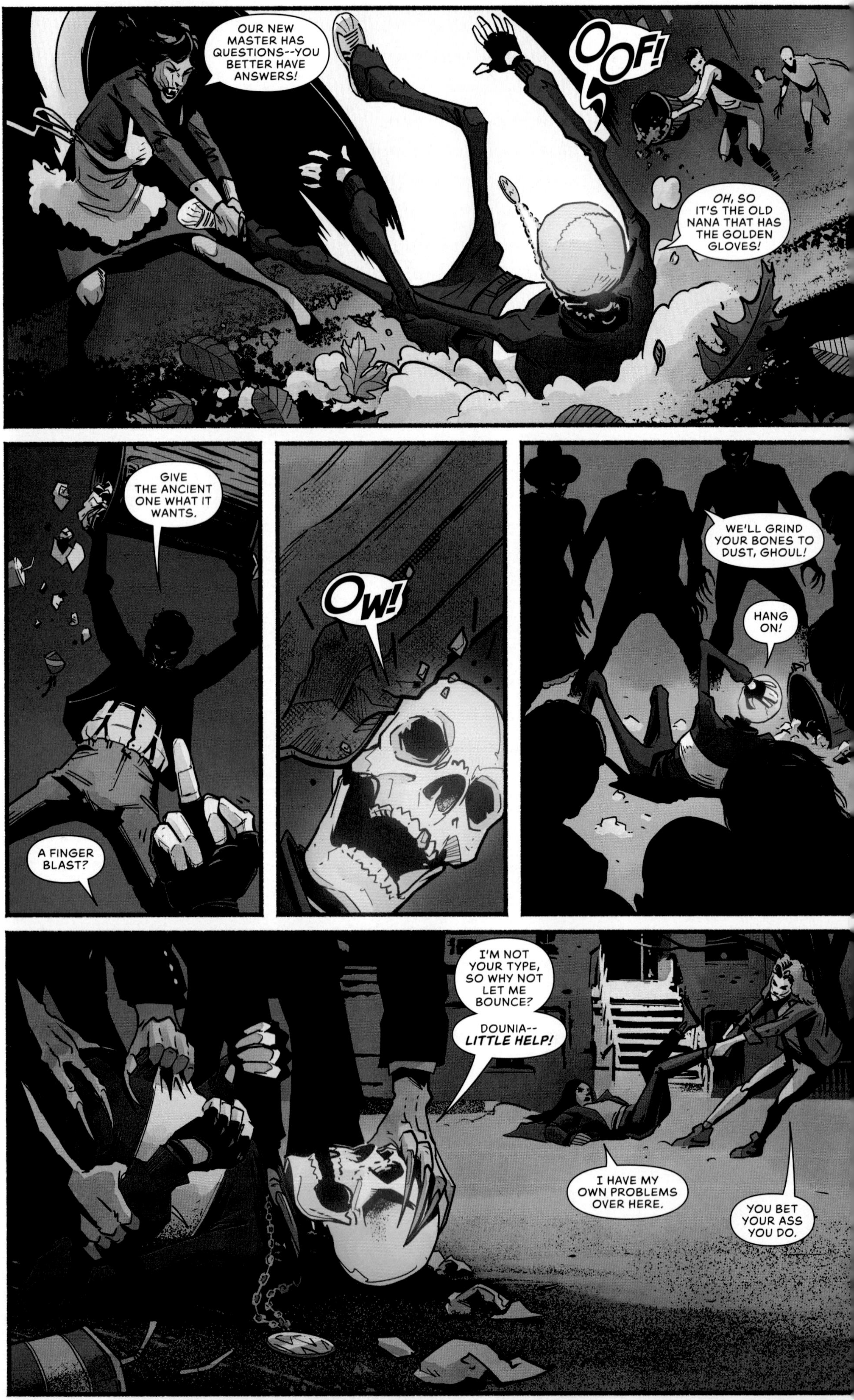
OUR NEW MASTER HAS QUESTIONS--YOU BETTER HAVE ANSWERS!
OOF!
OH, SO IT'S THE OLD NANA THAT HAS THE GOLDEN GLOVES!
GIVE THE ANCIENT ONE WHAT IT WANTS.
A FINGER BLAST?
OW!
WE'LL GRIND YOUR BONES TO DUST, GHOUL!
HANG ON!
I'M NOT YOUR TYPE, SO WHY NOT LET ME BOUNCE?
DOUNIA-- LITTLE HELP!
I HAVE MY OWN PROBLEMS OVER HERE.
YOU BET YOUR ASS YOU DO.

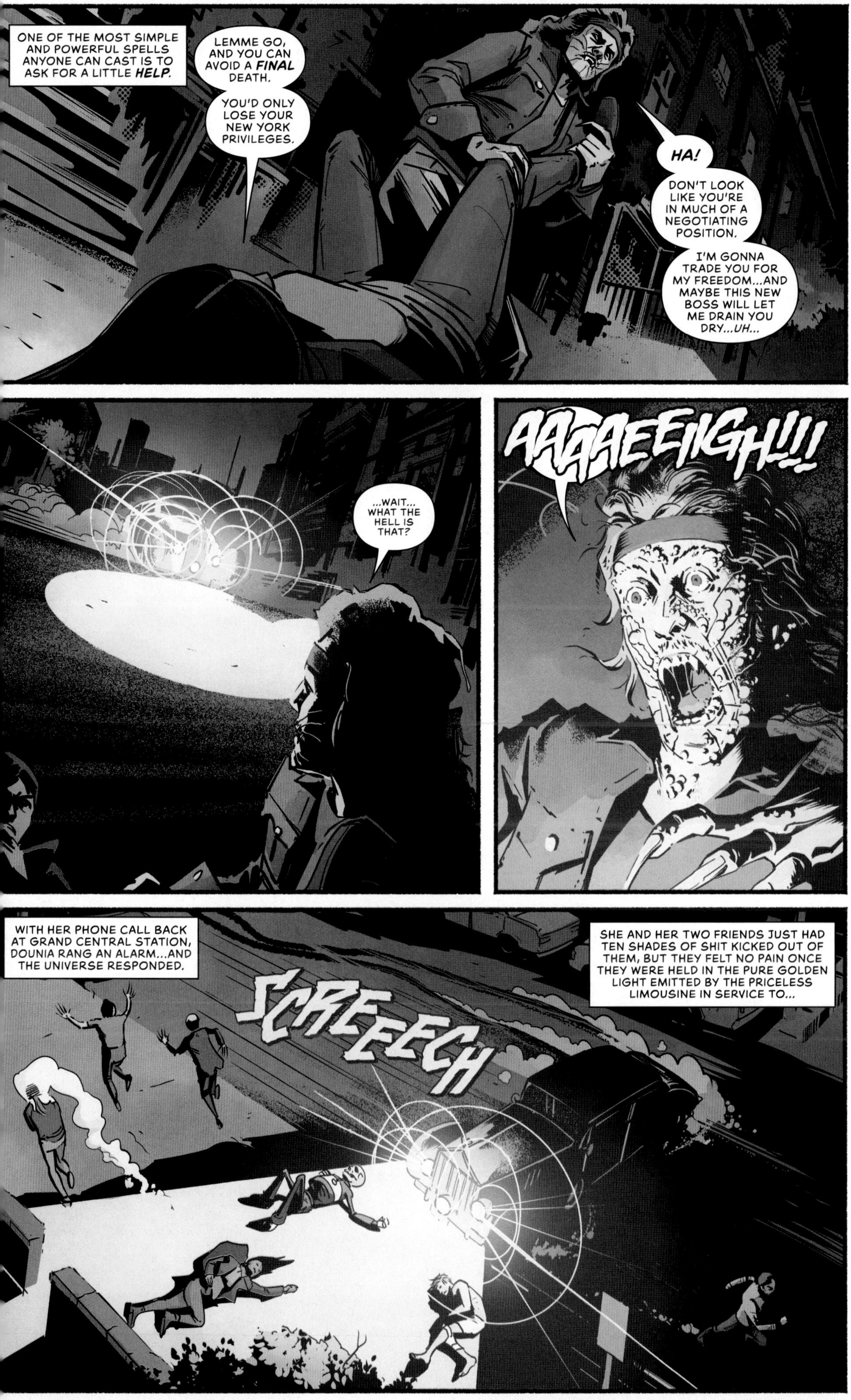
ONE OF THE MOST SIMPLE AND POWERFUL SPELLS ANYONE CAN CAST IS TO ASK FOR A LITTLE **HELP**.
LEMME GO, AND YOU CAN AVOID A ***FINAL*** DEATH.
YOU'D ONLY LOSE YOUR NEW YORK PRIVILEGES.
HA!
DON'T LOOK LIKE YOU'RE IN MUCH OF A NEGOTIATING POSITION.
I'M GONNA TRADE YOU FOR MY FREEDOM...AND MAYBE THIS NEW BOSS WILL LET ME DRAIN YOU DRY...*UH*...
...WAIT... WHAT THE HELL IS THAT?
AAAAEEIIGH!!!!
WITH HER PHONE CALL BACK AT GRAND CENTRAL STATION, DOUNIA RANG AN ALARM...AND THE UNIVERSE RESPONDED.
SCREEECH
SHE AND HER TWO FRIENDS JUST HAD TEN SHADES OF SHIT KICKED OUT OF THEM, BUT THEY FELT NO PAIN ONCE THEY WERE HELD IN THE PURE GOLDEN LIGHT EMITTED BY THE PRICELESS LIMOUSINE IN SERVICE TO...

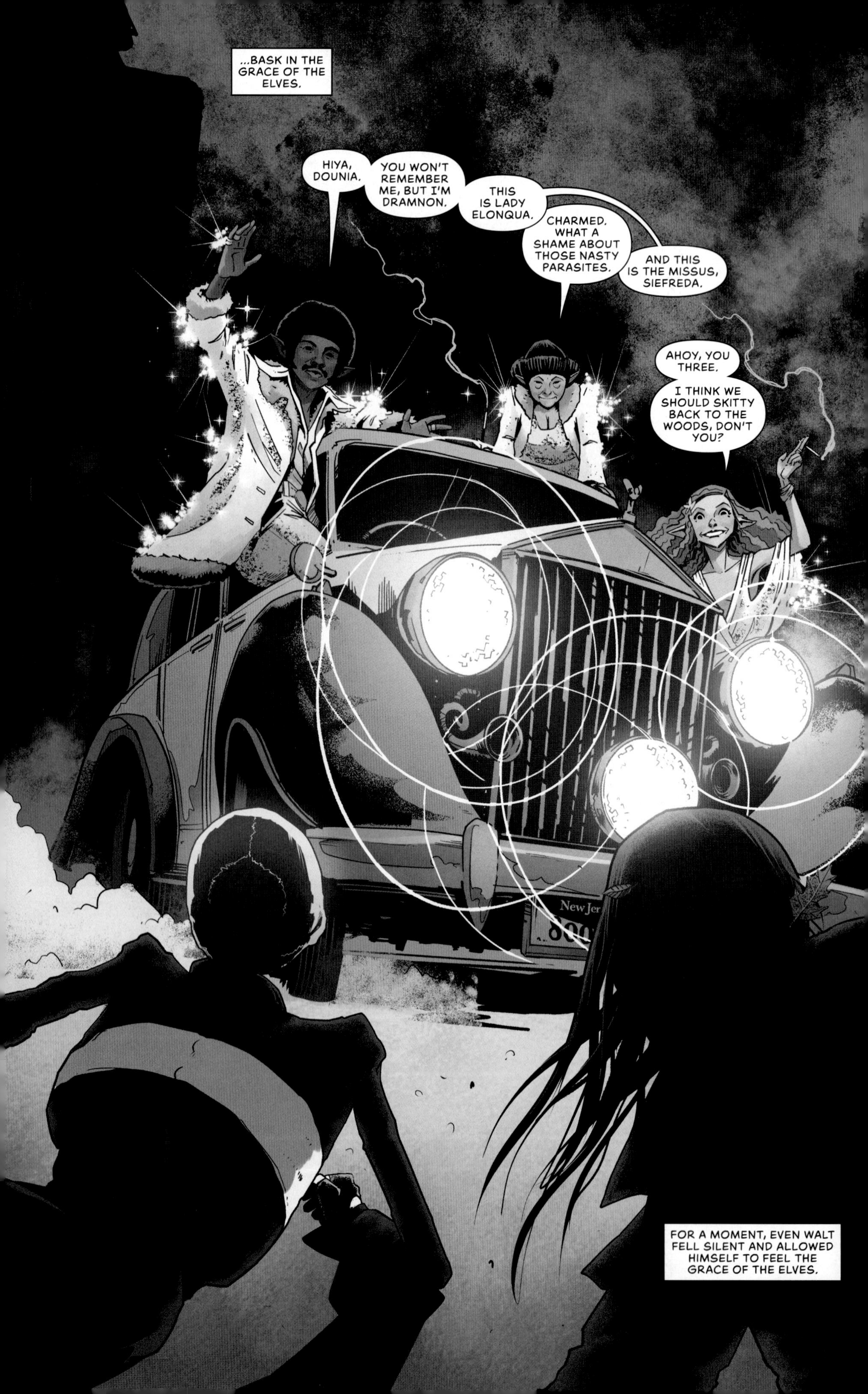
...BASK IN THE GRACE OF THE ELVES.
HIYA, DOUNIA.
YOU WON'T REMEMBER ME, BUT I'M DRAMNON.
THIS IS LADY ELONQUA.
CHARMED. WHAT A SHAME ABOUT THOSE NASTY PARASITES.
AND THIS IS THE MISSUS, SIEFREDA.
AHOY, YOU THREE.
I THINK WE SHOULD SKITTY BACK TO THE WOODS, DON'T YOU?
New Jer
FOR A MOMENT, EVEN WALT FELL SILENT AND ALLOWED HIMSELF TO FEEL THE GRACE OF THE ELVES.

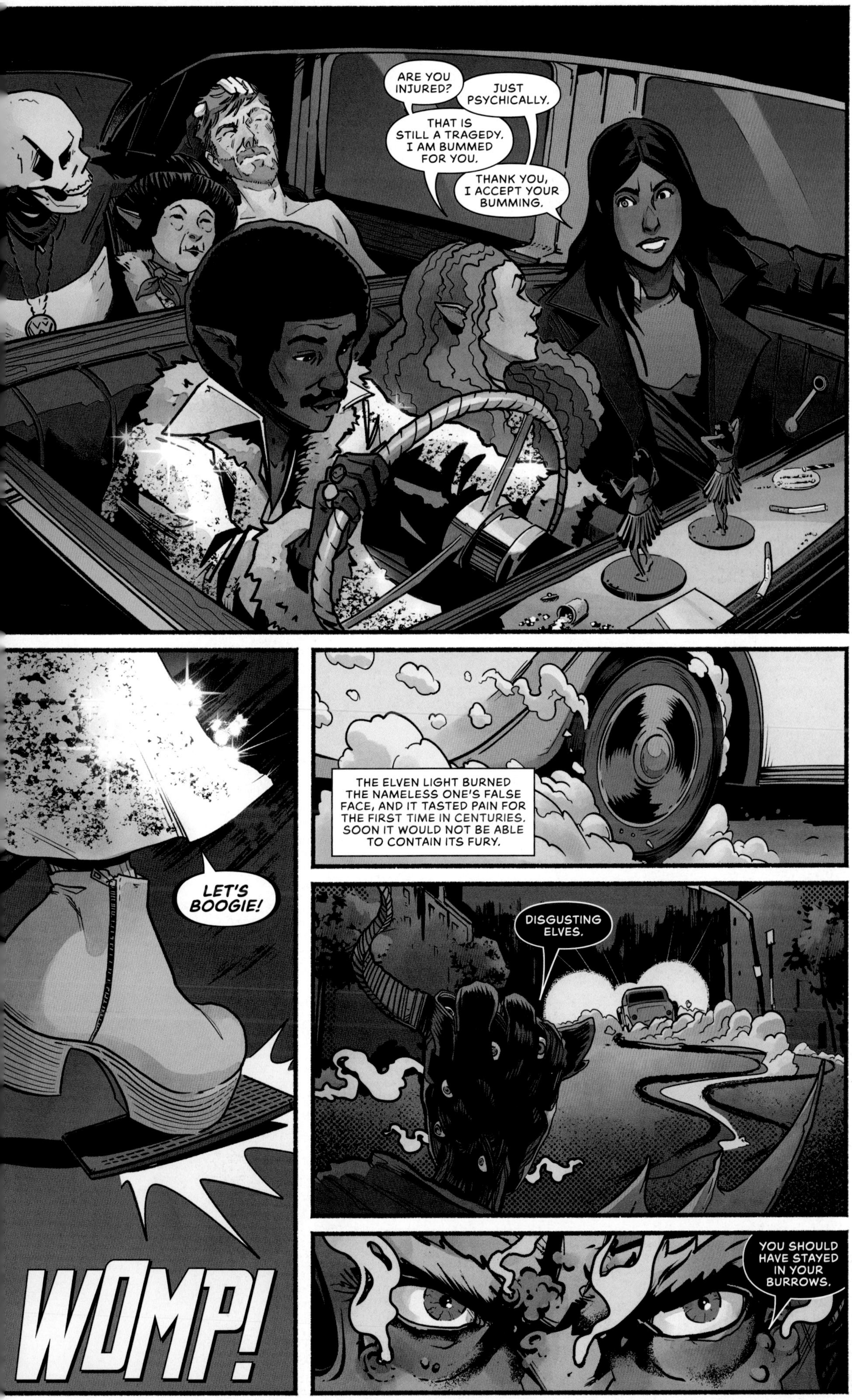
ARE YOU INJURED?
JUST PSYCHICALLY.
THAT IS STILL A TRAGEDY. I AM BUMMED FOR YOU.
THANK YOU, I ACCEPT YOUR BUMMING.
LET'S BOOGIE!
WOMP!
THE ELVEN LIGHT BURNED THE NAMELESS ONE'S FALSE FACE, AND IT TASTED PAIN FOR THE FIRST TIME IN CENTURIES. SOON IT WOULD NOT BE ABLE TO CONTAIN ITS FURY.
DISGUSTING ELVES.
YOU SHOULD HAVE STAYED IN YOUR BURROWS.

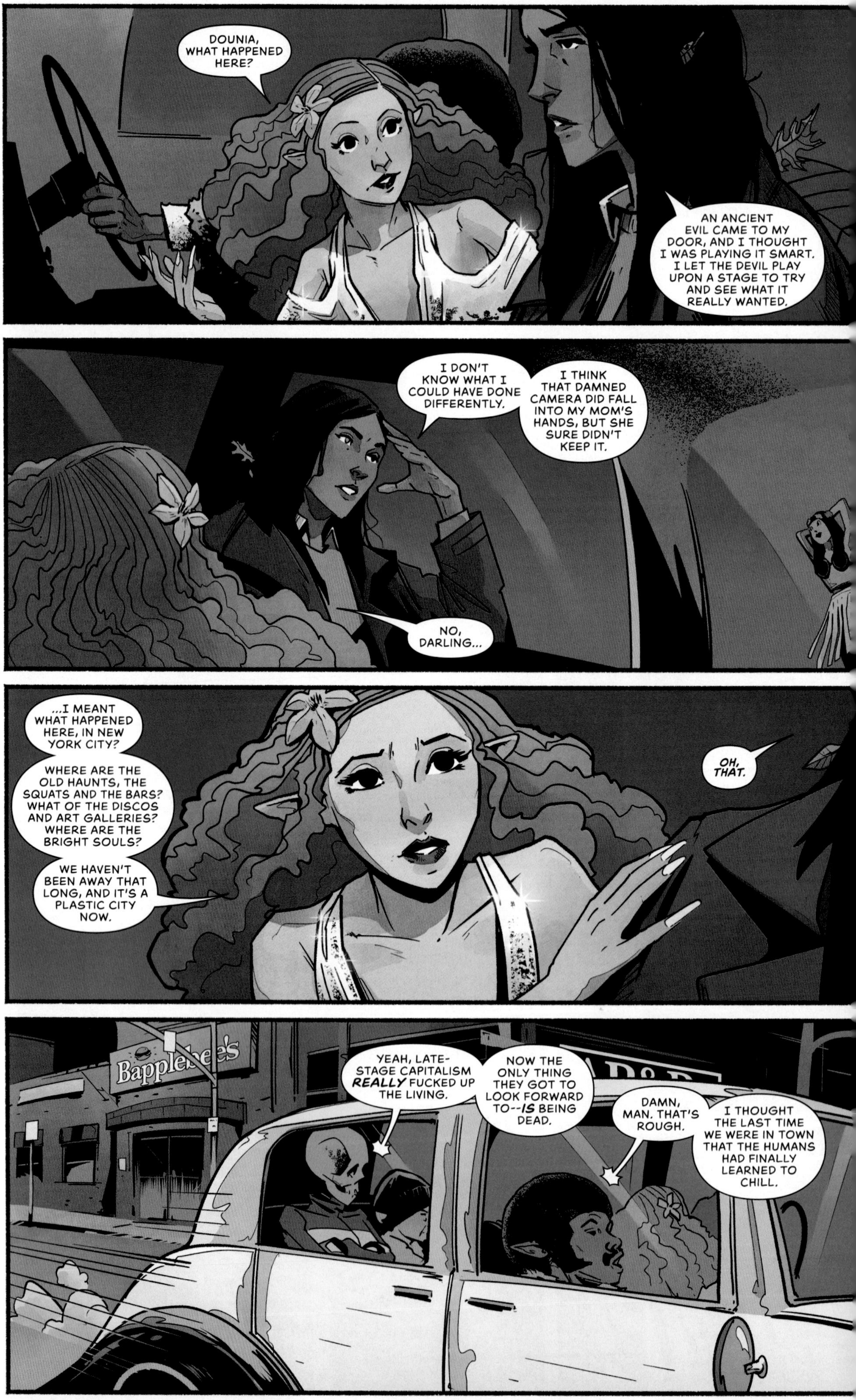
DOUNIA, WHAT HAPPENED HERE?
AN ANCIENT EVIL CAME TO MY DOOR, AND I THOUGHT I WAS PLAYING IT SMART. I LET THE DEVIL PLAY UPON A STAGE TO TRY AND SEE WHAT IT REALLY WANTED.
I DON'T KNOW WHAT I COULD HAVE DONE DIFFERENTLY.
I THINK THAT DAMNED CAMERA DID FALL INTO MY MOM'S HANDS, BUT SHE SURE DIDN'T KEEP IT.
NO, DARLING...
...I MEANT WHAT HAPPENED HERE, IN NEW YORK CITY?
WHERE ARE THE OLD HAUNTS, THE SQUATS AND THE BARS? WHAT OF THE DISCOS AND ART GALLERIES? WHERE ARE THE BRIGHT SOULS?
WE HAVEN'T BEEN AWAY THAT LONG, AND IT'S A PLASTIC CITY NOW.
OH, THAT.
Bapplebee's
YEAH, LATE-STAGE CAPITALISM ***REALLY*** FUCKED UP THE LIVING.
NOW THE ONLY THING THEY GOT TO LOOK FORWARD TO--***IS*** BEING DEAD.
DAMN, MAN, THAT'S ROUGH.
I THOUGHT THE LAST TIME WE WERE IN TOWN THAT THE HUMANS HAD FINALLY LEARNED TO CHILL.

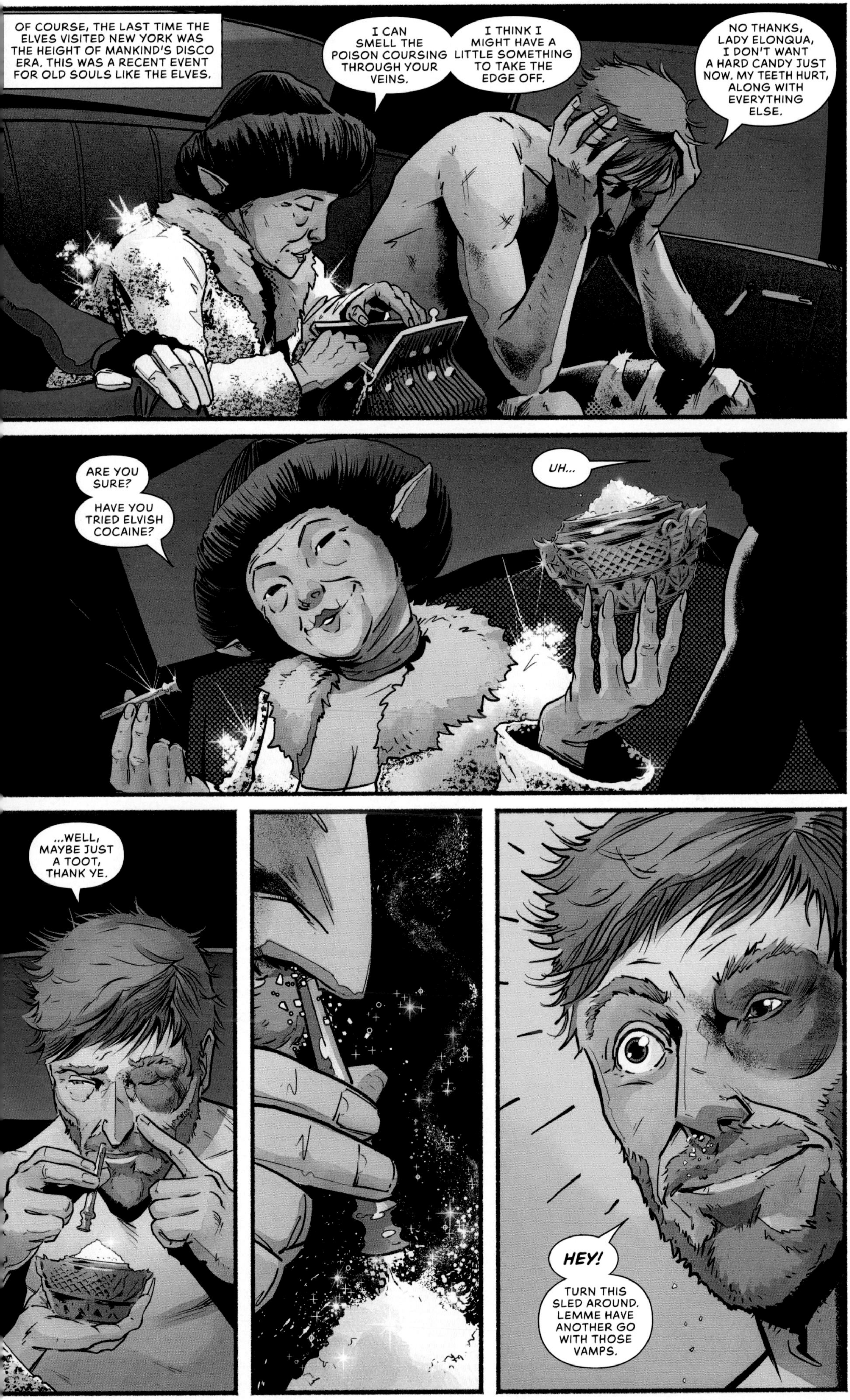
OF COURSE, THE LAST TIME THE ELVES VISITED NEW YORK WAS THE HEIGHT OF MANKIND'S DISCO ERA. THIS WAS A RECENT EVENT FOR OLD SOULS LIKE THE ELVES.
I CAN SMELL THE POISON COURSING THROUGH YOUR VEINS.
I THINK I MIGHT HAVE A LITTLE SOMETHING TO TAKE THE EDGE OFF.
NO THANKS, LADY ELONQUA, I DON'T WANT A HARD CANDY JUST NOW. MY TEETH HURT, ALONG WITH EVERYTHING ELSE.
ARE YOU SURE?
HAVE YOU TRIED ELVISH COCAINE?
UH...
...WELL, MAYBE JUST A TOOT, THANK YE.
HEY!
TURN THIS SLED AROUND. LEMME HAVE ANOTHER GO WITH THOSE VAMPS.

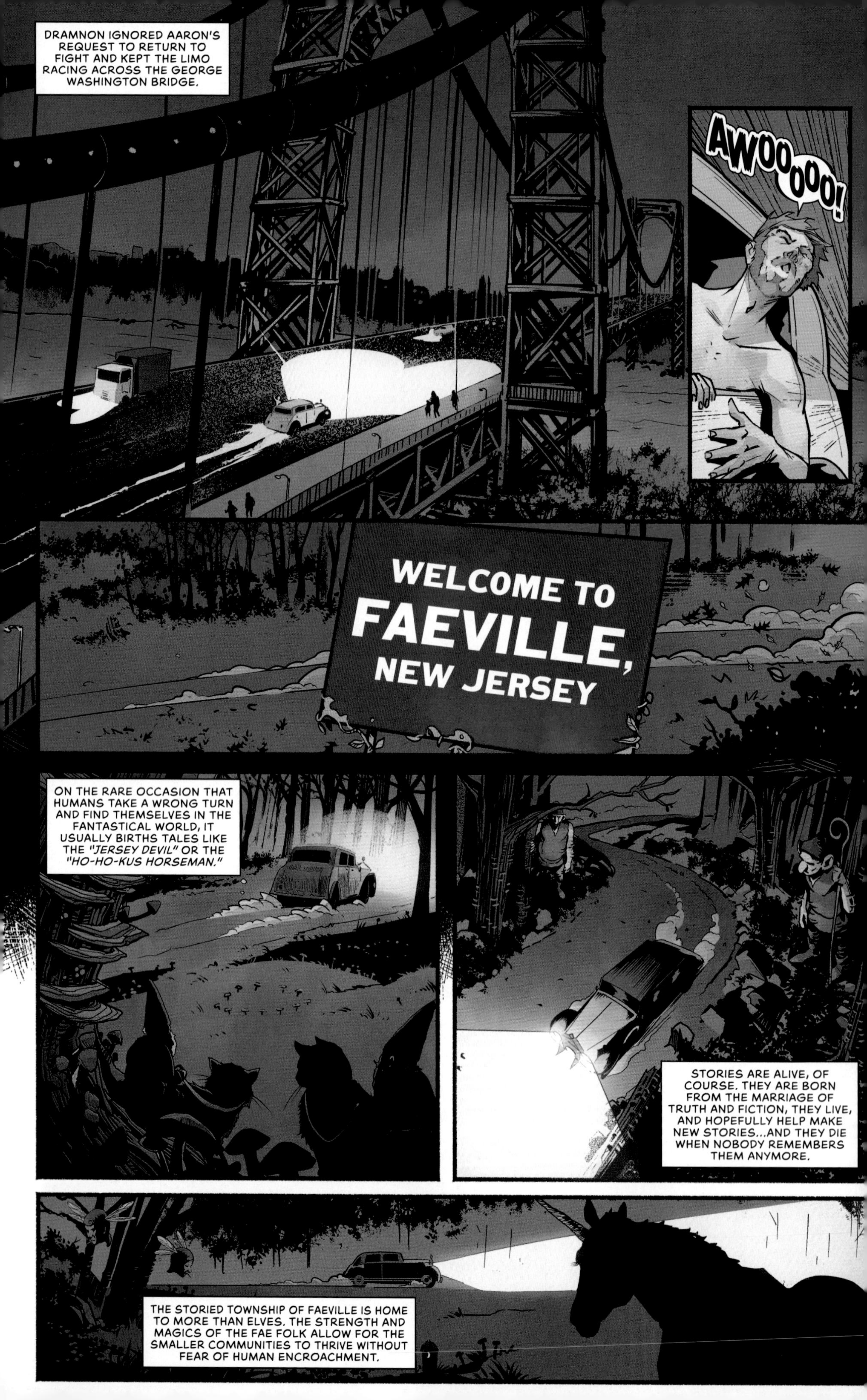
DRAMNON IGNORED AARON'S REQUEST TO RETURN TO FIGHT AND KEPT THE LIMO RACING ACROSS THE GEORGE WASHINGTON BRIDGE.
AWOOOOO!
WELCOME TO FAEVILLE, NEW JERSEY
ON THE RARE OCCASION THAT HUMANS TAKE A WRONG TURN AND FIND THEMSELVES IN THE FANTASTICAL WORLD, IT USUALLY BIRTHS TALES LIKE THE "JERSEY DEVIL" OR THE "HO-HO-KUS HORSEMAN."
STORIES ARE ALIVE, OF COURSE. THEY ARE BORN FROM THE MARRIAGE OF TRUTH AND FICTION, THEY LIVE, AND HOPEFULLY HELP MAKE NEW STORIES...AND THEY DIE WHEN NOBODY REMEMBERS THEM ANYMORE.
THE STORIED TOWNSHIP OF FAEVILLE IS HOME TO MORE THAN ELVES. THE STRENGTH AND MAGICS OF THE FAE FOLK ALLOW FOR THE SMALLER COMMUNITIES TO THRIVE WITHOUT FEAR OF HUMAN ENCROACHMENT.

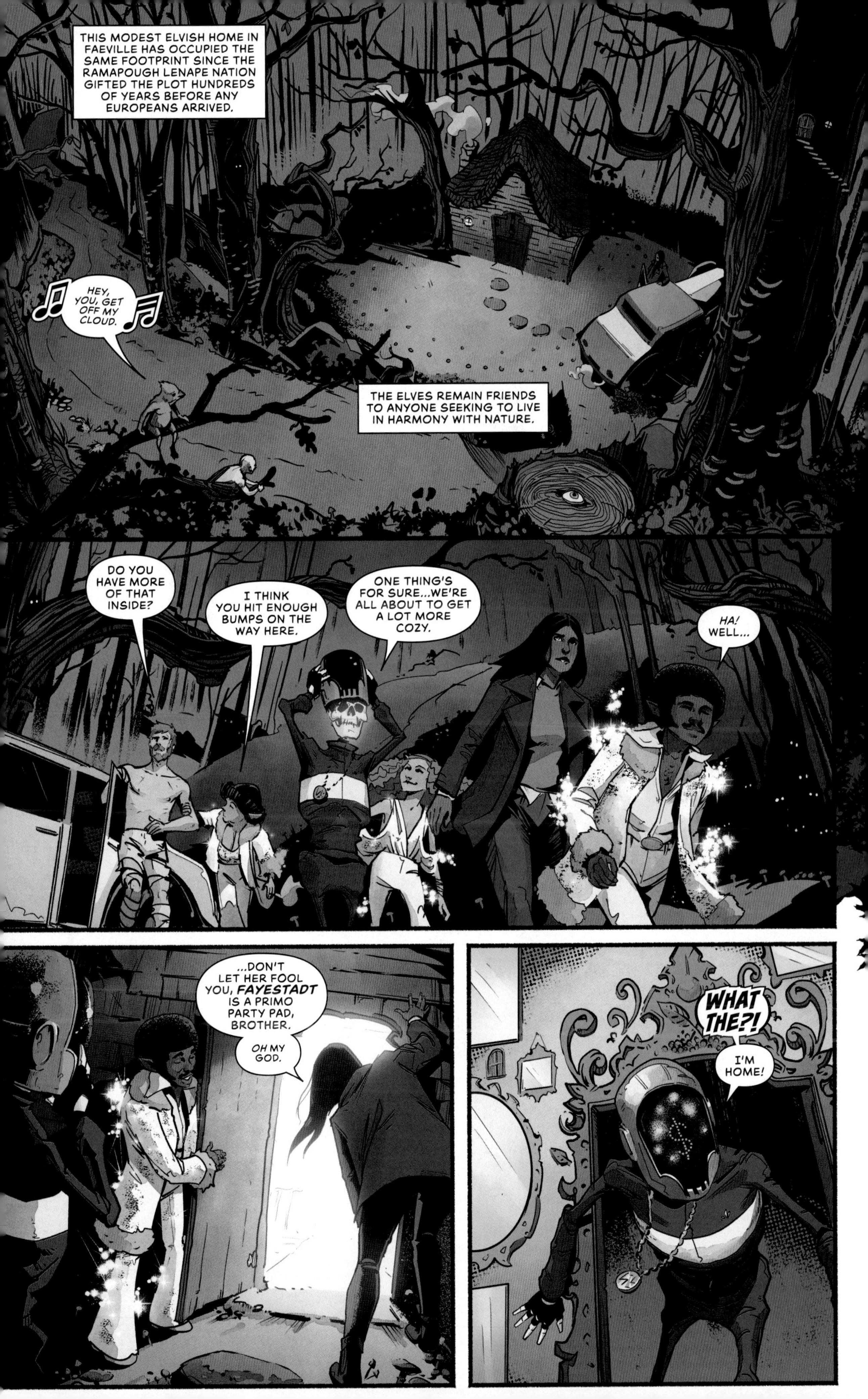
THIS MODEST ELVISH HOME IN FAEVILLE HAS OCCUPIED THE SAME FOOTPRINT SINCE THE RAMAPOUGH LENAPE NATION GIFTED THE PLOT HUNDREDS OF YEARS BEFORE ANY EUROPEANS ARRIVED.
HEY, YOU, GET OFF MY CLOUD.
THE ELVES REMAIN FRIENDS TO ANYONE SEEKING TO LIVE IN HARMONY WITH NATURE.
DO YOU HAVE MORE OF THAT INSIDE?
I THINK YOU HIT ENOUGH BUMPS ON THE WAY HERE.
ONE THING'S FOR SURE...WE'RE ALL ABOUT TO GET A LOT MORE COZY.
HA! WELL...
...DON'T LET HER FOOL YOU, FAYESTADT IS A PRIMO PARTY PAD, BROTHER.
OH MY GOD.
WHAT THE?!
I'M HOME!

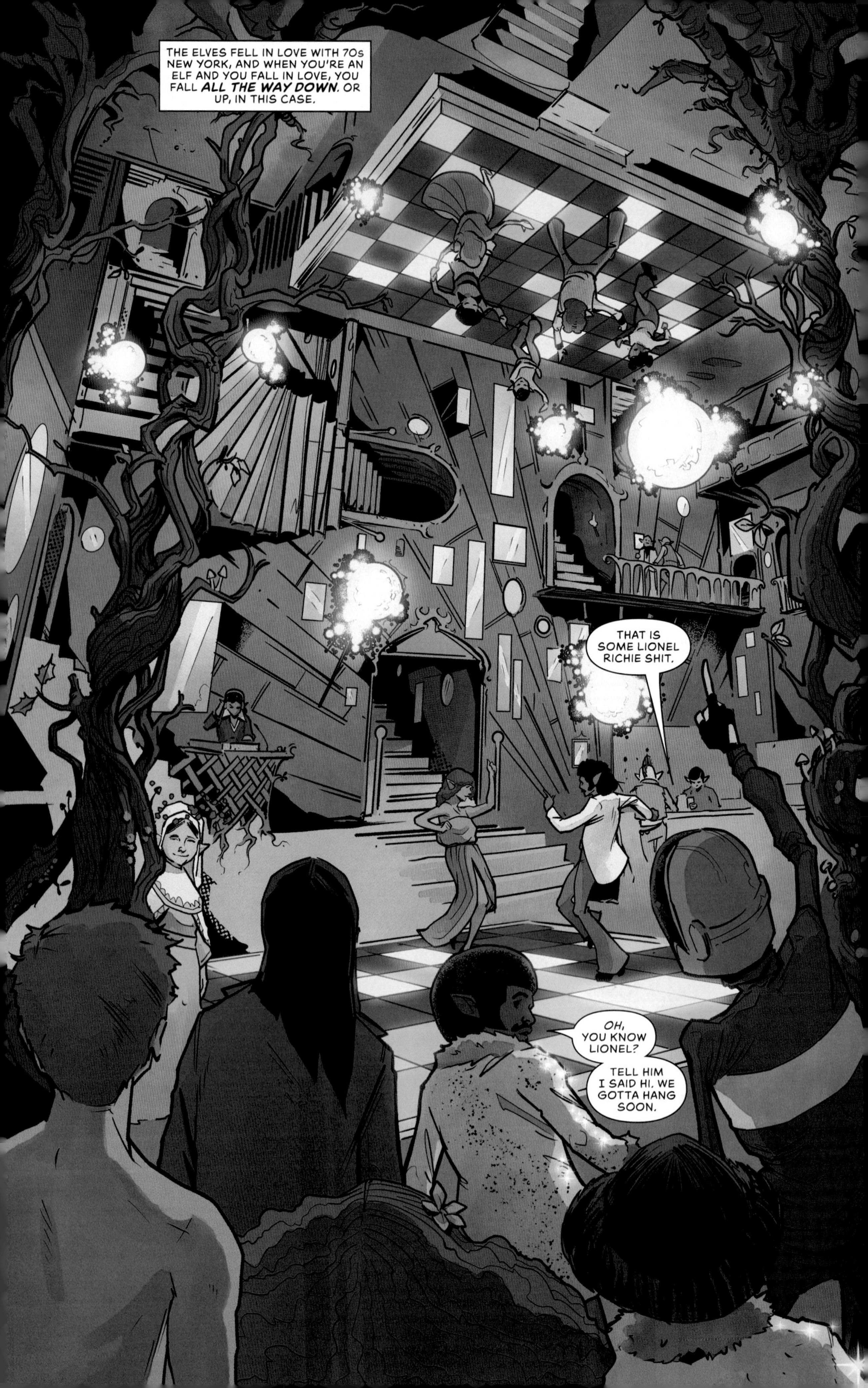
THE ELVES FELL IN LOVE WITH 70s NEW YORK, AND WHEN YOU'RE AN ELF AND YOU FALL IN LOVE, YOU FALL ALL THE WAY DOWN. OR UP, IN THIS CASE.
THAT IS SOME LIONEL RICHIE SHIT.
OH, YOU KNOW LIONEL?
TELL HIM I SAID HI. WE GOTTA HANG SOON.

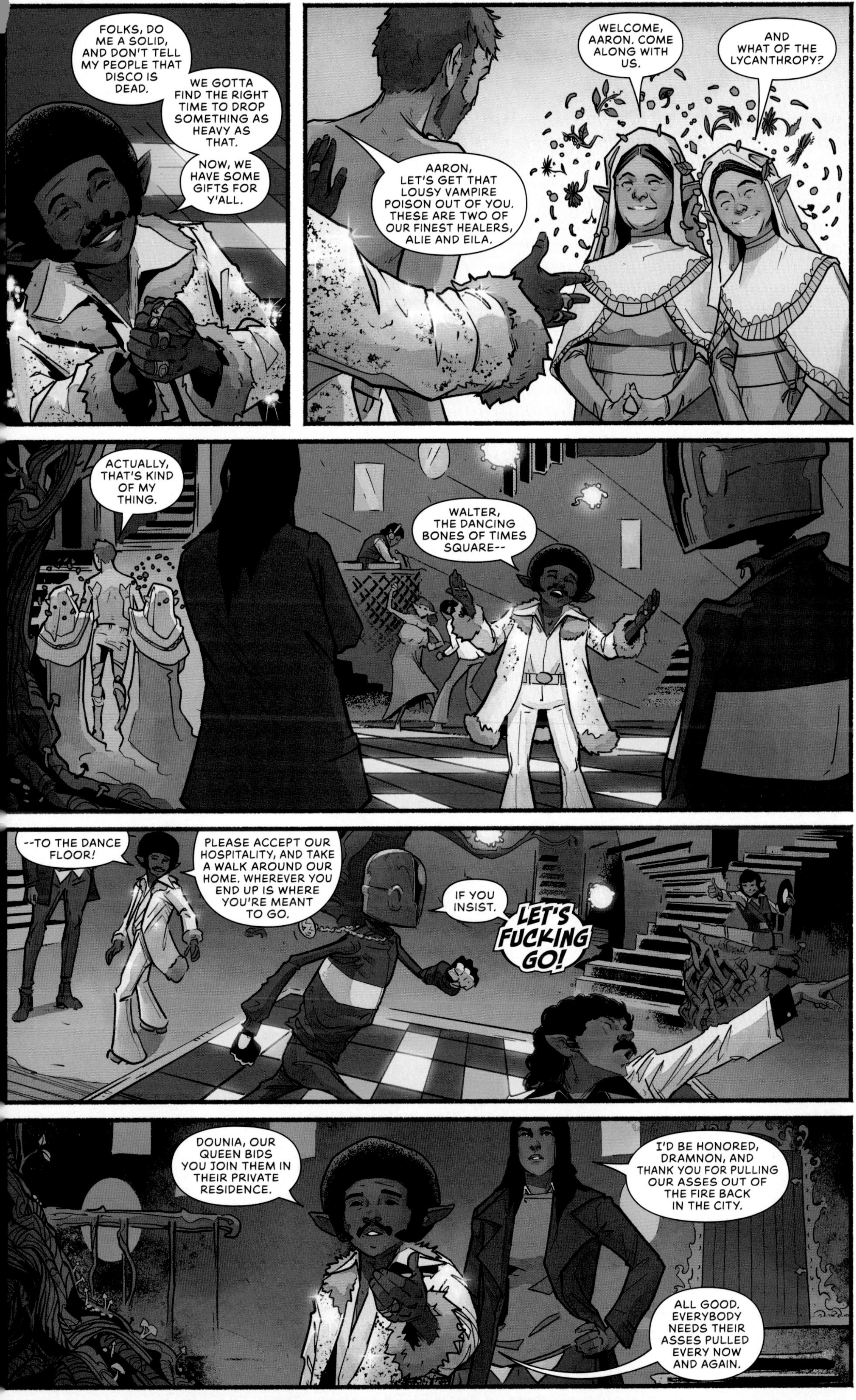
FOLKS, DO ME A SOLID, AND DON'T TELL MY PEOPLE THAT DISCO IS DEAD.
WE GOTTA FIND THE RIGHT TIME TO DROP SOMETHING AS HEAVY AS THAT.
NOW, WE HAVE SOME GIFTS FOR Y'ALL.
AARON, LET'S GET THAT LOUSY VAMPIRE POISON OUT OF YOU. THESE ARE TWO OF OUR FINEST HEALERS, ALIE AND EILA.
WELCOME, AARON. COME ALONG WITH US.
AND WHAT OF THE LYCANTHROPY?
ACTUALLY, THAT'S KIND OF MY THING.
WALTER, THE DANCING BONES OF TIMES SQUARE--
--TO THE DANCE FLOOR!
PLEASE ACCEPT OUR HOSPITALITY, AND TAKE A WALK AROUND OUR HOME. WHEREVER YOU END UP IS WHERE YOU'RE MEANT TO GO.
IF YOU INSIST.
LET'S FUCKING GO!
DOUNIA, OUR QUEEN BIDS YOU JOIN THEM IN THEIR PRIVATE RESIDENCE.
I'D BE HONORED, DRAMNON, AND THANK YOU FOR PULLING OUR ASSES OUT OF THE FIRE BACK IN THE CITY.
ALL GOOD. EVERYBODY NEEDS THEIR ASSES PULLED EVERY NOW AND AGAIN.

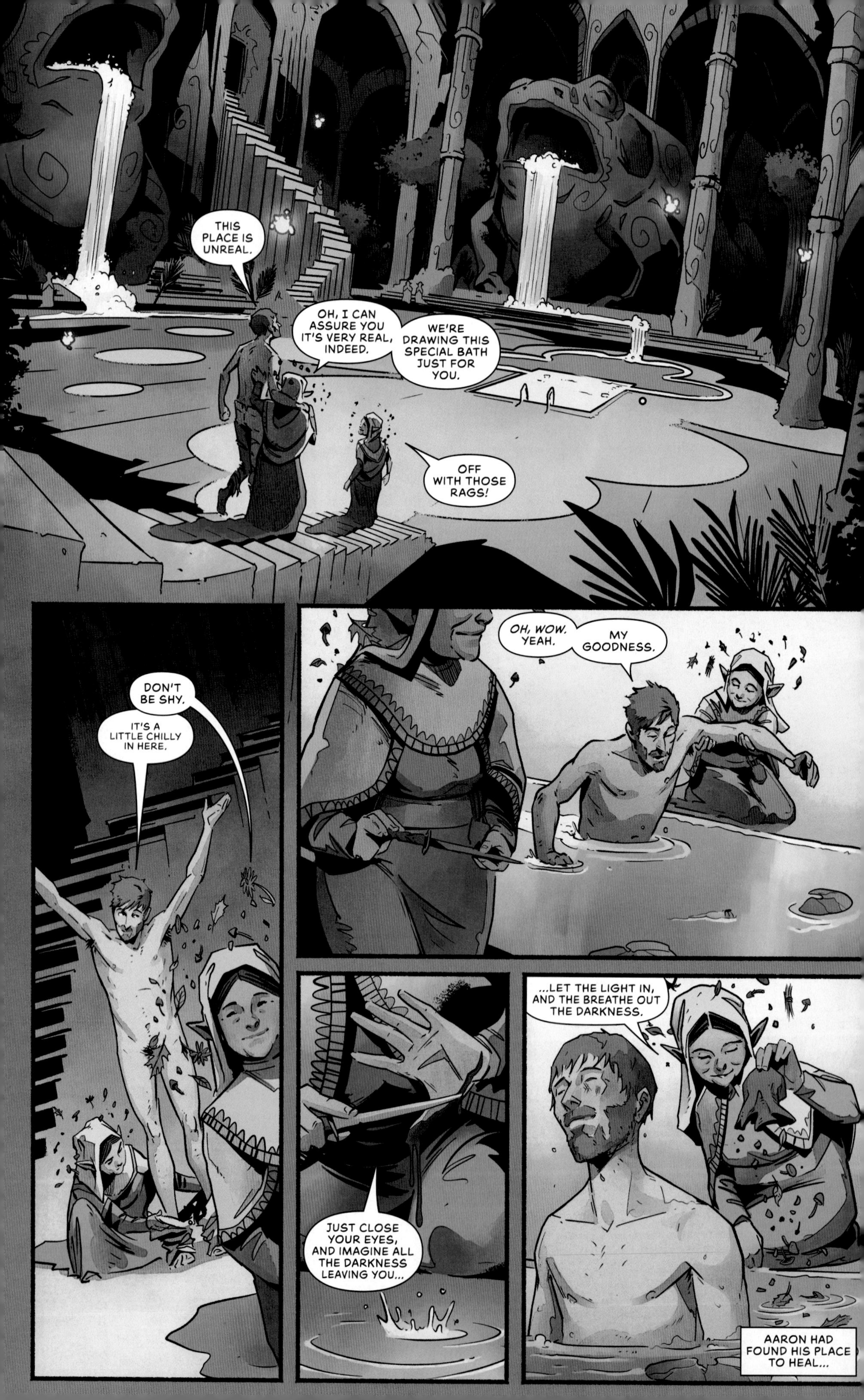
THIS PLACE IS UNREAL.
OH, I CAN ASSURE YOU IT'S VERY REAL, INDEED.
WE'RE DRAWING THIS SPECIAL BATH JUST FOR YOU.
OFF WITH THOSE RAGS!
DON'T BE SHY.
IT'S A LITTLE CHILLY IN HERE.
OH, WOW. YEAH.
MY GOODNESS.
JUST CLOSE YOUR EYES, AND IMAGINE ALL THE DARKNESS LEAVING YOU...
...LET THE LIGHT IN, AND THE BREATHE OUT THE DARKNESS.
AARON HAD FOUND HIS PLACE TO HEAL...

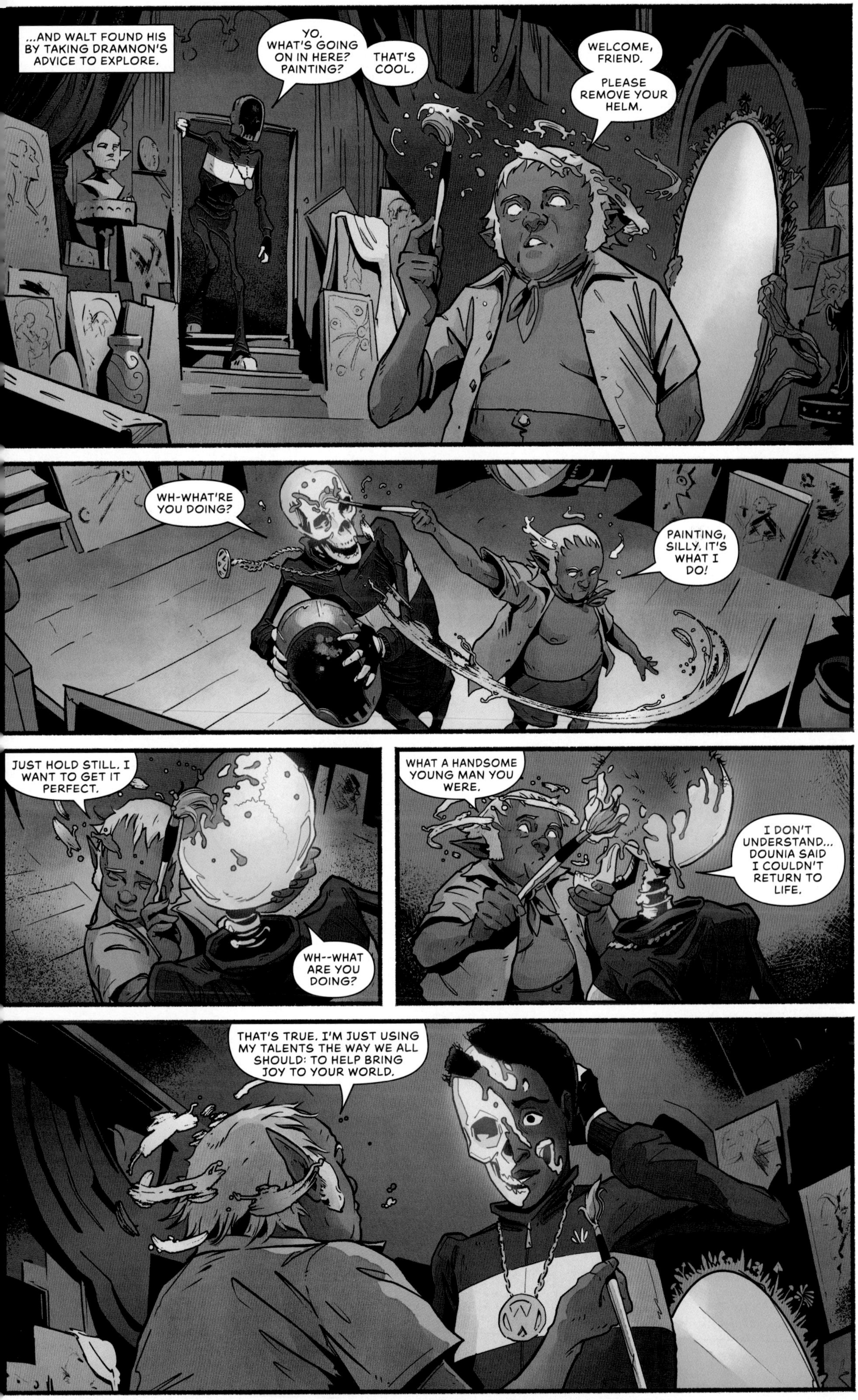
...AND WALT FOUND HIS BY TAKING DRAMNON'S ADVICE TO EXPLORE.
YO. WHAT'S GOING ON IN HERE? PAINTING?
THAT'S COOL.
WELCOME, FRIEND.
PLEASE REMOVE YOUR HELM.
WH-WHAT'RE YOU DOING?
PAINTING, SILLY. IT'S WHAT I DO!
JUST HOLD STILL. I WANT TO GET IT PERFECT.
WH--WHAT ARE YOU DOING?
WHAT A HANDSOME YOUNG MAN YOU WERE.
I DON'T UNDERSTAND... DOUNIA SAID I COULDN'T RETURN TO LIFE.
THAT'S TRUE. I'M JUST USING MY TALENTS THE WAY WE ALL SHOULD: TO HELP BRING JOY TO YOUR WORLD.

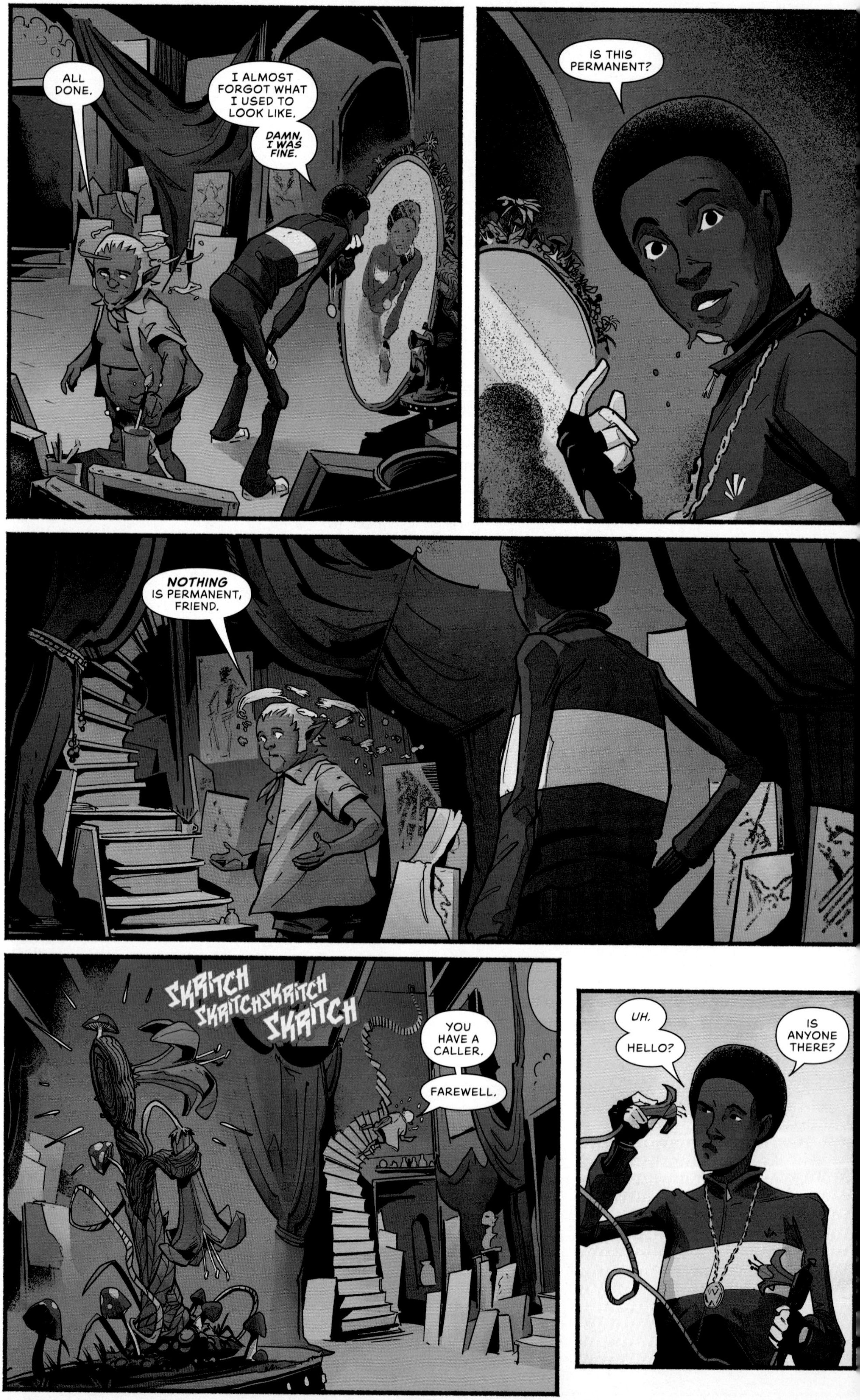
ALL DONE.
I ALMOST FORGOT WHAT I USED TO LOOK LIKE.
DAMN, I WAS FINE.
IS THIS PERMANENT?
NOTHING IS PERMANENT, FRIEND.
SKRITCH SKRITCHSKRITCH SKRITCH
YOU HAVE A CALLER.
FAREWELL.
UH.
HELLO?
IS ANYONE THERE?

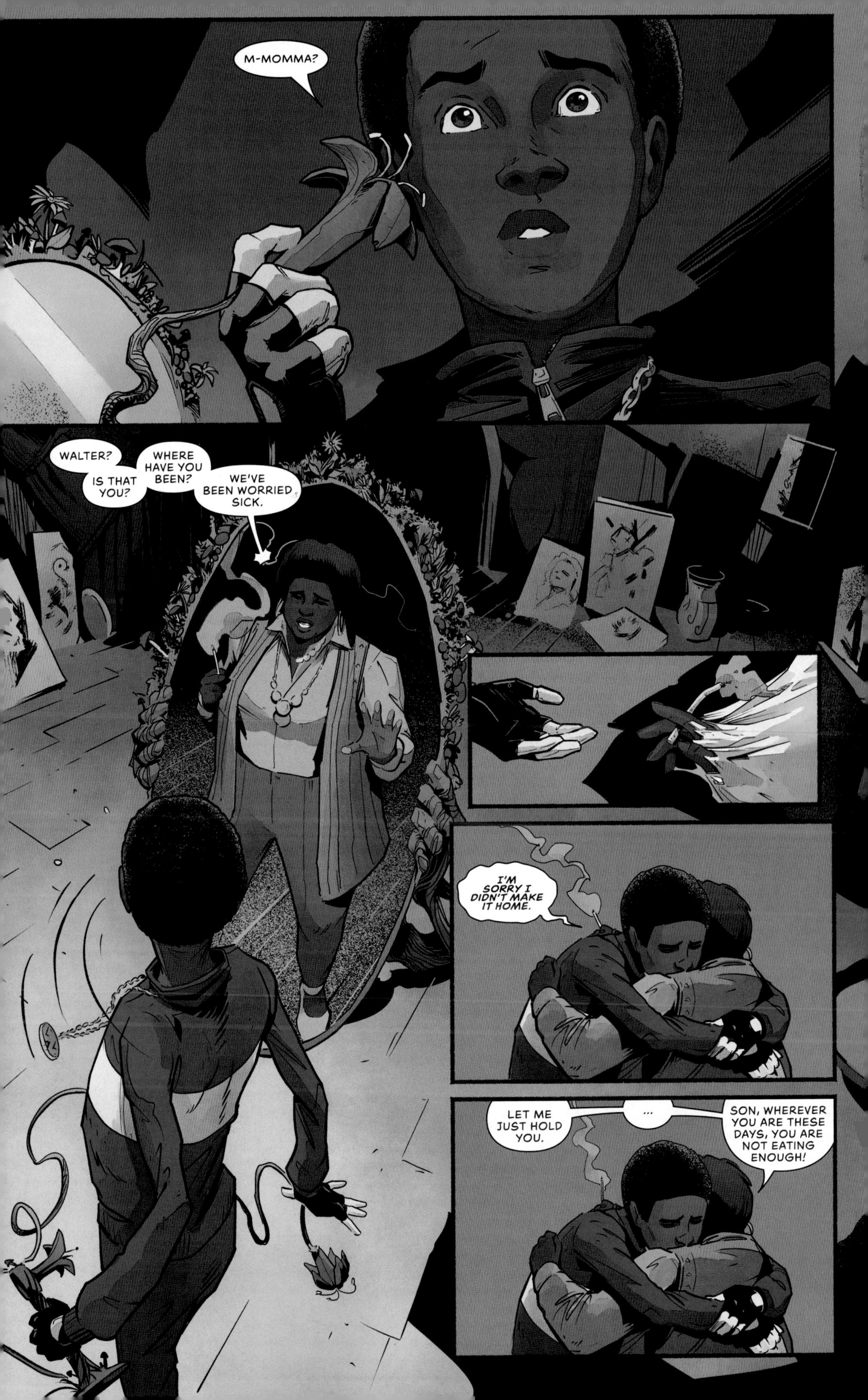
M-MOMMA?
WALTER?
IS THAT YOU?
WHERE HAVE YOU BEEN?
WE'VE BEEN WORRIED SICK.
I'M SORRY I DIDN'T MAKE IT HOME.
LET ME JUST HOLD YOU.
...
SON, WHEREVER YOU ARE THESE DAYS, YOU ARE NOT EATING ENOUGH!

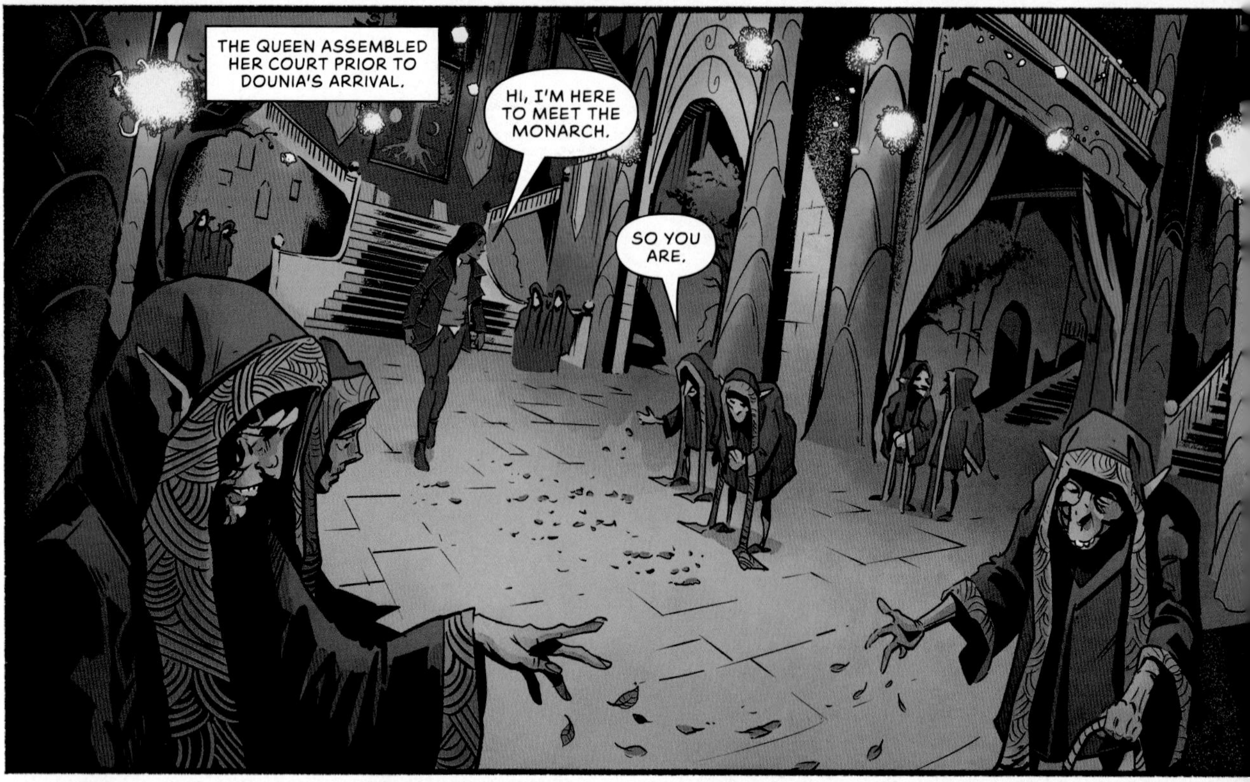
THE QUEEN ASSEMBLED HER COURT PRIOR TO DOUNIA'S ARRIVAL.
HI, I'M HERE TO MEET THE MONARCH.
SO YOU ARE.

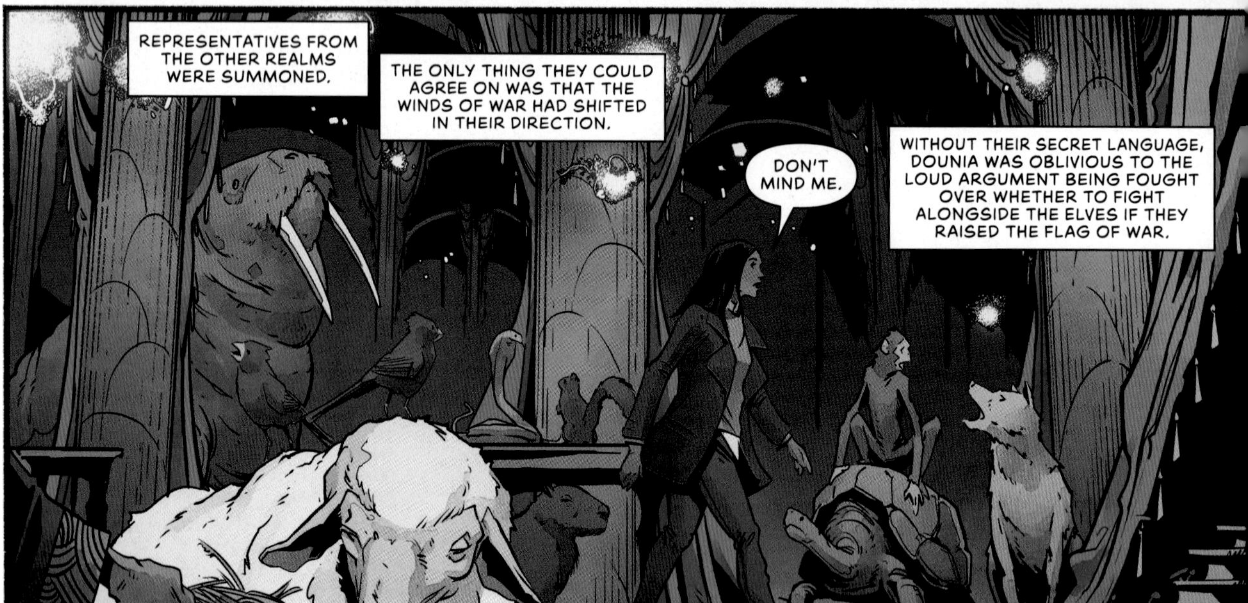
REPRESENTATIVES FROM THE OTHER REALMS WERE SUMMONED.
THE ONLY THING THEY COULD AGREE ON WAS THAT THE WINDS OF WAR HAD SHIFTED IN THEIR DIRECTION.
DON'T MIND ME.
WITHOUT THEIR SECRET LANGUAGE, DOUNIA WAS OBLIVIOUS TO THE LOUD ARGUMENT BEING FOUGHT OVER WHETHER TO FIGHT ALONGSIDE THE ELVES IF THEY RAISED THE FLAG OF WAR.

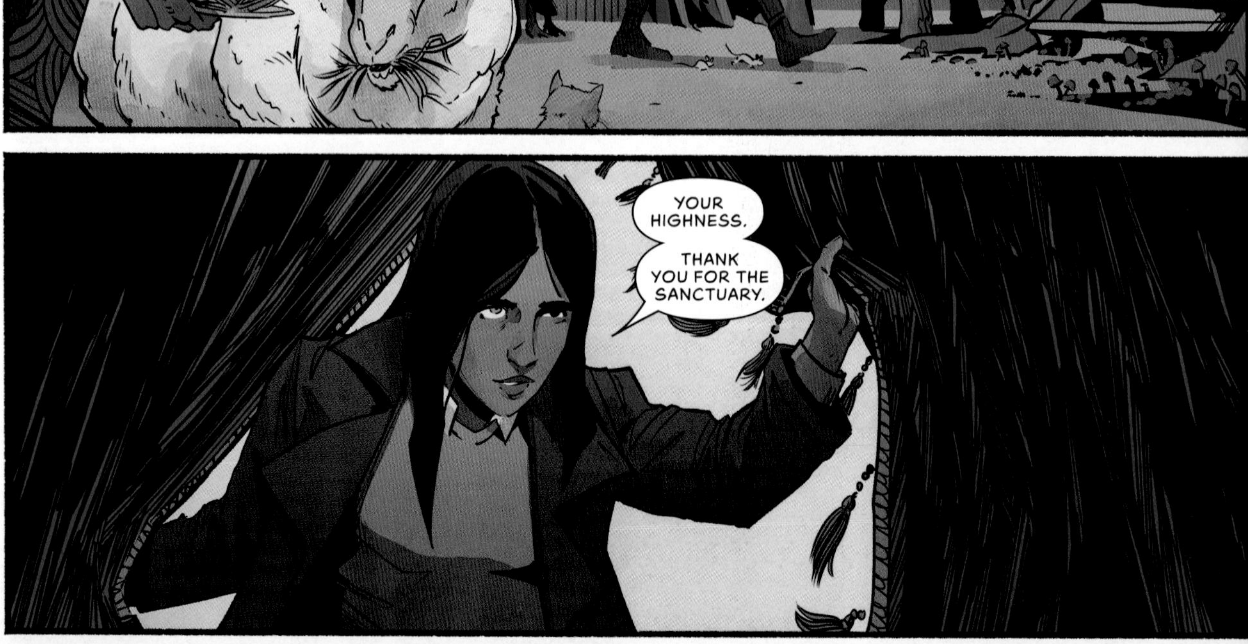
YOUR HIGHNESS.
THANK YOU FOR THE SANCTUARY.

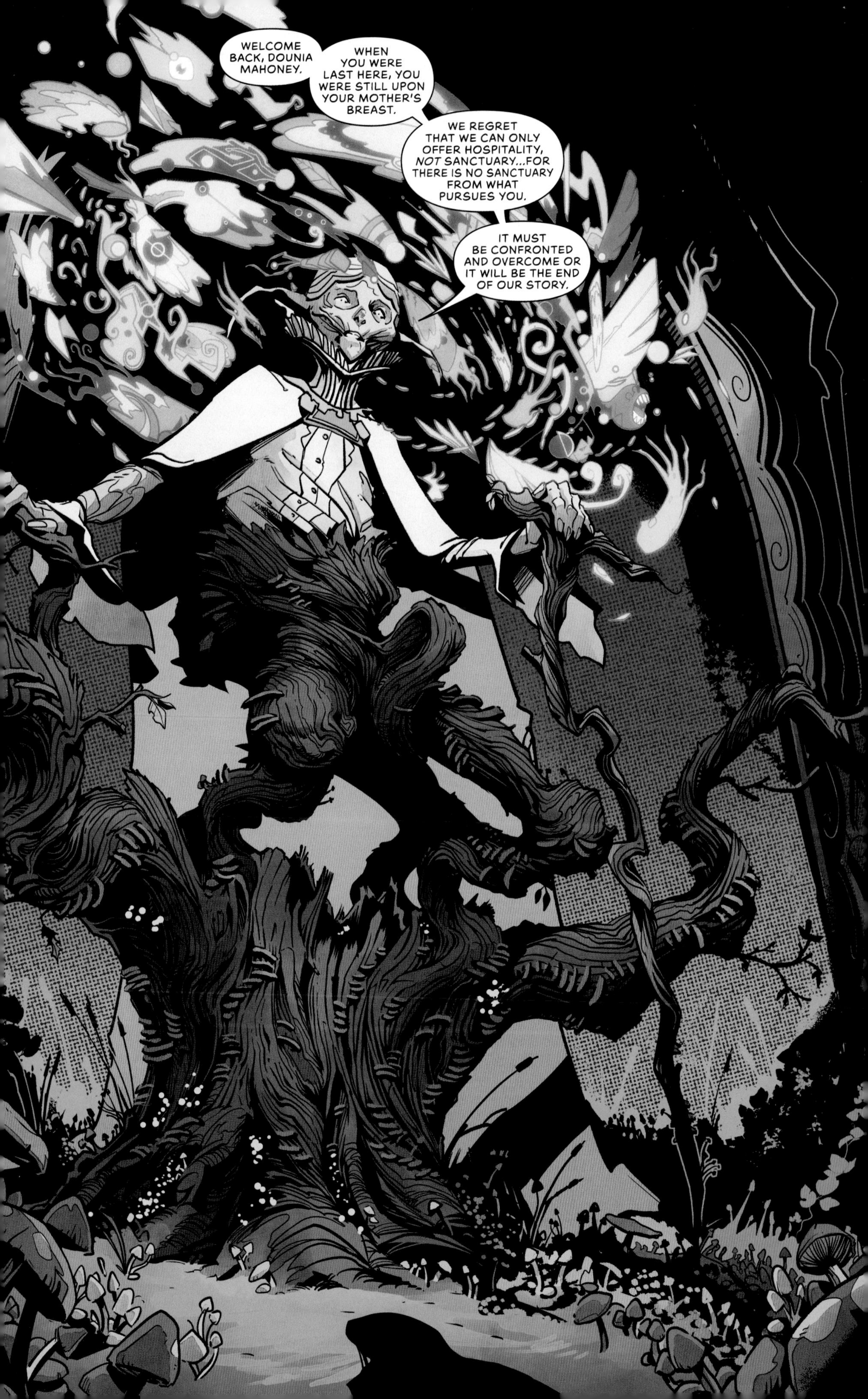
WELCOME BACK, DOUNIA MAHONEY.
WHEN YOU WERE LAST HERE, YOU WERE STILL UPON YOUR MOTHER'S BREAST.
WE REGRET THAT WE CAN ONLY OFFER HOSPITALITY, *NOT* SANCTUARY...FOR THERE IS NO SANCTUARY FROM WHAT PURSUES YOU.
IT MUST BE CONFRONTED AND OVERCOME OR IT WILL BE THE END OF OUR STORY.

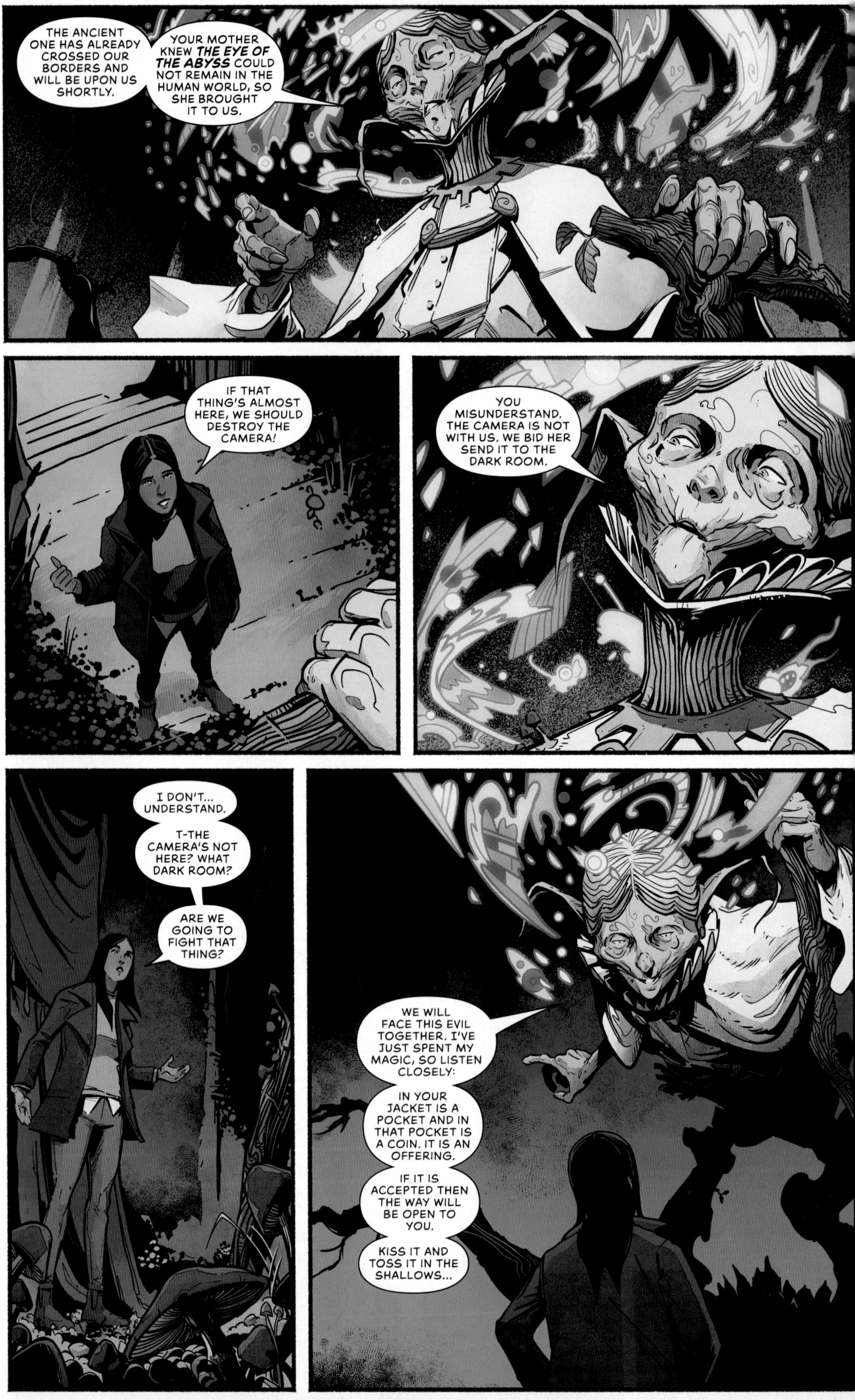
THE ANCIENT ONE HAS ALREADY CROSSED OUR BORDERS AND WILL BE UPON US SHORTLY.
YOUR MOTHER KNEW ***THE EYE OF THE ABYSS*** COULD NOT REMAIN IN THE HUMAN WORLD, SO SHE BROUGHT IT TO US.
IF THAT THING'S ALMOST HERE, WE SHOULD DESTROY THE CAMERA!
YOU MISUNDERSTAND. THE CAMERA IS NOT WITH US. WE BID HER SEND IT TO THE DARK ROOM.
I DON'T... UNDERSTAND.
T-THE CAMERA'S NOT HERE? WHAT DARK ROOM?
ARE WE GOING TO FIGHT THAT THING?
WE WILL FACE THIS EVIL TOGETHER. I'VE JUST SPENT MY MAGIC, SO LISTEN CLOSELY:
IN YOUR JACKET IS A POCKET AND IN THAT POCKET IS A COIN. IT IS AN OFFERING.
IF IT IS ACCEPTED THEN THE WAY WILL BE OPEN TO YOU.
KISS IT AND TOSS IT IN THE SHALLOWS...

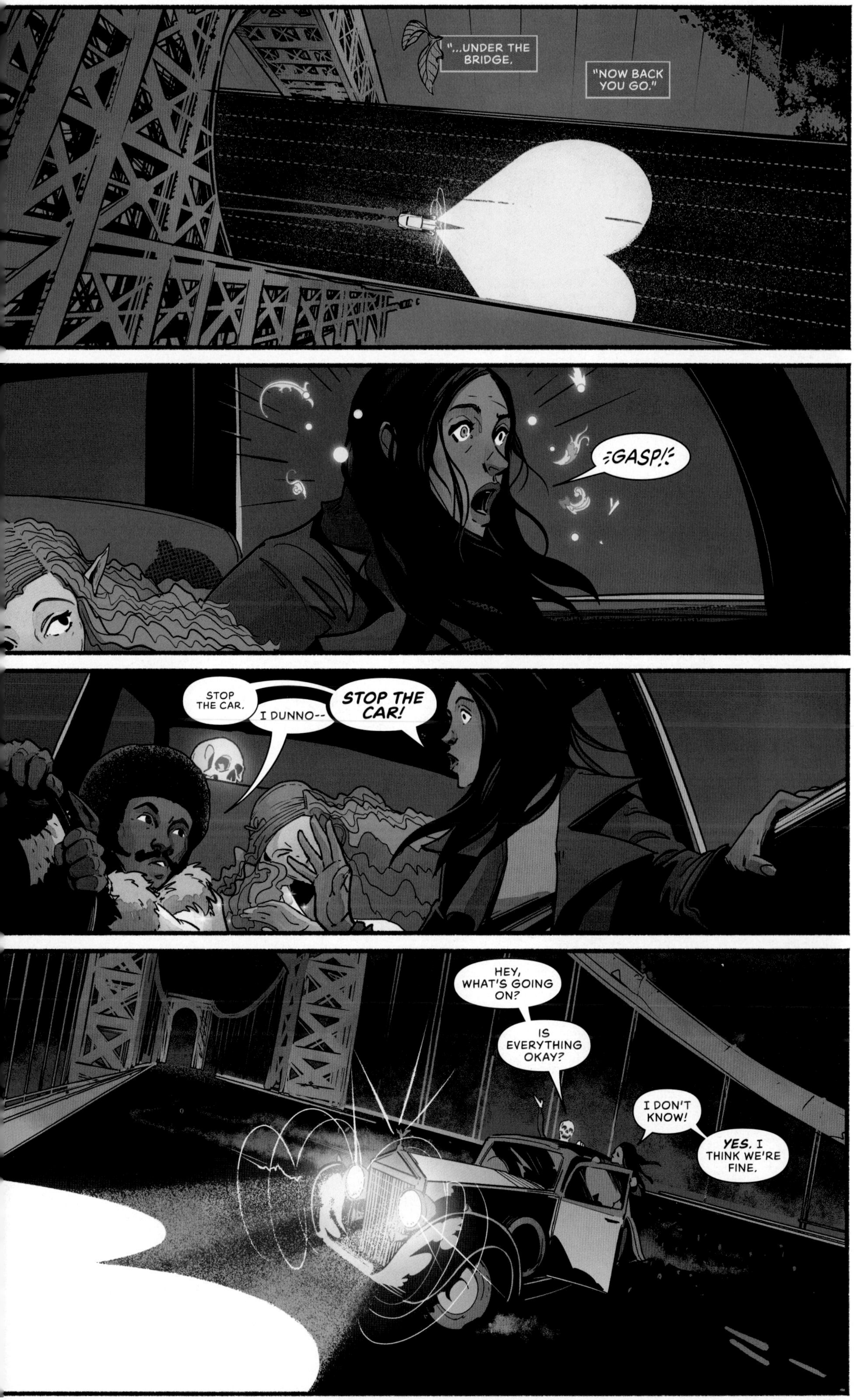
"...UNDER THE BRIDGE.
"NOW BACK YOU GO."
GASP!
STOP THE CAR.
I DUNNO--
STOP THE CAR!
HEY, WHAT'S GOING ON?
IS EVERYTHING OKAY?
I DON'T KNOW!
YES. I THINK WE'RE FINE.

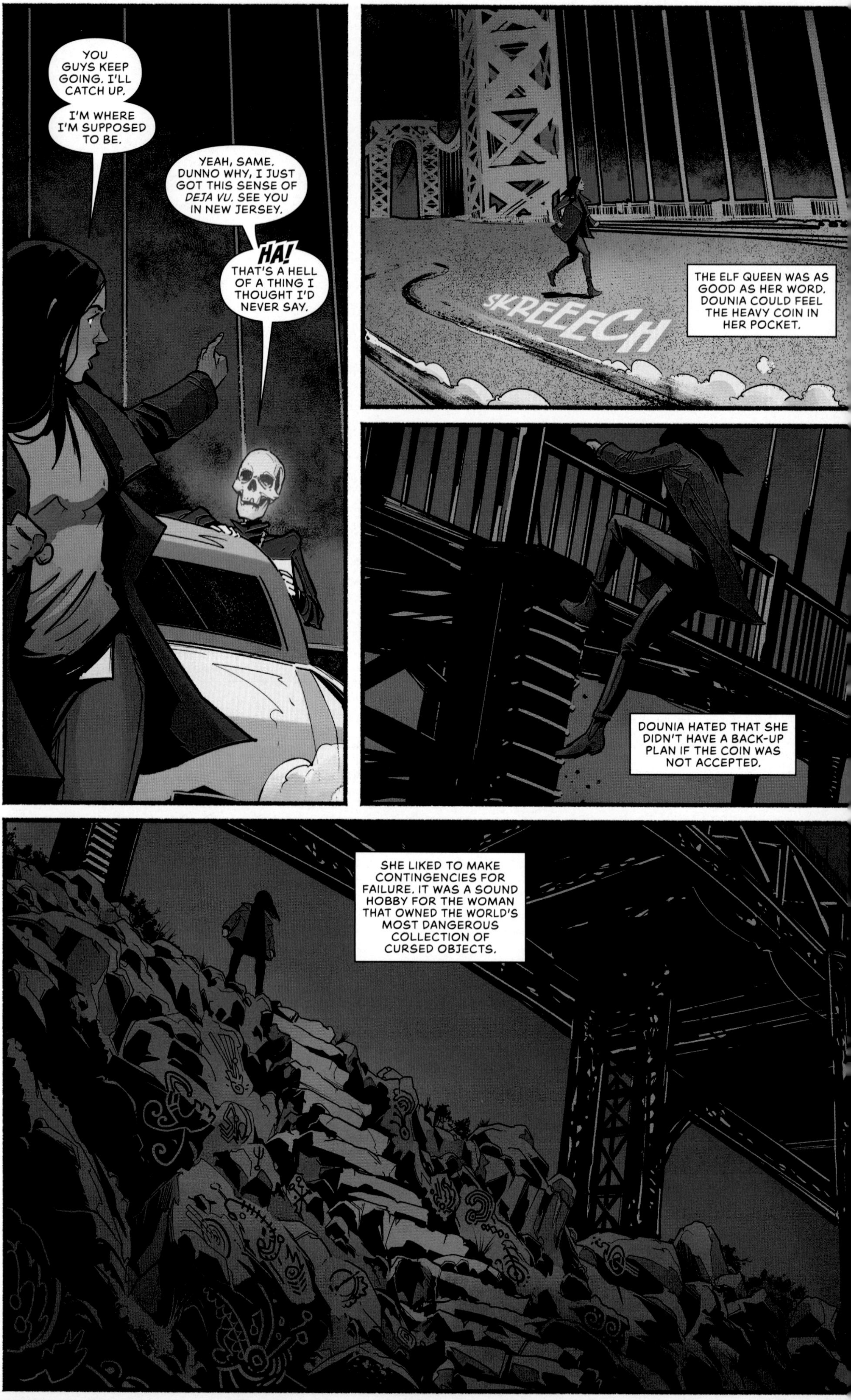
YOU GUYS KEEP GOING. I'LL CATCH UP.
I'M WHERE I'M SUPPOSED TO BE.
YEAH, SAME. DUNNO WHY, I JUST GOT THIS SENSE OF *DEJA VU*. SEE YOU IN NEW JERSEY.
HA!
THAT'S A HELL OF A THING I THOUGHT I'D NEVER SAY.
SKREEEECH
THE ELF QUEEN WAS AS GOOD AS HER WORD. DOUNIA COULD FEEL THE HEAVY COIN IN HER POCKET.
DOUNIA HATED THAT SHE DIDN'T HAVE A BACK-UP PLAN IF THE COIN WAS NOT ACCEPTED.
SHE LIKED TO MAKE CONTINGENCIES FOR FAILURE. IT WAS A SOUND HOBBY FOR THE WOMAN THAT OWNED THE WORLD'S MOST DANGEROUS COLLECTION OF CURSED OBJECTS.

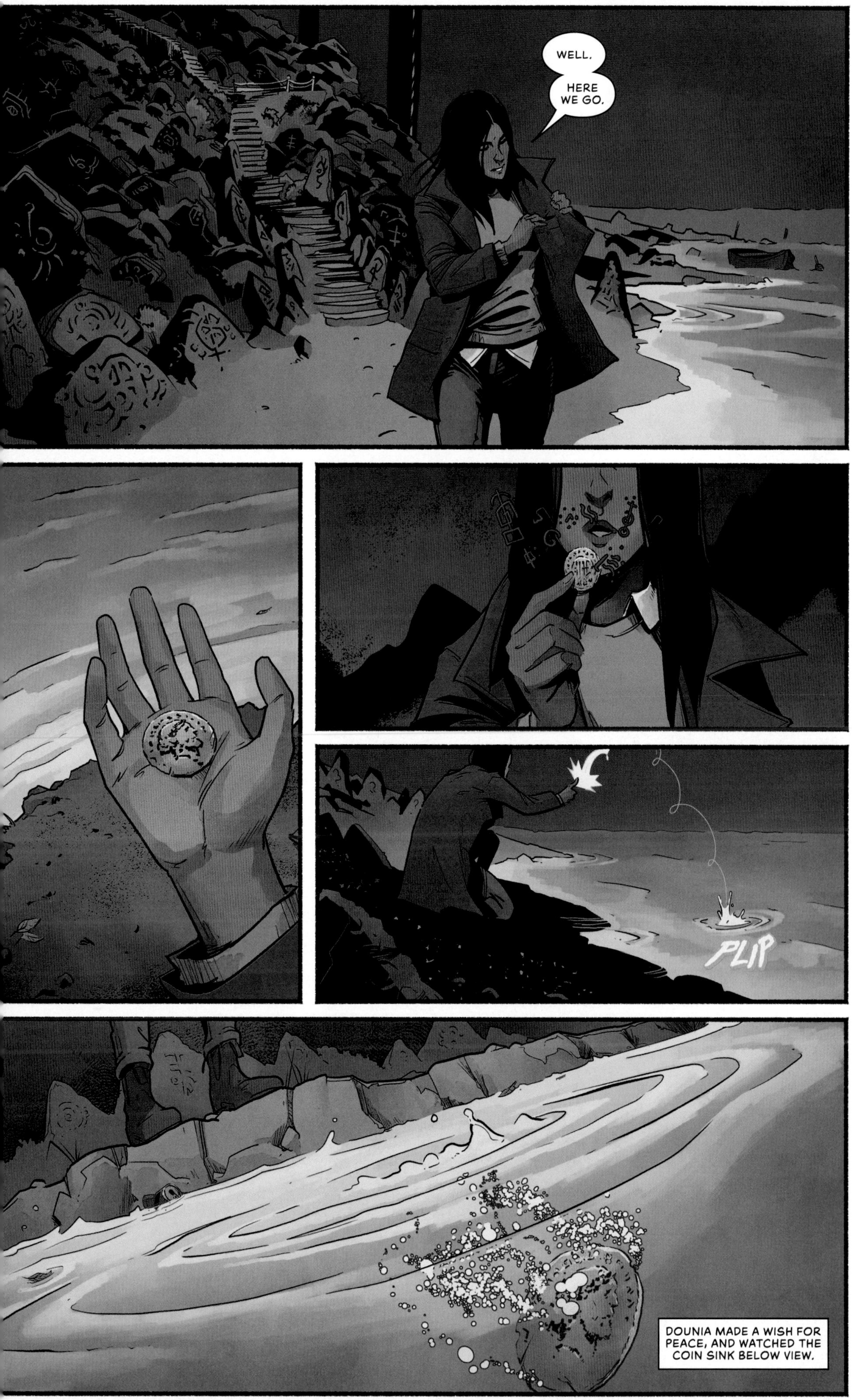
WELL,
HERE WE GO.
PLIP
DOUNIA MADE A WISH FOR PEACE, AND WATCHED THE COIN SINK BELOW VIEW.

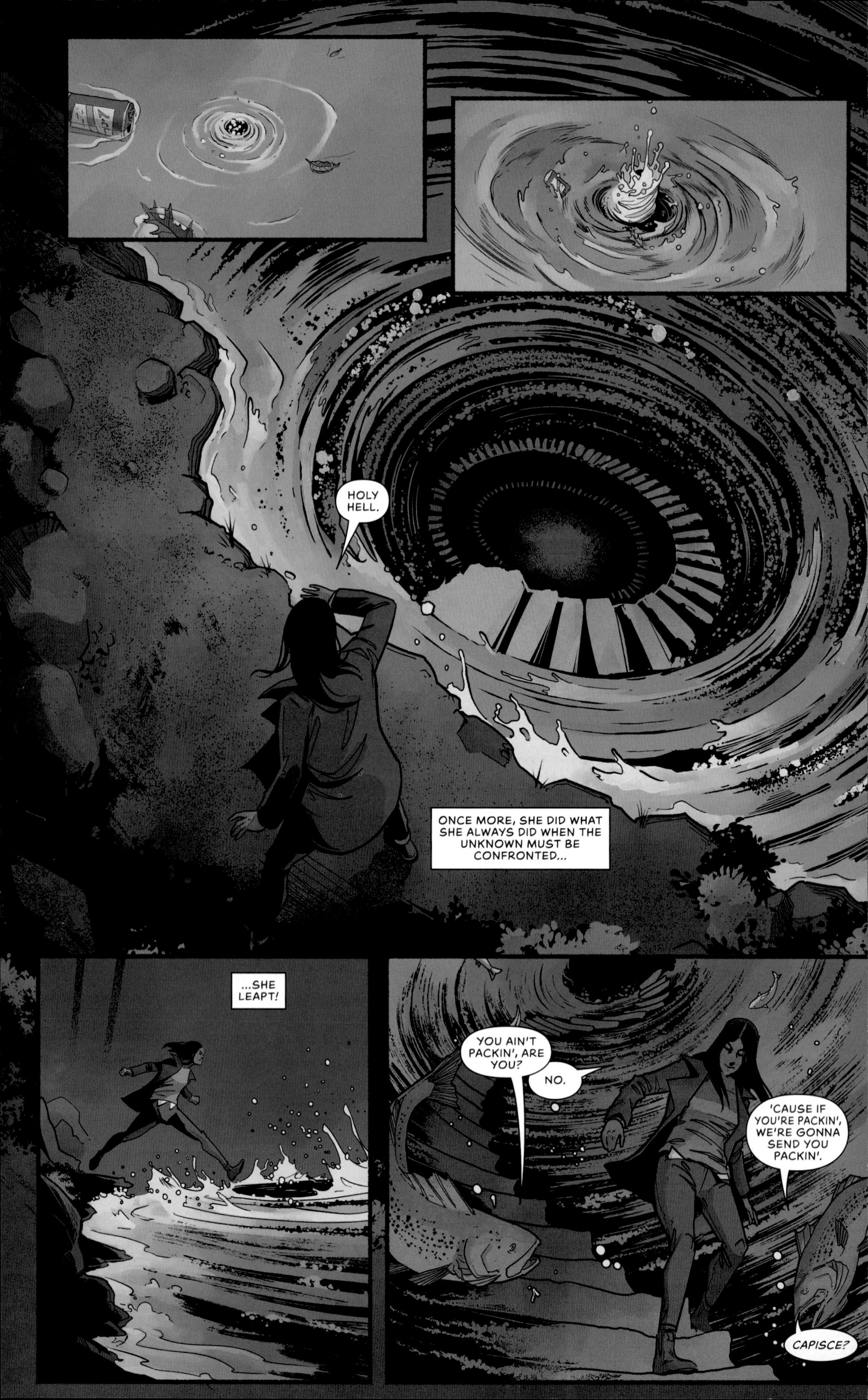
HOLY HELL.
ONCE MORE, SHE DID WHAT SHE ALWAYS DID WHEN THE UNKNOWN MUST BE CONFRONTED...
...SHE LEAPT!
YOU AIN'T PACKIN', ARE YOU?
NO.
'CAUSE IF YOU'RE PACKIN', WE'RE GONNA SEND YOU PACKIN'.
CAPISCE?

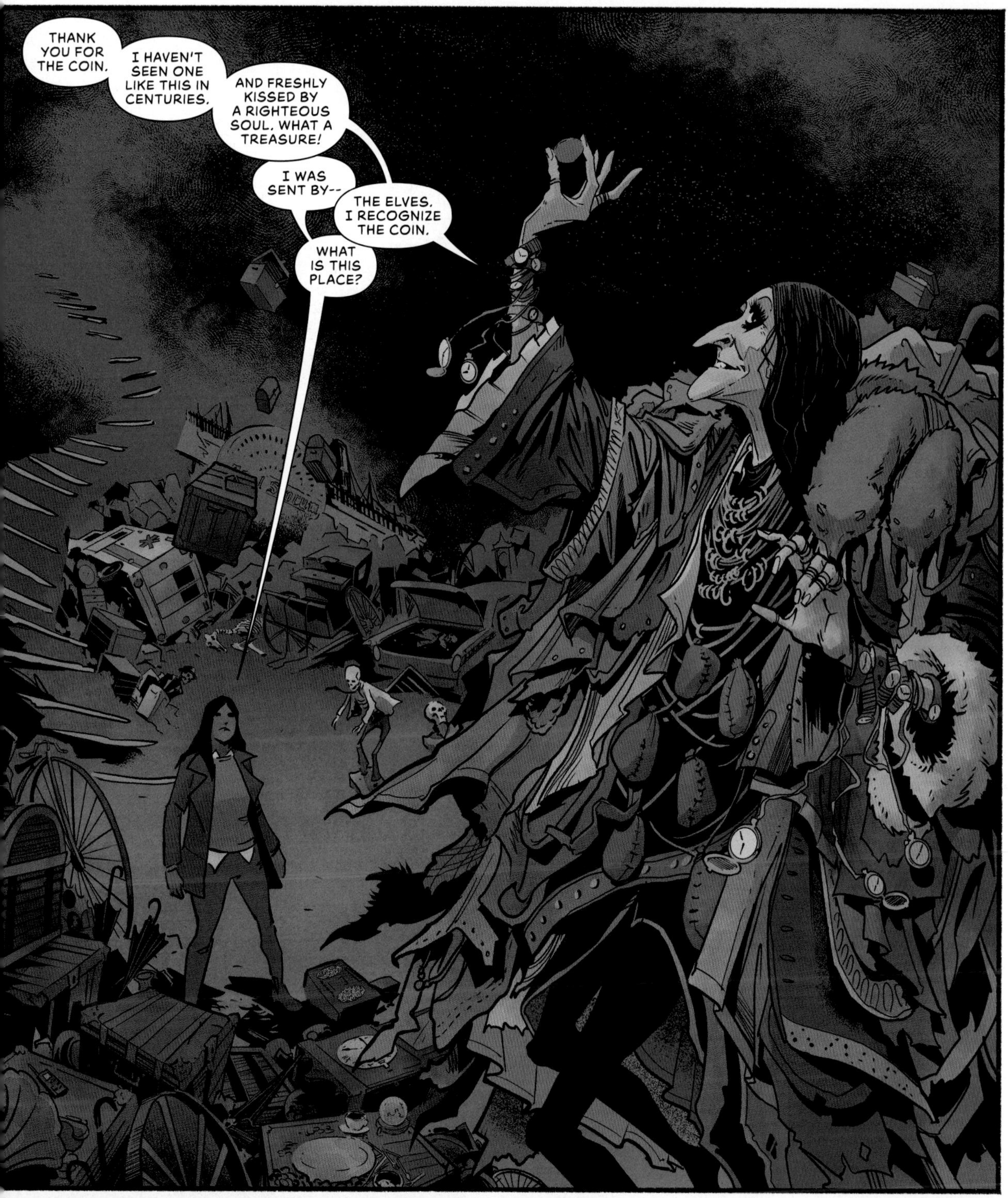
THANK YOU FOR THE COIN.
I HAVEN'T SEEN ONE LIKE THIS IN CENTURIES.
AND FRESHLY KISSED BY A RIGHTEOUS SOUL. WHAT A TREASURE!
I WAS SENT BY--
THE ELVES. I RECOGNIZE THE COIN.
WHAT IS THIS PLACE?

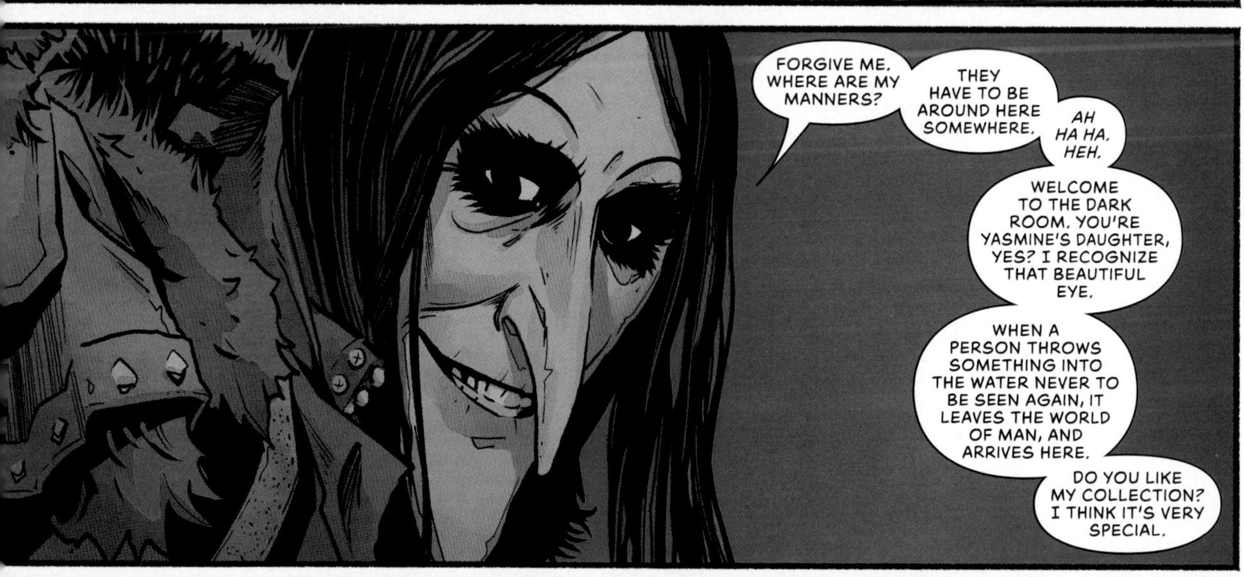
FORGIVE ME. WHERE ARE MY MANNERS?
THEY HAVE TO BE AROUND HERE SOMEWHERE.
AH HA HA, HEH.
WELCOME TO THE DARK ROOM. YOU'RE YASMINE'S DAUGHTER, YES? I RECOGNIZE THAT BEAUTIFUL EYE.
WHEN A PERSON THROWS SOMETHING INTO THE WATER NEVER TO BE SEEN AGAIN, IT LEAVES THE WORLD OF MAN, AND ARRIVES HERE.
DO YOU LIKE MY COLLECTION? I THINK IT'S VERY SPECIAL.

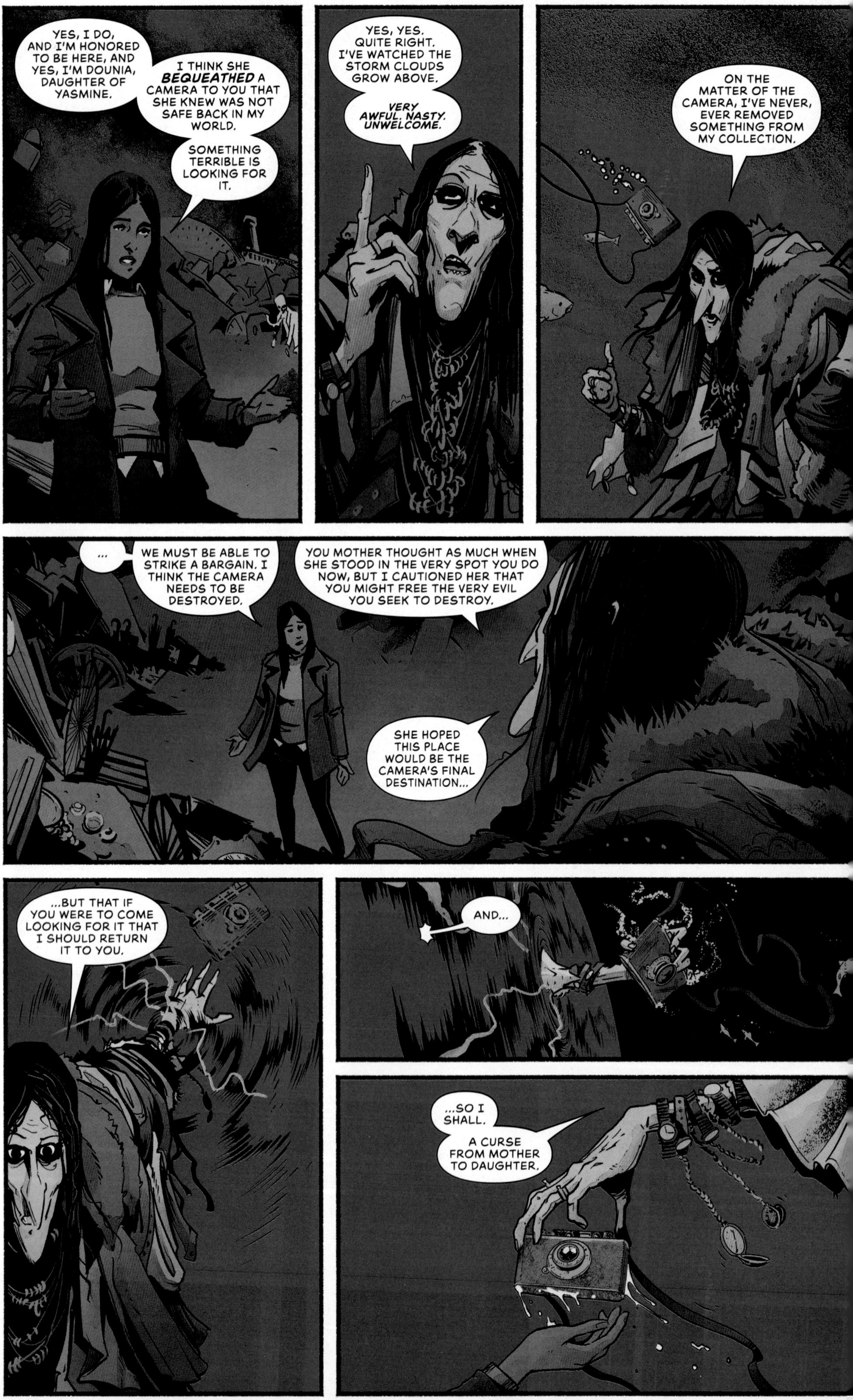
YES, I DO, AND I'M HONORED TO BE HERE, AND YES, I'M DOUNIA, DAUGHTER OF YASMINE.
I THINK SHE ***BEQUEATHED*** A CAMERA TO YOU THAT SHE KNEW WAS NOT SAFE BACK IN MY WORLD.
SOMETHING TERRIBLE IS LOOKING FOR IT.
YES, YES. QUITE RIGHT. I'VE WATCHED THE STORM CLOUDS GROW ABOVE.
VERY AWFUL. NASTY. UNWELCOME.
ON THE MATTER OF THE CAMERA, I'VE NEVER, EVER REMOVED SOMETHING FROM MY COLLECTION.
...
WE MUST BE ABLE TO STRIKE A BARGAIN. I THINK THE CAMERA NEEDS TO BE DESTROYED.
YOU MOTHER THOUGHT AS MUCH WHEN SHE STOOD IN THE VERY SPOT YOU DO NOW, BUT I CAUTIONED HER THAT YOU MIGHT FREE THE VERY EVIL YOU SEEK TO DESTROY.
SHE HOPED THIS PLACE WOULD BE THE CAMERA'S FINAL DESTINATION...
...BUT THAT IF YOU WERE TO COME LOOKING FOR IT THAT I SHOULD RETURN IT TO YOU.
AND...
...SO I SHALL.
A CURSE FROM MOTHER TO DAUGHTER.

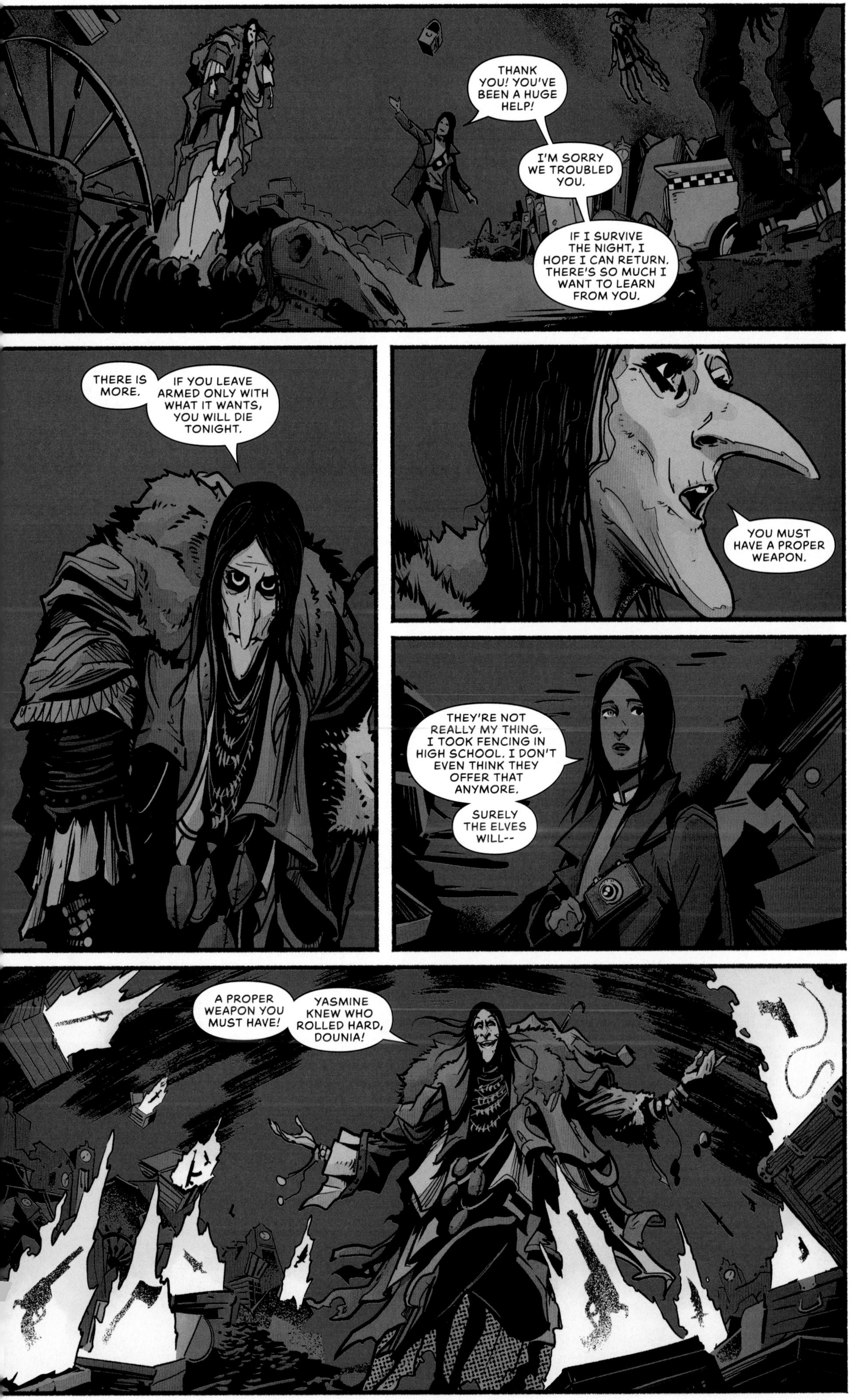
THANK YOU! YOU'VE BEEN A HUGE HELP!
I'M SORRY WE TROUBLED YOU.
IF I SURVIVE THE NIGHT, I HOPE I CAN RETURN. THERE'S SO MUCH I WANT TO LEARN FROM YOU.
THERE IS MORE.
IF YOU LEAVE ARMED ONLY WITH WHAT IT WANTS, YOU WILL DIE TONIGHT.
YOU MUST HAVE A PROPER WEAPON.
THEY'RE NOT REALLY MY THING. I TOOK FENCING IN HIGH SCHOOL. I DON'T EVEN THINK THEY OFFER THAT ANYMORE.
SURELY THE ELVES WILL--
A PROPER WEAPON YOU MUST HAVE!
YASMINE KNEW WHO ROLLED HARD, DOUNIA!

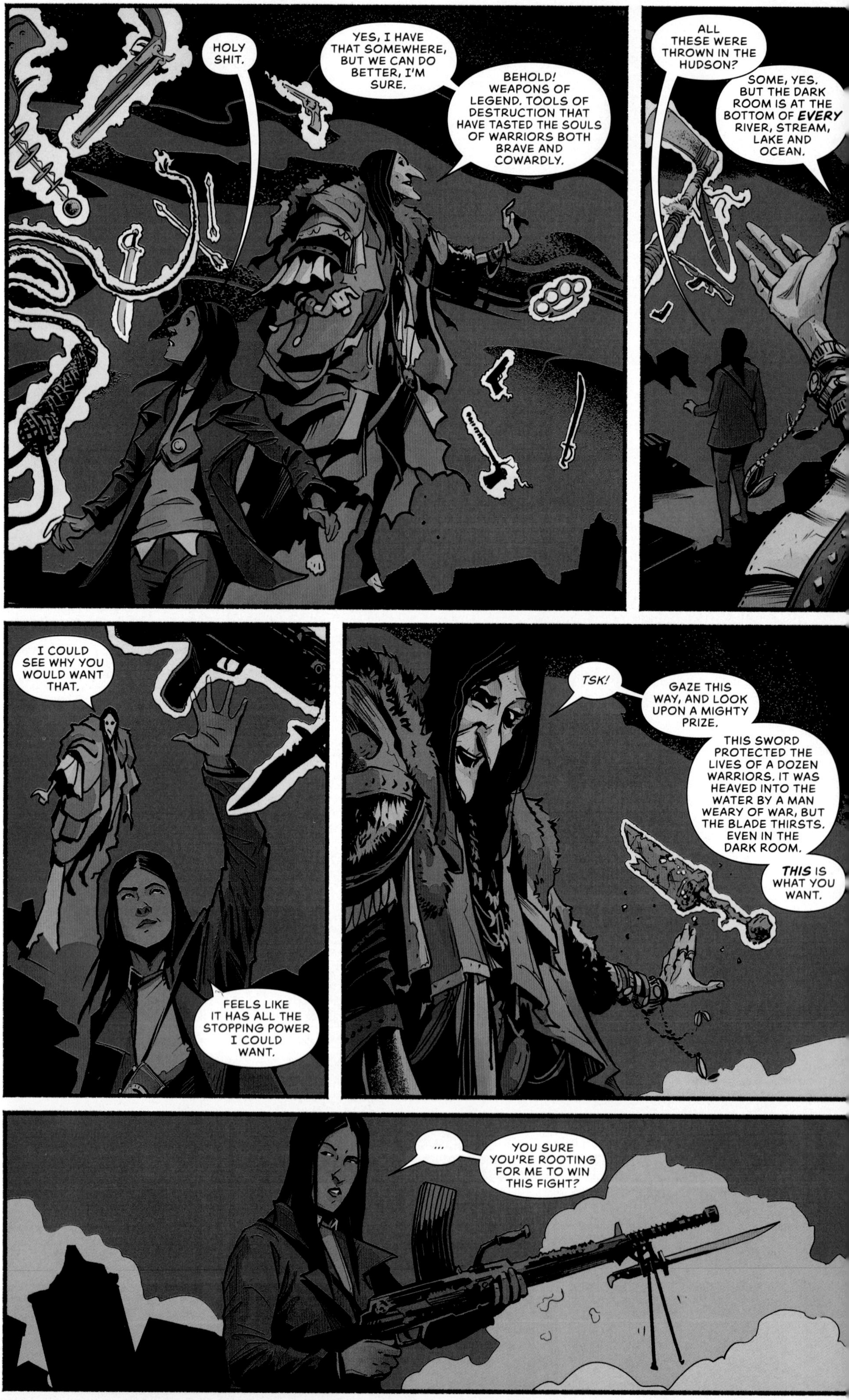
HOLY SHIT.
YES, I HAVE THAT SOMEWHERE, BUT WE CAN DO BETTER, I'M SURE.
BEHOLD! WEAPONS OF LEGEND. TOOLS OF DESTRUCTION THAT HAVE TASTED THE SOULS OF WARRIORS BOTH BRAVE AND COWARDLY.
ALL THESE WERE THROWN IN THE HUDSON?
SOME, YES. BUT THE DARK ROOM IS AT THE BOTTOM OF ***EVERY*** RIVER, STREAM, LAKE AND OCEAN.
I COULD SEE WHY YOU WOULD WANT THAT.
FEELS LIKE IT HAS ALL THE STOPPING POWER I COULD WANT.
TSK!
GAZE THIS WAY, AND LOOK UPON A MIGHTY PRIZE.
THIS SWORD PROTECTED THE LIVES OF A DOZEN WARRIORS. IT WAS HEAVED INTO THE WATER BY A MAN WEARY OF WAR, BUT THE BLADE THIRSTS, EVEN IN THE DARK ROOM.
THIS IS WHAT YOU WANT.
...
YOU SURE YOU'RE ROOTING FOR ME TO WIN THIS FIGHT?

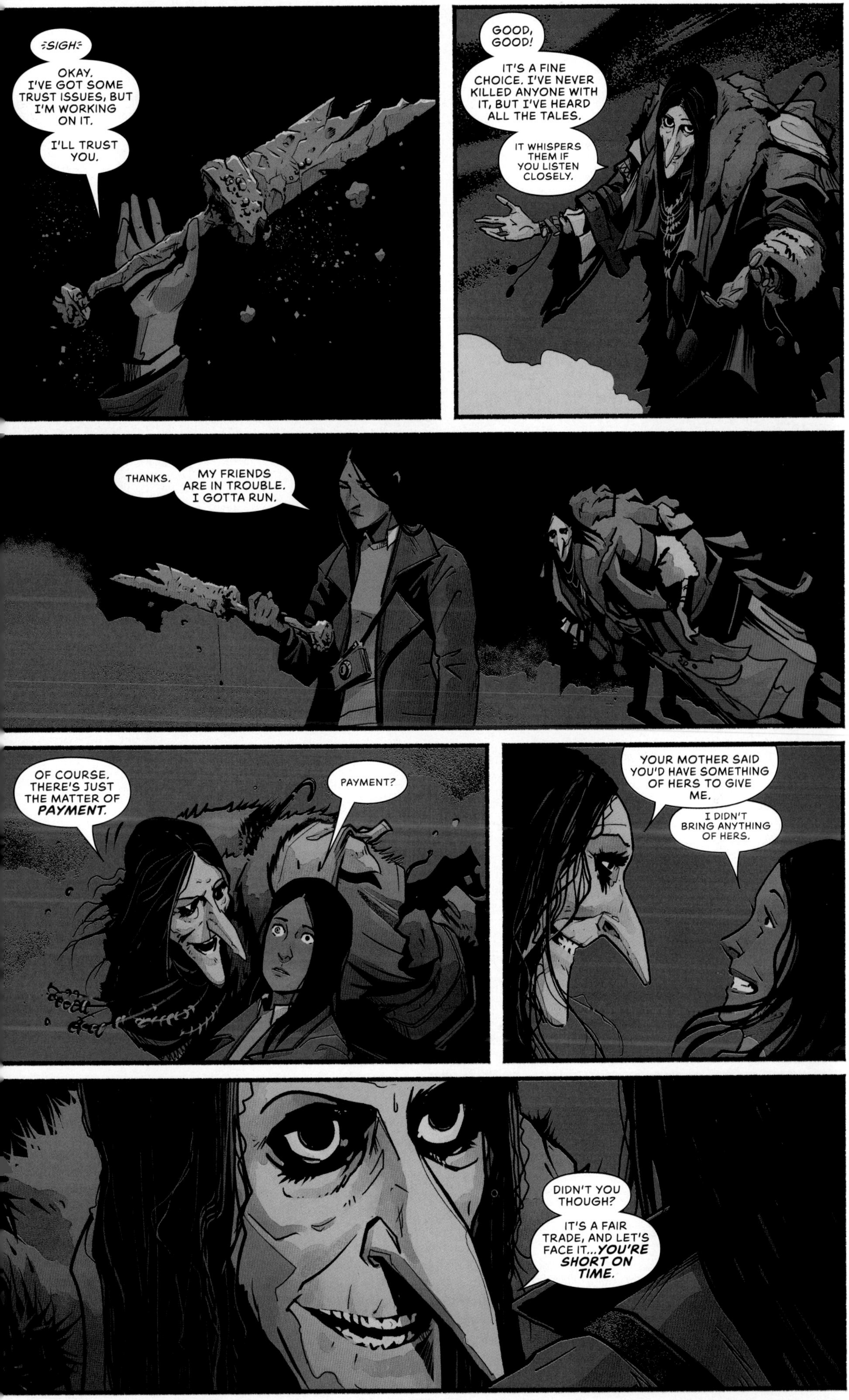

=SIGH=
OKAY. I'VE GOT SOME TRUST ISSUES, BUT I'M WORKING ON IT.
I'LL TRUST YOU.
GOOD, GOOD!
IT'S A FINE CHOICE. I'VE NEVER KILLED ANYONE WITH IT, BUT I'VE HEARD ALL THE TALES.
IT WHISPERS THEM IF YOU LISTEN CLOSELY.
THANKS.
MY FRIENDS ARE IN TROUBLE. I GOTTA RUN.
OF COURSE. THERE'S JUST THE MATTER OF ***PAYMENT***.
PAYMENT?
YOUR MOTHER SAID YOU'D HAVE SOMETHING OF HERS TO GIVE ME.
I DIDN'T BRING ANYTHING OF HERS.
DIDN'T YOU THOUGH?
IT'S A FAIR TRADE, AND LET'S FACE IT... ***YOU'RE SHORT ON TIME.***

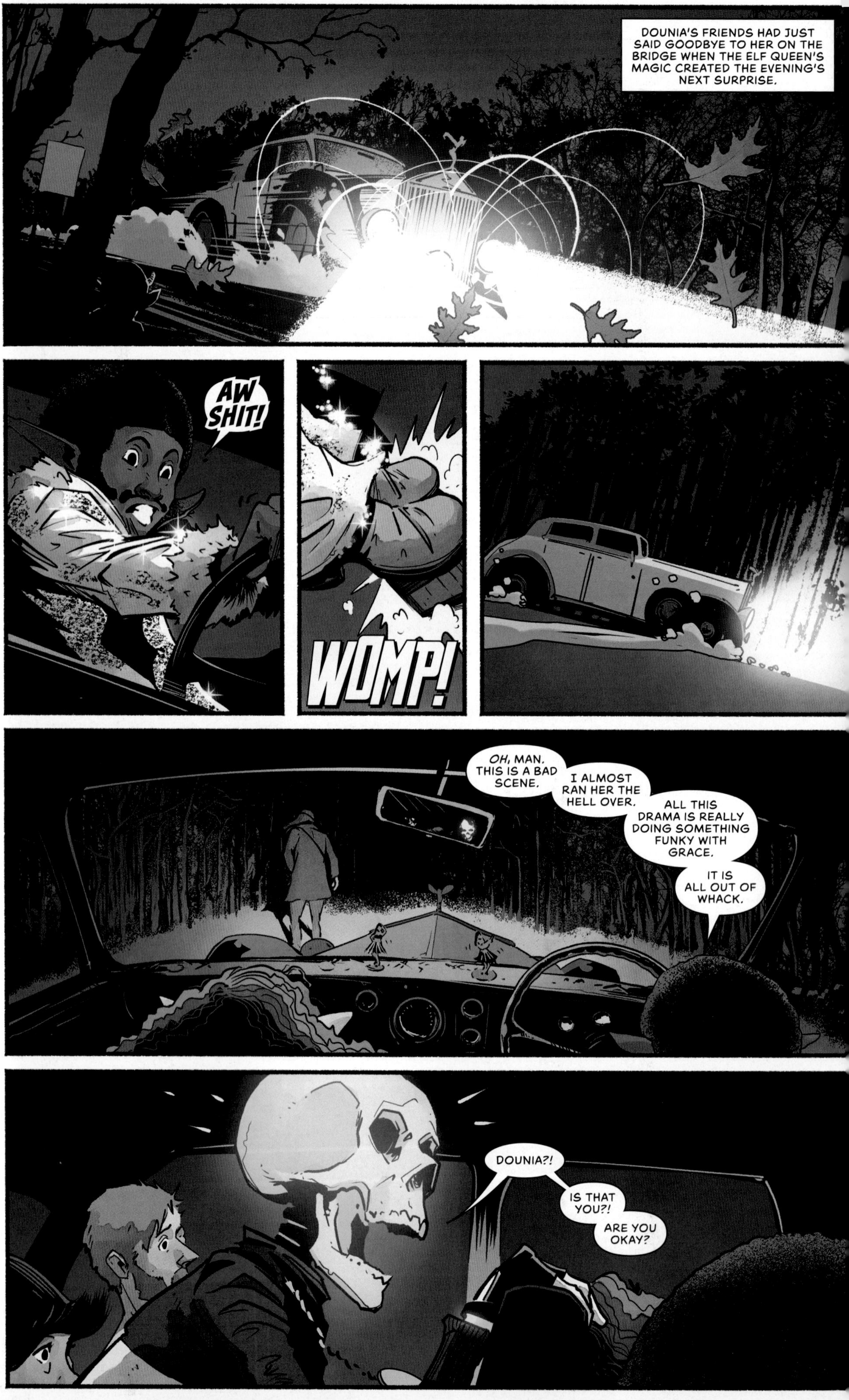
DOUNIA'S FRIENDS HAD JUST SAID GOODBYE TO HER ON THE BRIDGE WHEN THE ELF QUEEN'S MAGIC CREATED THE EVENING'S NEXT SURPRISE.
AW SHIT!
WOMP!
OH, MAN. THIS IS A BAD SCENE.
I ALMOST RAN HER THE HELL OVER.
ALL THIS DRAMA IS REALLY DOING SOMETHING FUNKY WITH GRACE.
IT IS ALL OUT OF WHACK.
DOUNIA?!
IS THAT YOU?!
ARE YOU OKAY?

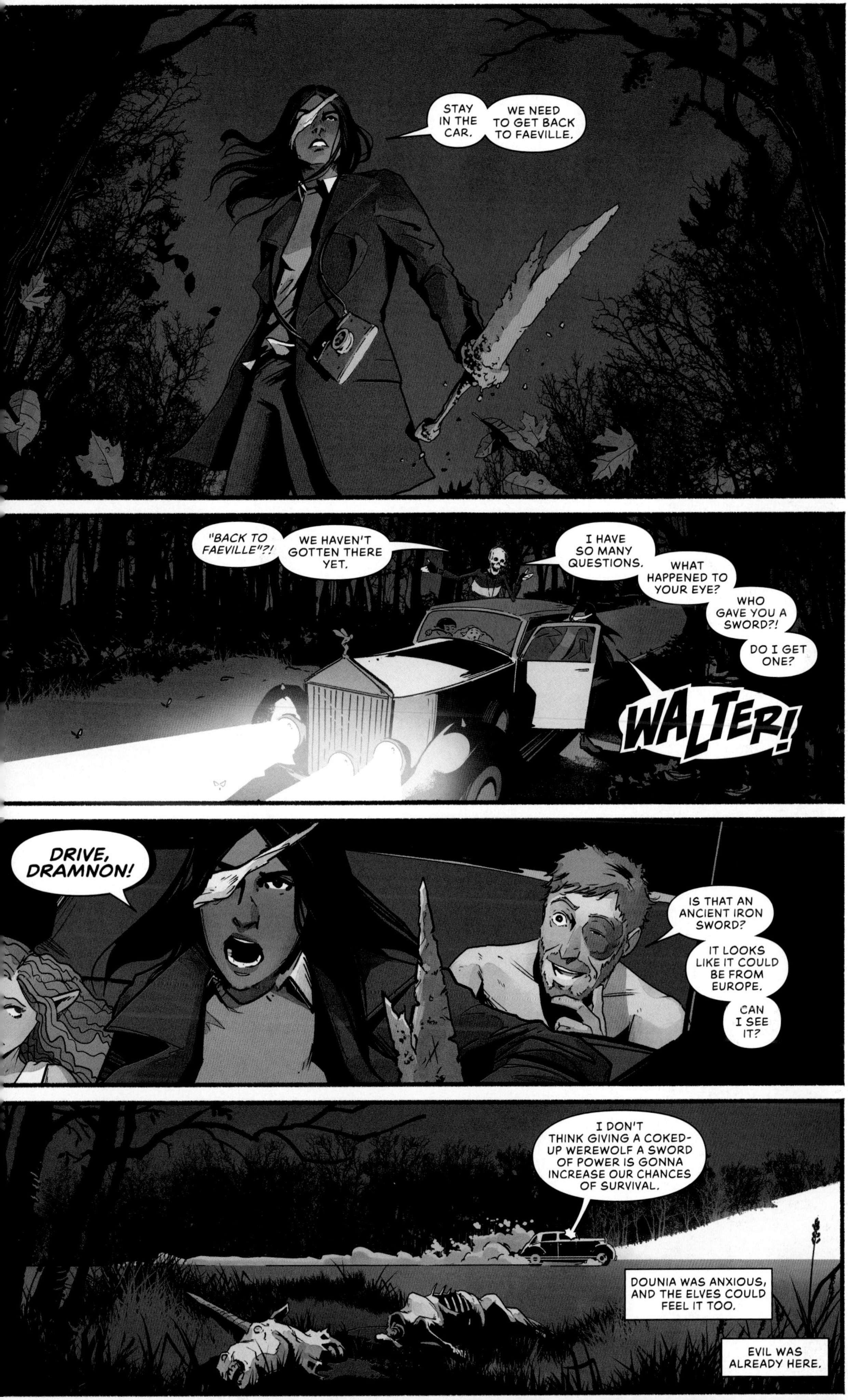
STAY IN THE CAR.
WE NEED TO GET BACK TO FAEVILLE.
"BACK TO FAEVILLE"?!
WE HAVEN'T GOTTEN THERE YET.
I HAVE SO MANY QUESTIONS.
WHAT HAPPENED TO YOUR EYE?
WHO GAVE YOU A SWORD?!
DO I GET ONE?
WALTER!
DRIVE, DRAMNON!
IS THAT AN ANCIENT IRON SWORD?
IT LOOKS LIKE IT COULD BE FROM EUROPE.
CAN I SEE IT?
I DON'T THINK GIVING A COKED-UP WEREWOLF A SWORD OF POWER IS GONNA INCREASE OUR CHANCES OF SURVIVAL.
DOUNIA WAS ANXIOUS, AND THE ELVES COULD FEEL IT TOO.
EVIL WAS ALREADY HERE.

CHAPTER THREE

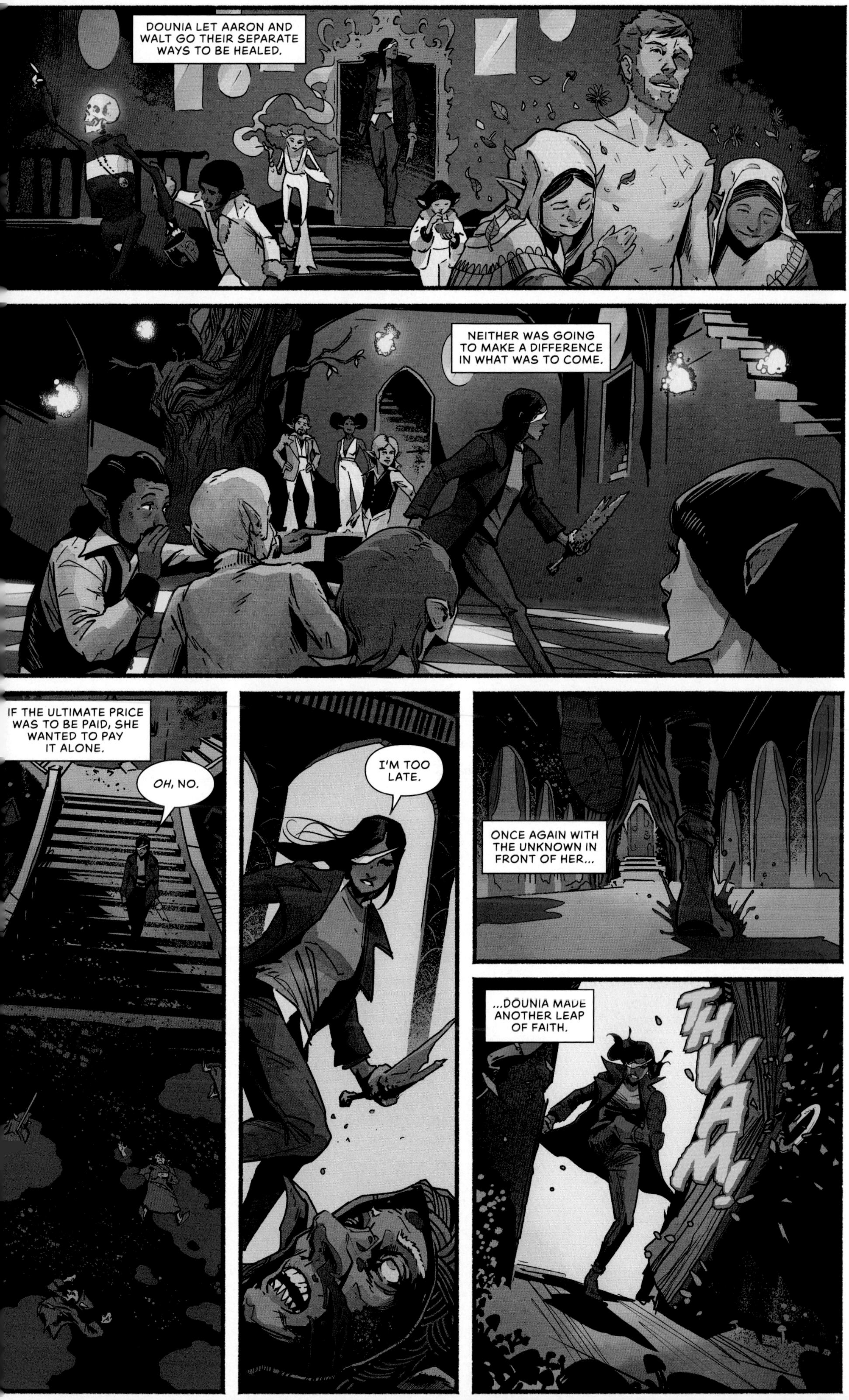
DOUNIA LET AARON AND WALT GO THEIR SEPARATE WAYS TO BE HEALED.
NEITHER WAS GOING TO MAKE A DIFFERENCE IN WHAT WAS TO COME.
IF THE ULTIMATE PRICE WAS TO BE PAID, SHE WANTED TO PAY IT ALONE.
OH, NO.
I'M TOO LATE.
ONCE AGAIN WITH THE UNKNOWN IN FRONT OF HER...
...DOUNIA MADE ANOTHER LEAP OF FAITH.
THWAM!

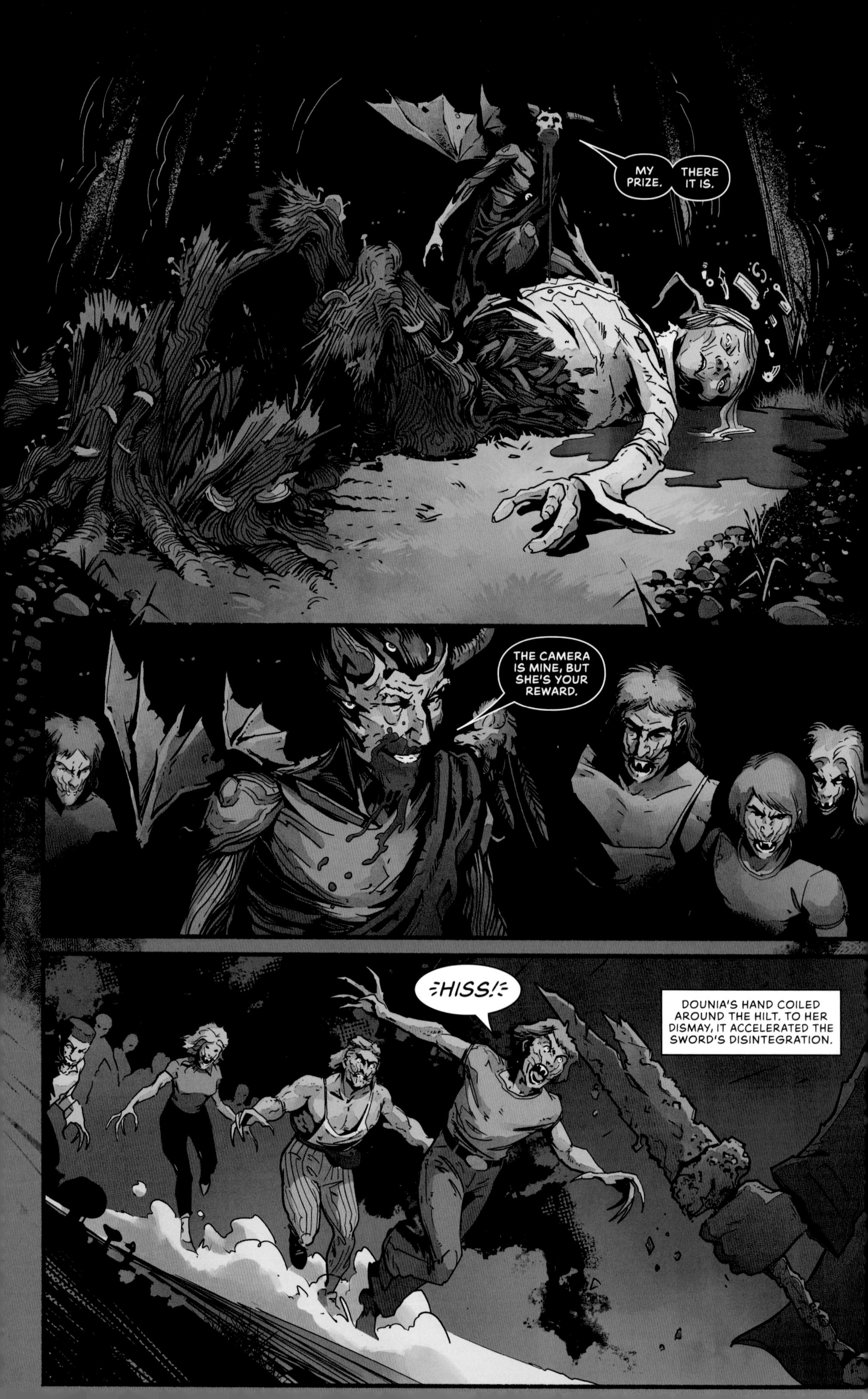
MY PRIZE.
THERE IT IS.
THE CAMERA IS MINE, BUT SHE'S YOUR REWARD.
HISS!
DOUNIA'S HAND COILED AROUND THE HILT. TO HER DISMAY, IT ACCELERATED THE SWORD'S DISINTEGRATION.

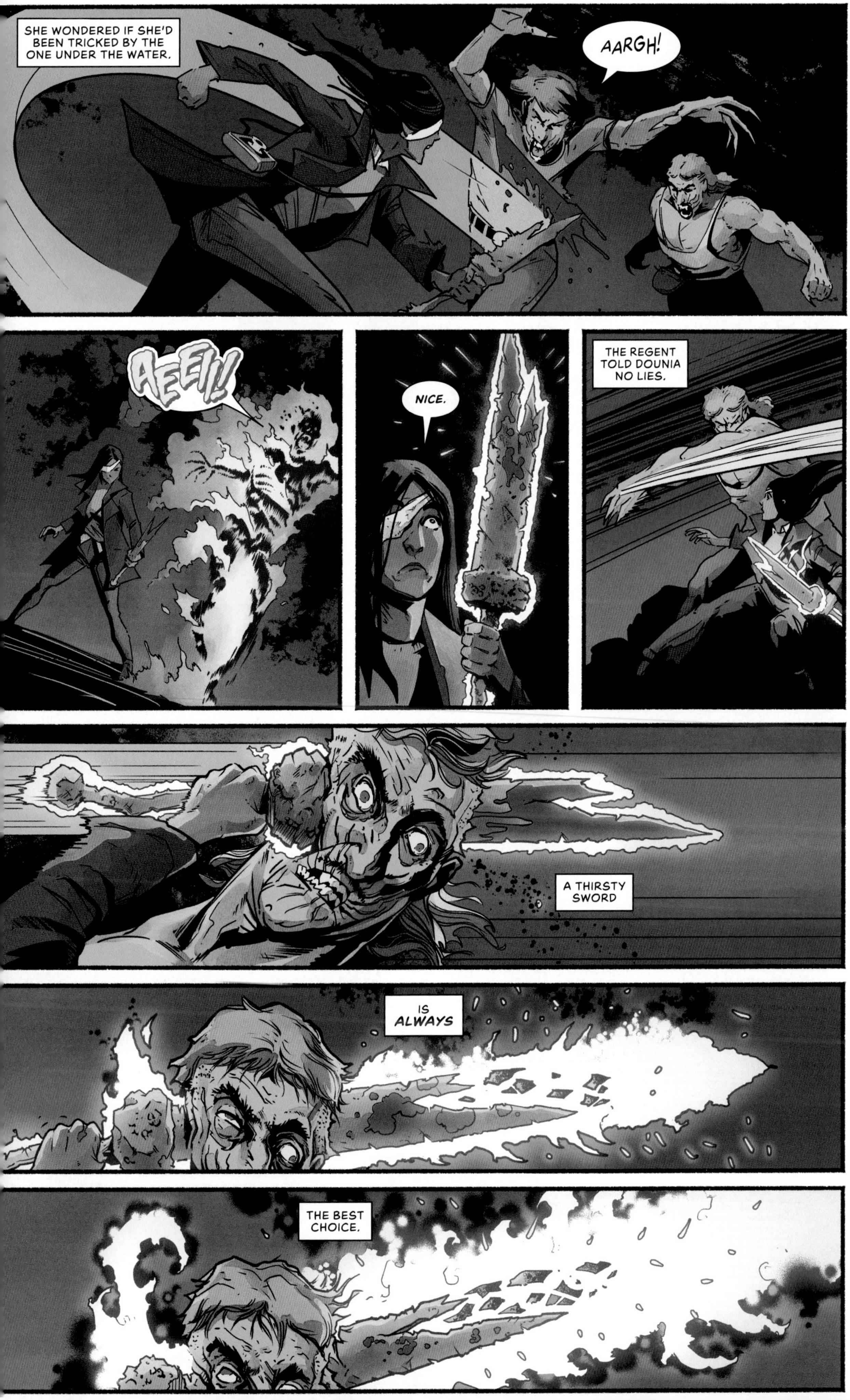
SHE WONDERED IF SHE'D BEEN TRICKED BY THE ONE UNDER THE WATER.
AARGH!
AEEII!
NICE.
THE REGENT TOLD DOUNIA NO LIES.
A THIRSTY SWORD
IS ALWAYS
THE BEST CHOICE.

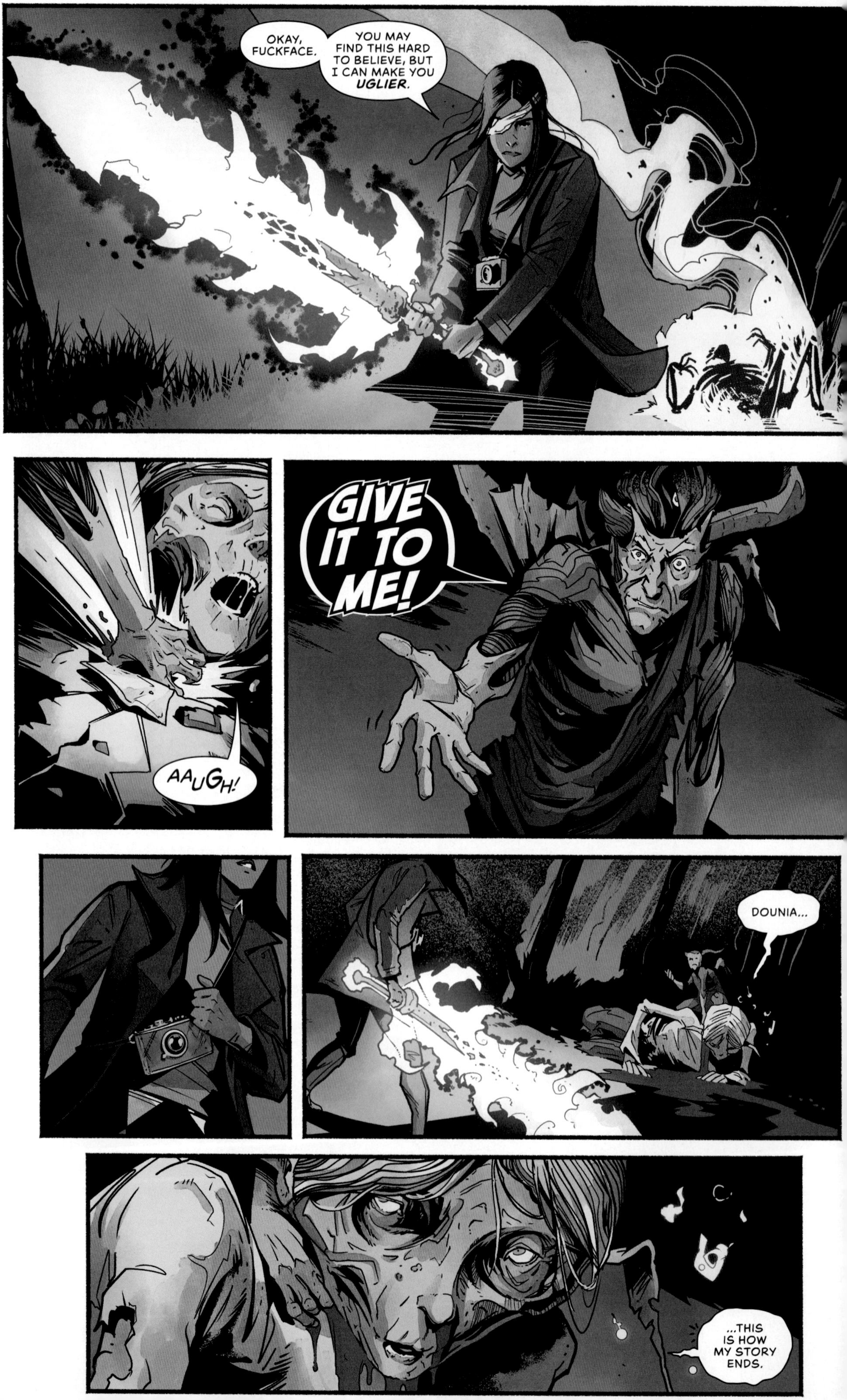
OKAY, FUCKFACE.
YOU MAY FIND THIS HARD TO BELIEVE, BUT I CAN MAKE YOU *UGLIER.*
AAUGH!
GIVE IT TO ME!
DOUNIA...
...THIS IS HOW MY STORY ENDS.

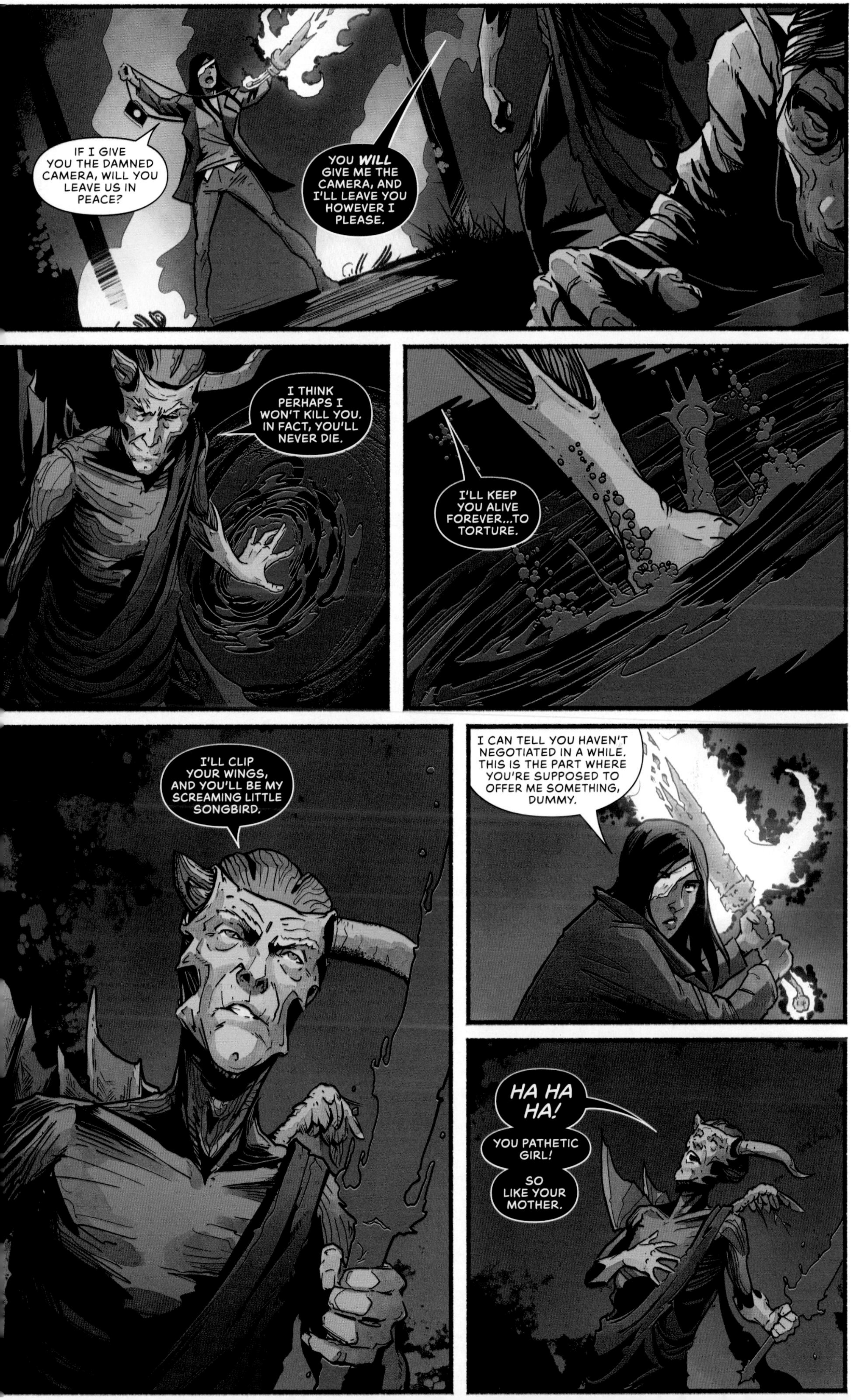
IF I GIVE YOU THE DAMNED CAMERA, WILL YOU LEAVE US IN PEACE?
YOU *WILL* GIVE ME THE CAMERA, AND I'LL LEAVE YOU HOWEVER I PLEASE.
I THINK PERHAPS I WON'T KILL YOU. IN FACT, YOU'LL NEVER DIE.
I'LL KEEP YOU ALIVE FOREVER...TO TORTURE.
I'LL CLIP YOUR WINGS, AND YOU'LL BE MY SCREAMING LITTLE SONGBIRD.
I CAN TELL YOU HAVEN'T NEGOTIATED IN A WHILE. THIS IS THE PART WHERE YOU'RE SUPPOSED TO OFFER ME SOMETHING, DUMMY.
HA HA HA!
YOU PATHETIC GIRL!
SO LIKE YOUR MOTHER.

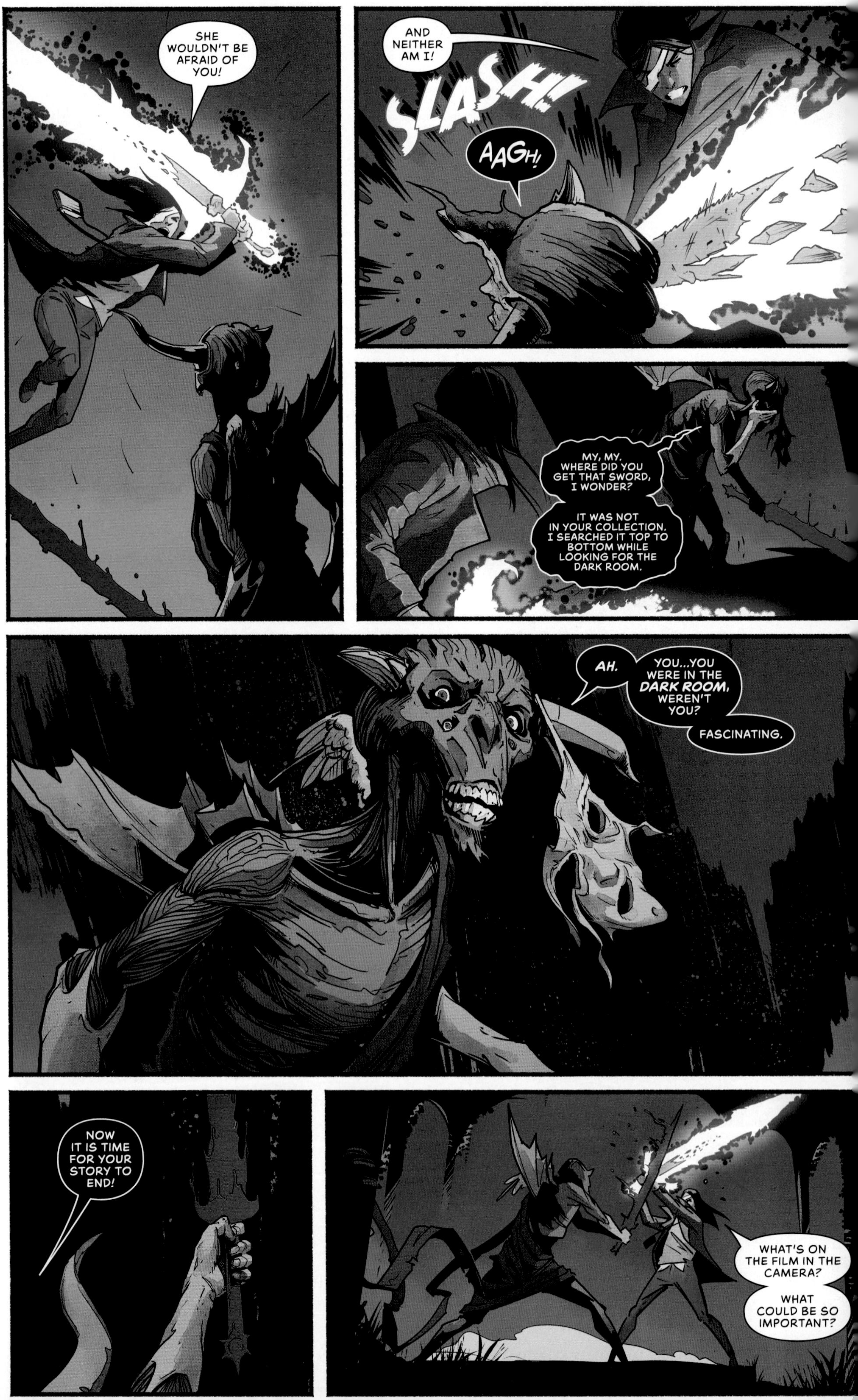
SHE WOULDN'T BE AFRAID OF YOU!
AND NEITHER AM I!
SLASH!
AAGH!
MY, MY. WHERE DID YOU GET THAT SWORD, I WONDER?
IT WAS NOT IN YOUR COLLECTION. I SEARCHED IT TOP TO BOTTOM WHILE LOOKING FOR THE DARK ROOM.
AH.
YOU...YOU WERE IN THE DARK ROOM, WEREN'T YOU?
FASCINATING.
NOW IT IS TIME FOR YOUR STORY TO END!
WHAT'S ON THE FILM IN THE CAMERA?
WHAT COULD BE SO IMPORTANT?

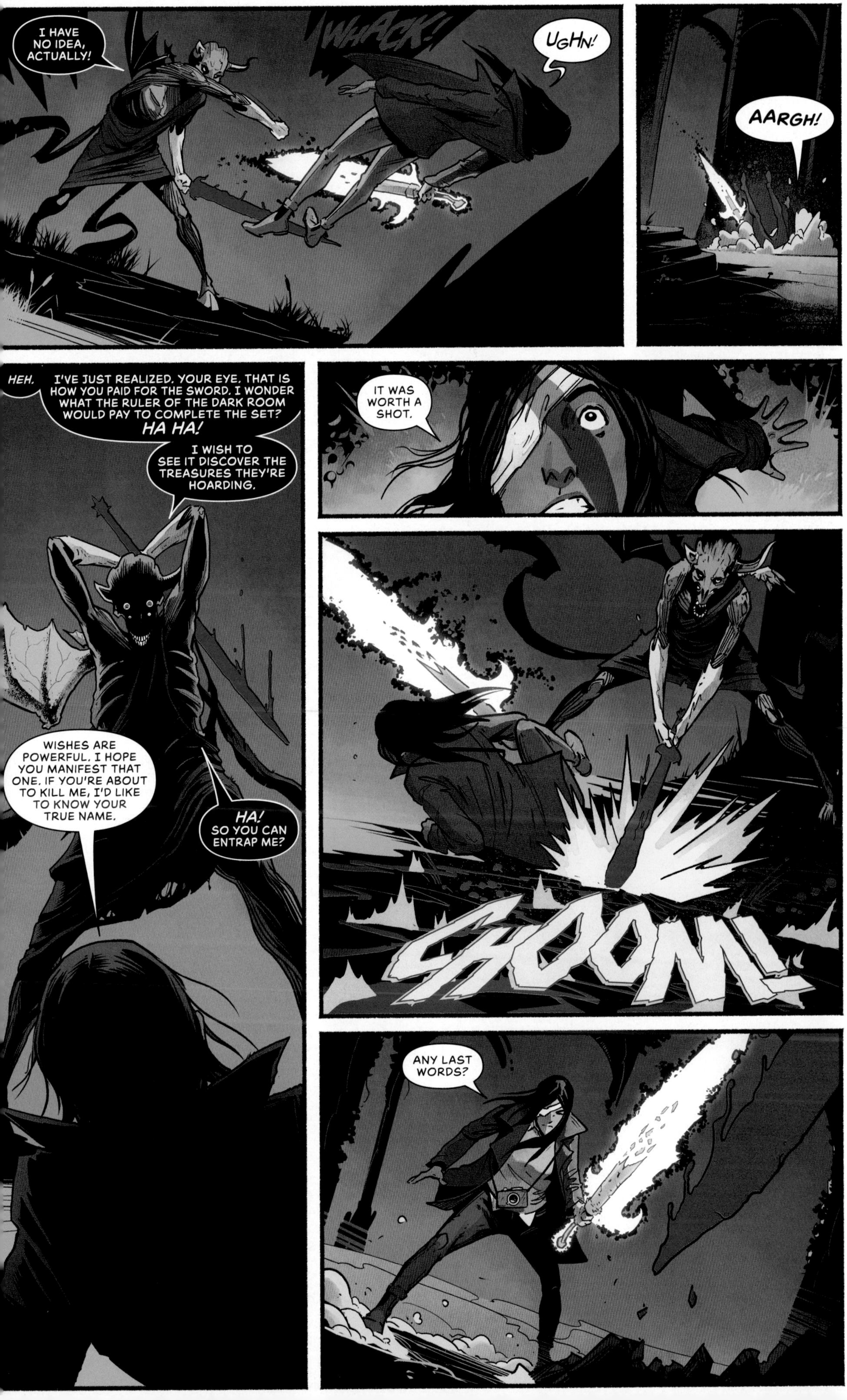

I HAVE NO IDEA, ACTUALLY!
WHACK!
UGHN!
AARGH!
HEH.
I'VE JUST REALIZED. YOUR EYE. THAT IS HOW YOU PAID FOR THE SWORD. I WONDER WHAT THE RULER OF THE DARK ROOM WOULD PAY TO COMPLETE THE SET? HA HA!
I WISH TO SEE IT DISCOVER THE TREASURES THEY'RE HOARDING.
WISHES ARE POWERFUL. I HOPE YOU MANIFEST THAT ONE. IF YOU'RE ABOUT TO KILL ME, I'D LIKE TO KNOW YOUR TRUE NAME.
HA! SO YOU CAN ENTRAP ME?
IT WAS WORTH A SHOT.
CHOOM!
ANY LAST WORDS?

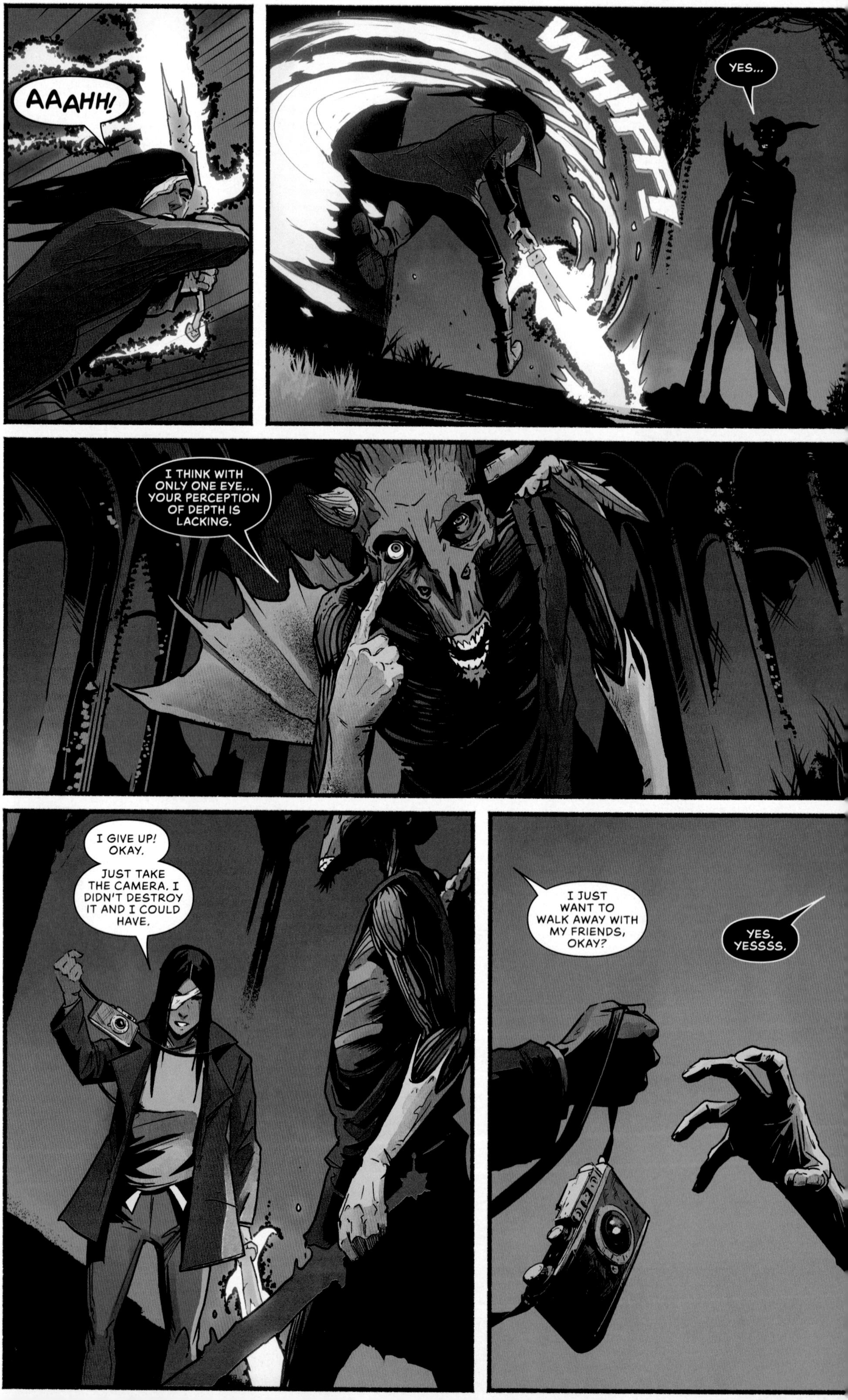
AAAHH!
WHIFF!
YES...
I THINK WITH ONLY ONE EYE... YOUR PERCEPTION OF DEPTH IS LACKING.
I GIVE UP! OKAY.
JUST TAKE THE CAMERA. I DIDN'T DESTROY IT AND I COULD HAVE.
I JUST WANT TO WALK AWAY WITH MY FRIENDS, OKAY?
YES. YESSSS.

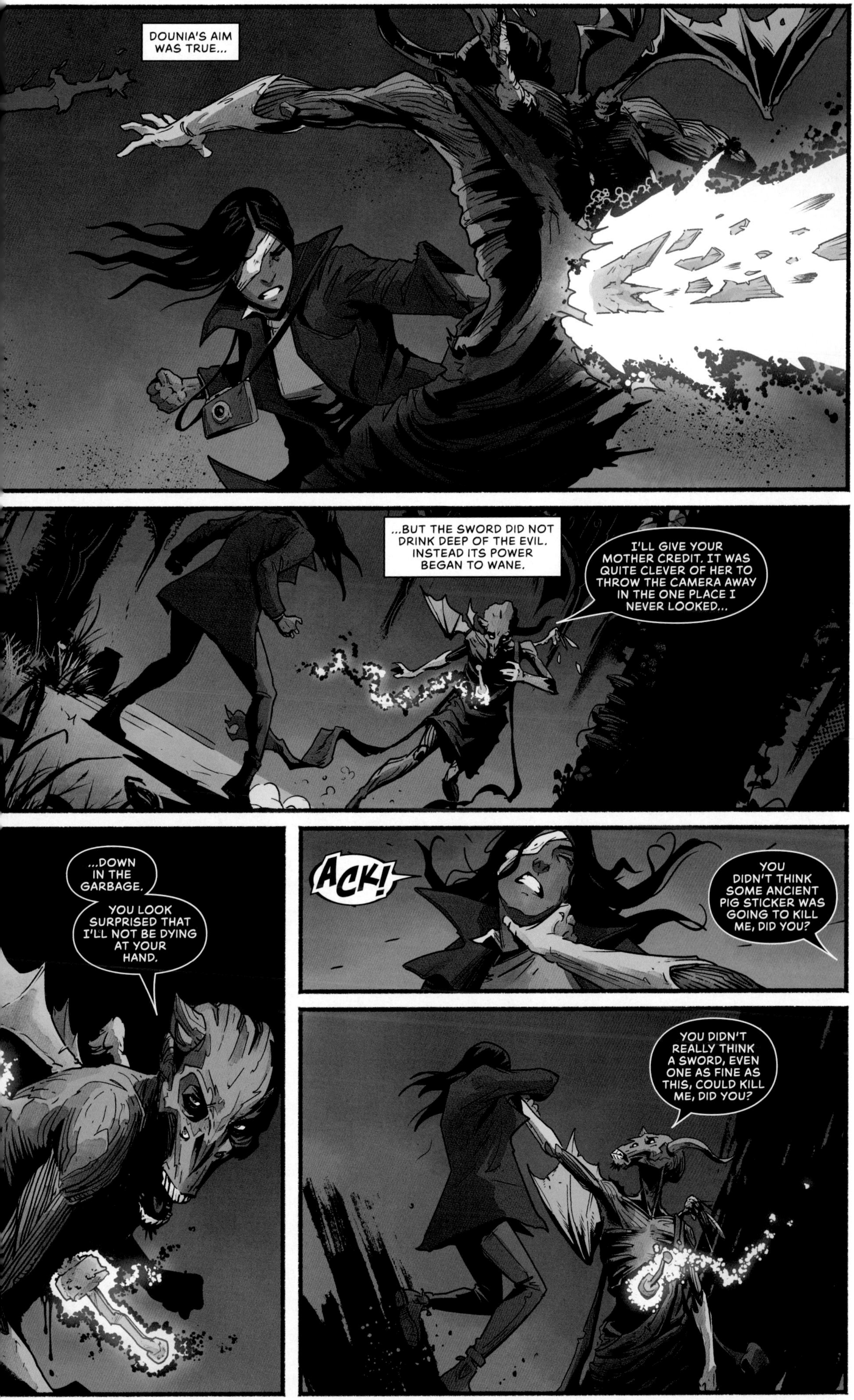
DOUNIA'S AIM WAS TRUE...
...BUT THE SWORD DID NOT DRINK DEEP OF THE EVIL. INSTEAD ITS POWER BEGAN TO WANE.
I'LL GIVE YOUR MOTHER CREDIT. IT WAS QUITE CLEVER OF HER TO THROW THE CAMERA AWAY IN THE ONE PLACE I NEVER LOOKED...
...DOWN IN THE GARBAGE.
YOU LOOK SURPRISED THAT I'LL NOT BE DYING AT YOUR HAND.
ACK!
YOU DIDN'T THINK SOME ANCIENT PIG STICKER WAS GOING TO KILL ME, DID YOU?
YOU DIDN'T REALLY THINK A SWORD, EVEN ONE AS FINE AS THIS, COULD KILL ME, DID YOU?

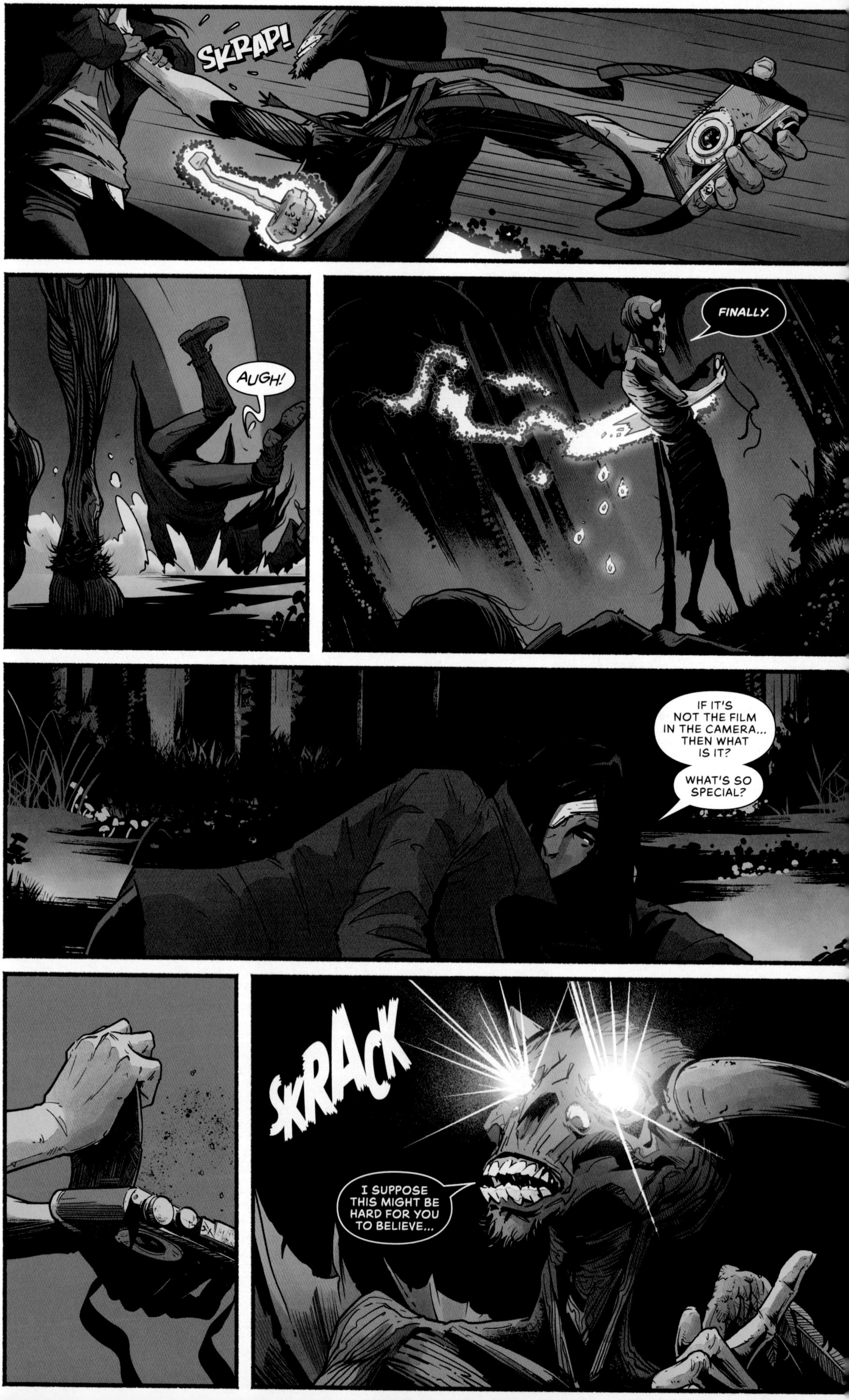
SKRAP!
AUGH!
FINALLY.
IF IT'S NOT THE FILM IN THE CAMERA... THEN WHAT IS IT?
WHAT'S SO SPECIAL?
SKRACK
I SUPPOSE THIS MIGHT BE HARD FOR YOU TO BELIEVE...

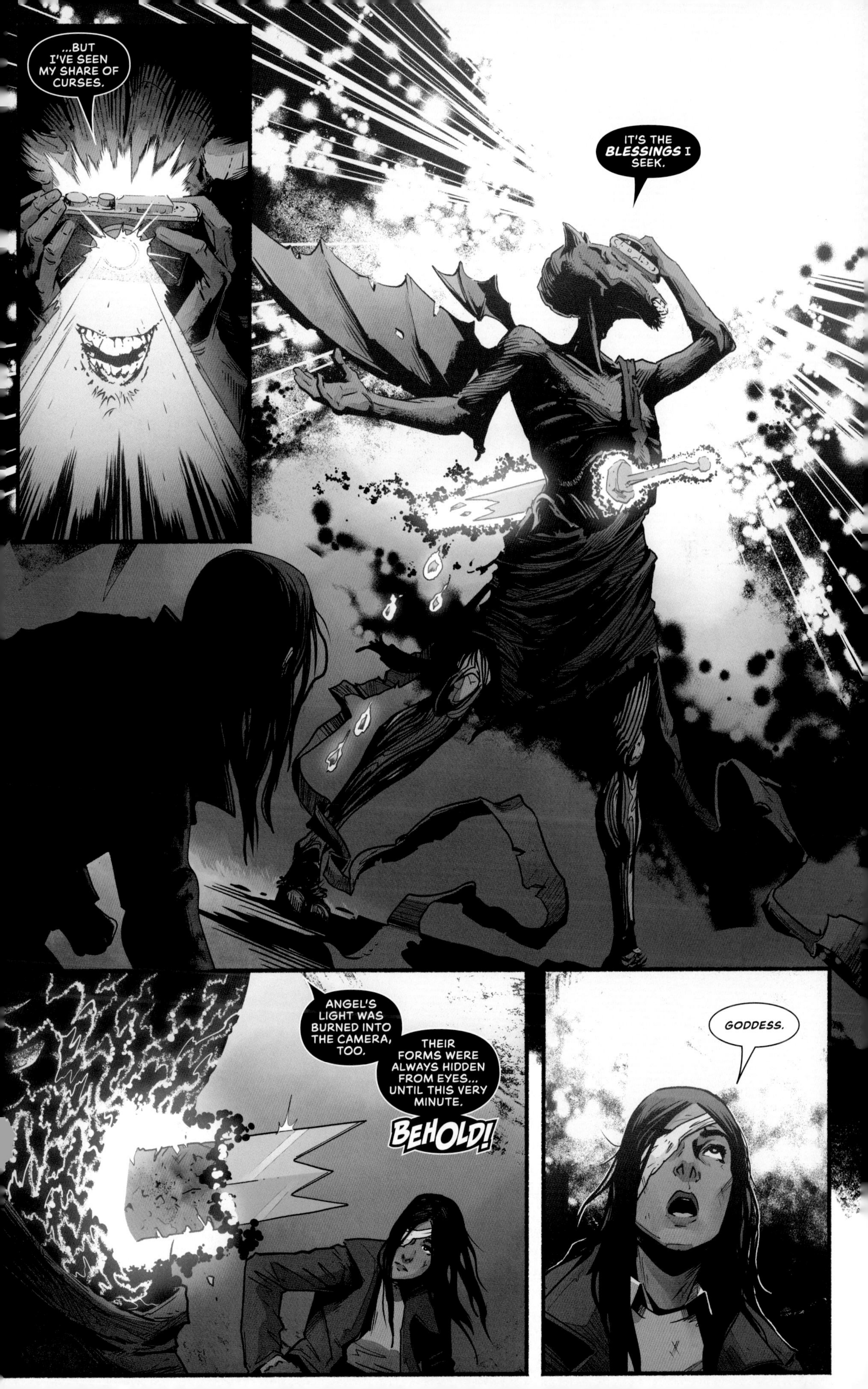
...BUT I'VE SEEN MY SHARE OF CURSES.
IT'S THE *BLESSINGS* I SEEK.
ANGEL'S LIGHT WAS BURNED INTO THE CAMERA, TOO.
THEIR FORMS WERE ALWAYS HIDDEN FROM EYES... UNTIL THIS VERY MINUTE.
BEHOLD!
GODDESS.

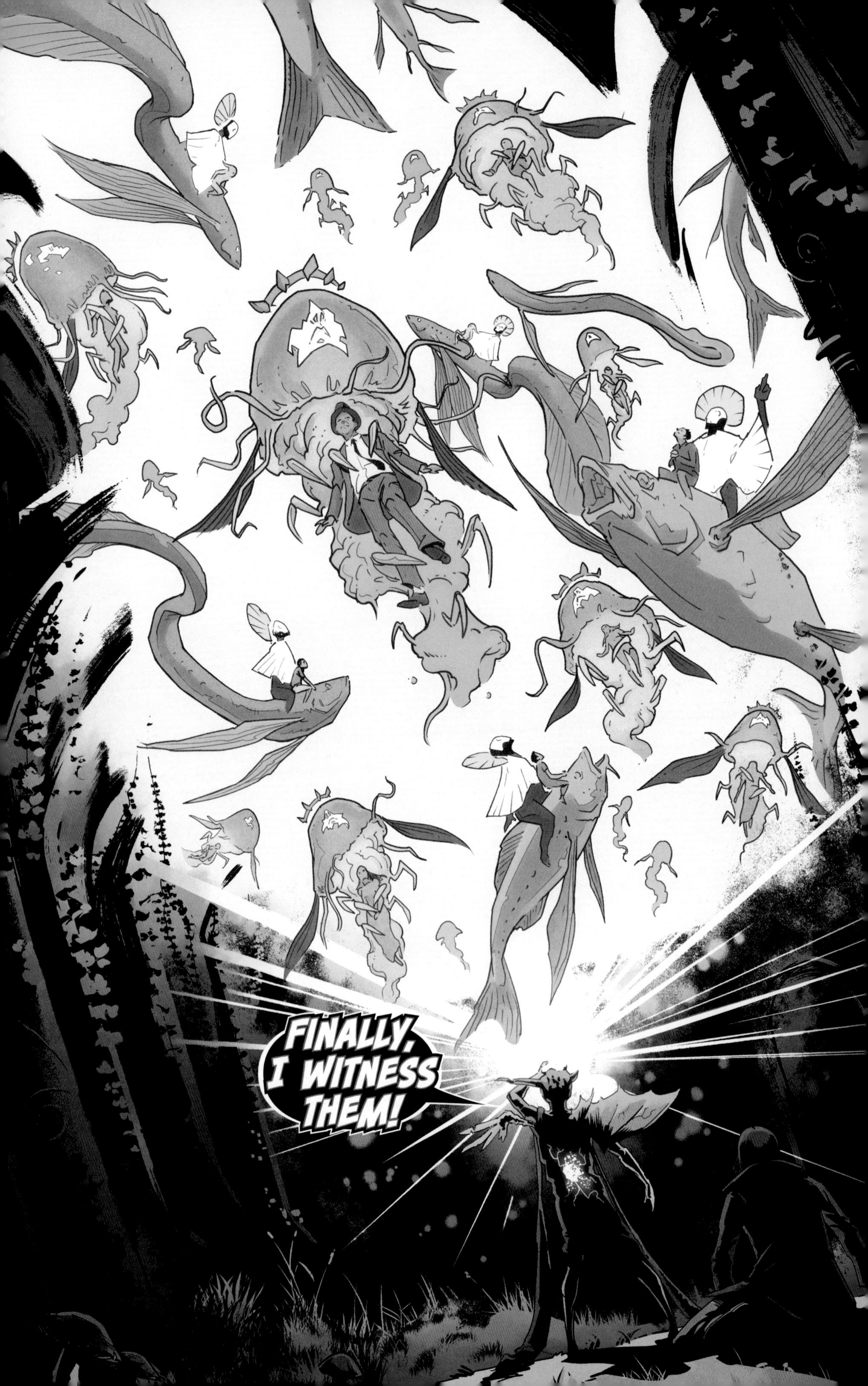
FINALLY, I WITNESS THEM!

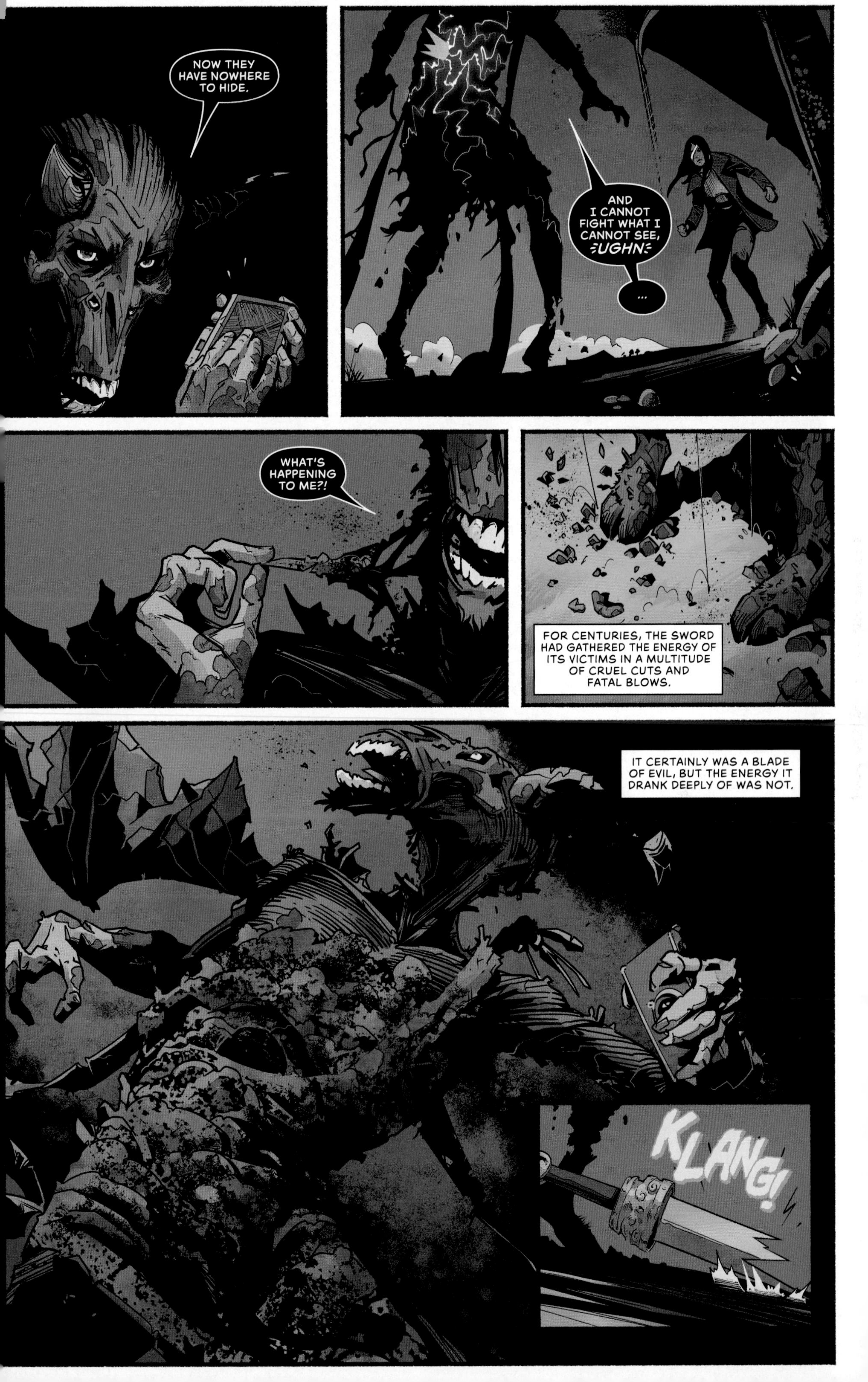
NOW THEY HAVE NOWHERE TO HIDE.
AND I CANNOT FIGHT WHAT I CANNOT SEE, UGHN
...
WHAT'S HAPPENING TO ME?!
FOR CENTURIES, THE SWORD HAD GATHERED THE ENERGY OF ITS VICTIMS IN A MULTITUDE OF CRUEL CUTS AND FATAL BLOWS.
IT CERTAINLY WAS A BLADE OF EVIL, BUT THE ENERGY IT DRANK DEEPLY OF WAS NOT.
KLANG!

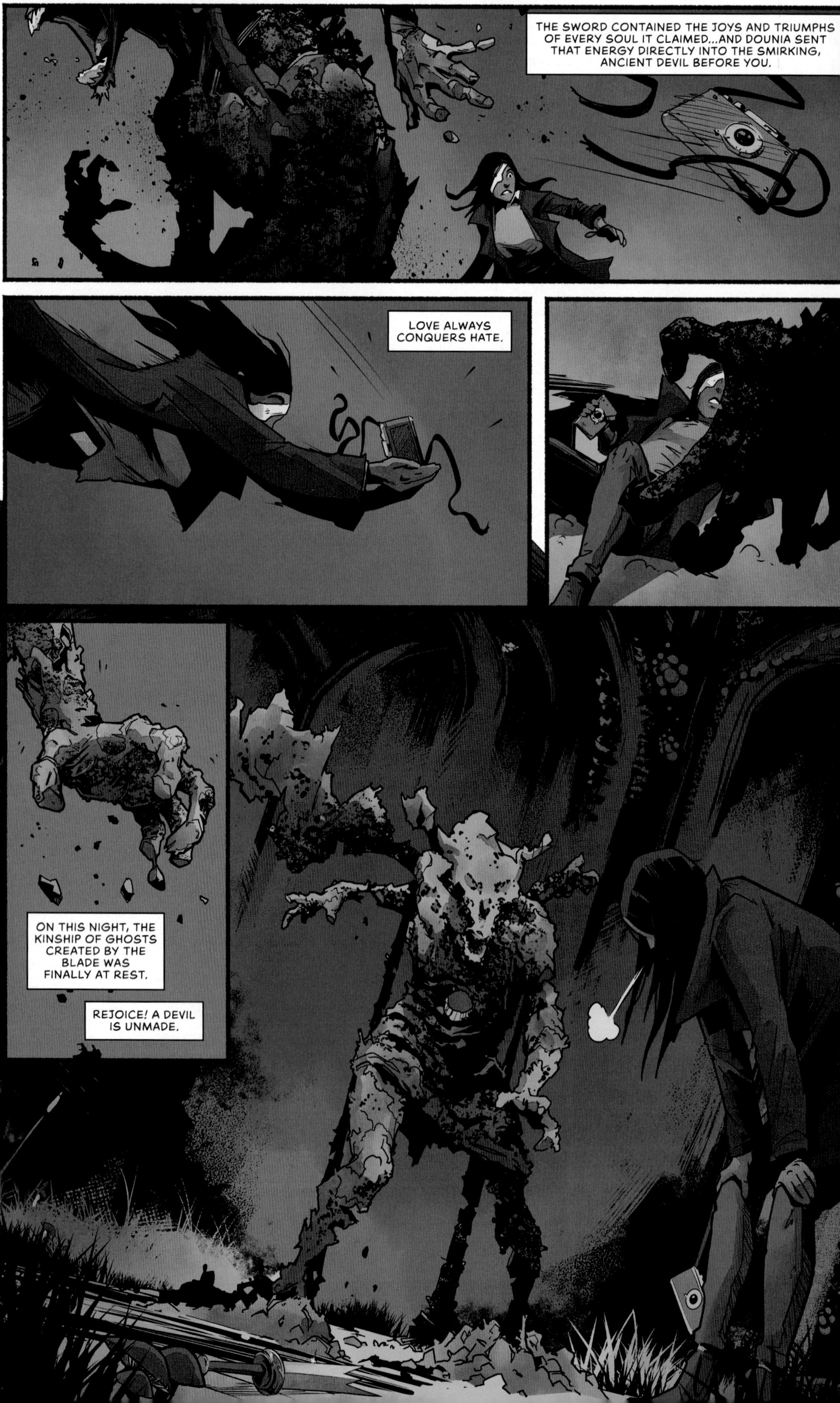
THE SWORD CONTAINED THE JOYS AND TRIUMPHS OF EVERY SOUL IT CLAIMED...AND DOUNIA SENT THAT ENERGY DIRECTLY INTO THE SMIRKING, ANCIENT DEVIL BEFORE YOU.
LOVE ALWAYS CONQUERS HATE.
ON THIS NIGHT, THE KINSHIP OF GHOSTS CREATED BY THE BLADE WAS FINALLY AT REST.
REJOICE! A DEVIL IS UNMADE.

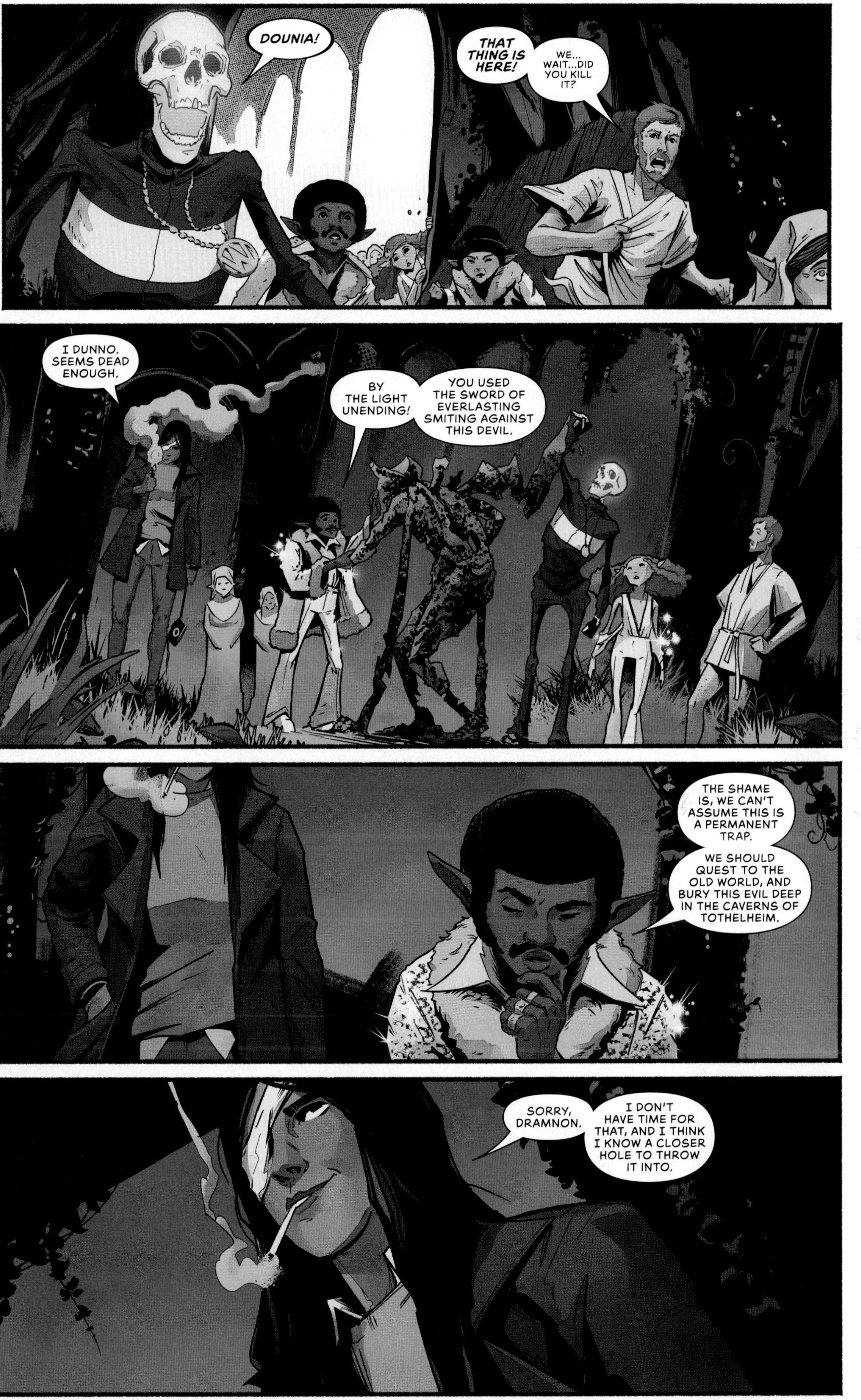
DOUNIA!
THAT THING IS HERE!
WE... WAIT...DID YOU KILL IT?
I DUNNO. SEEMS DEAD ENOUGH.
BY THE LIGHT UNENDING!
YOU USED THE SWORD OF EVERLASTING SMITING AGAINST THIS DEVIL.
THE SHAME IS, WE CAN'T ASSUME THIS IS A PERMANENT TRAP.
WE SHOULD QUEST TO THE OLD WORLD, AND BURY THIS EVIL DEEP IN THE CAVERNS OF TOTHELHEIM.
SORRY, DRAMNON.
I DON'T HAVE TIME FOR THAT, AND I THINK I KNOW A CLOSER HOLE TO THROW IT INTO.

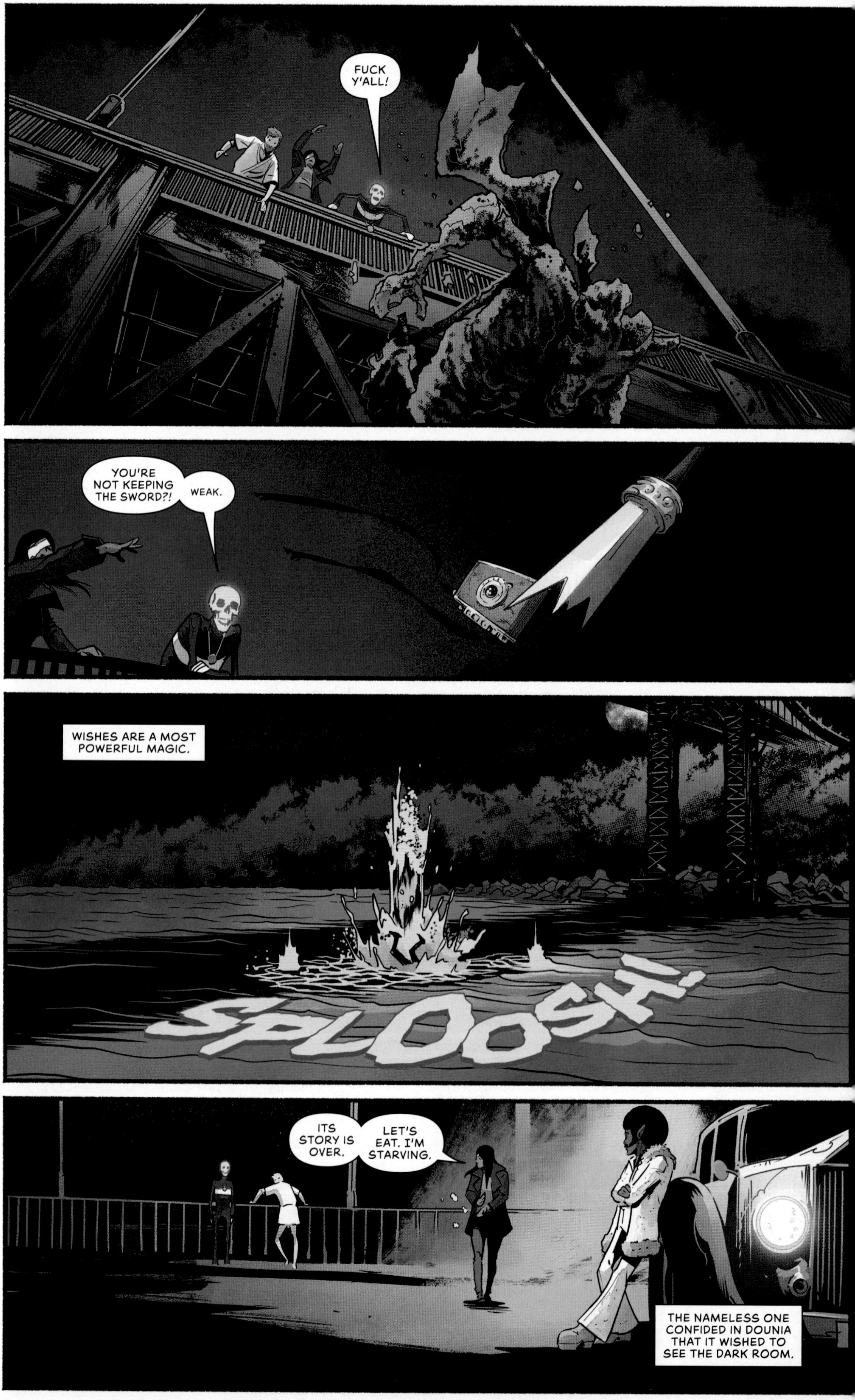
FUCK Y'ALL!
YOU'RE NOT KEEPING THE SWORD?!
WEAK.
WISHES ARE A MOST POWERFUL MAGIC.
SPLOOSH!
ITS STORY IS OVER.
LET'S EAT. I'M STARVING.
THE NAMELESS ONE CONFIDED IN DOUNIA THAT IT WISHED TO SEE THE DARK ROOM.

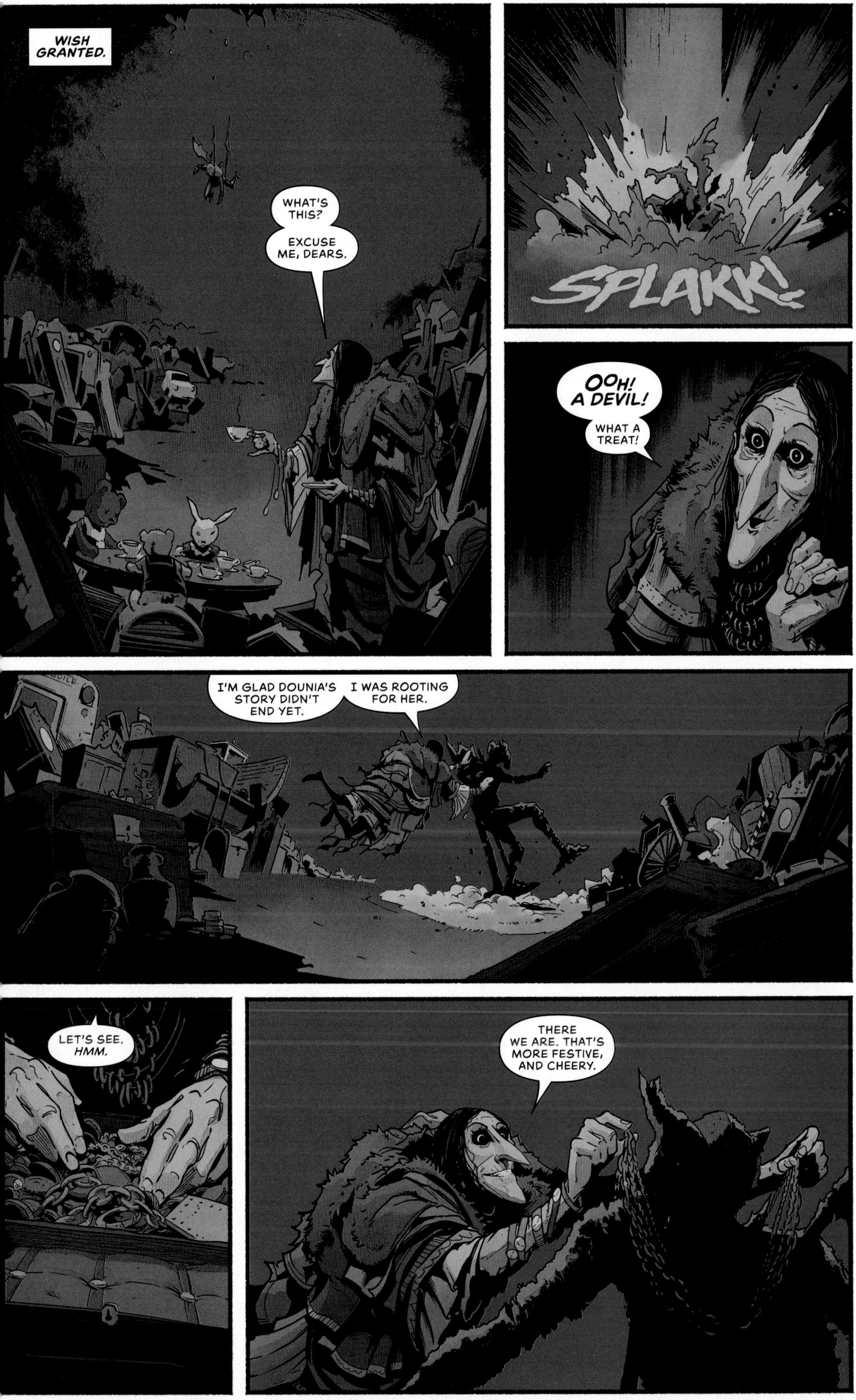
WISH GRANTED.
WHAT'S THIS?
EXCUSE ME, DEARS.
SPLAKK!
OOH! A DEVIL!
WHAT A TREAT!
I'M GLAD DOUNIA'S STORY DIDN'T END YET.
I WAS ROOTING FOR HER.
LET'S SEE. HMM.
THERE WE ARE. THAT'S MORE FESTIVE, AND CHEERY.

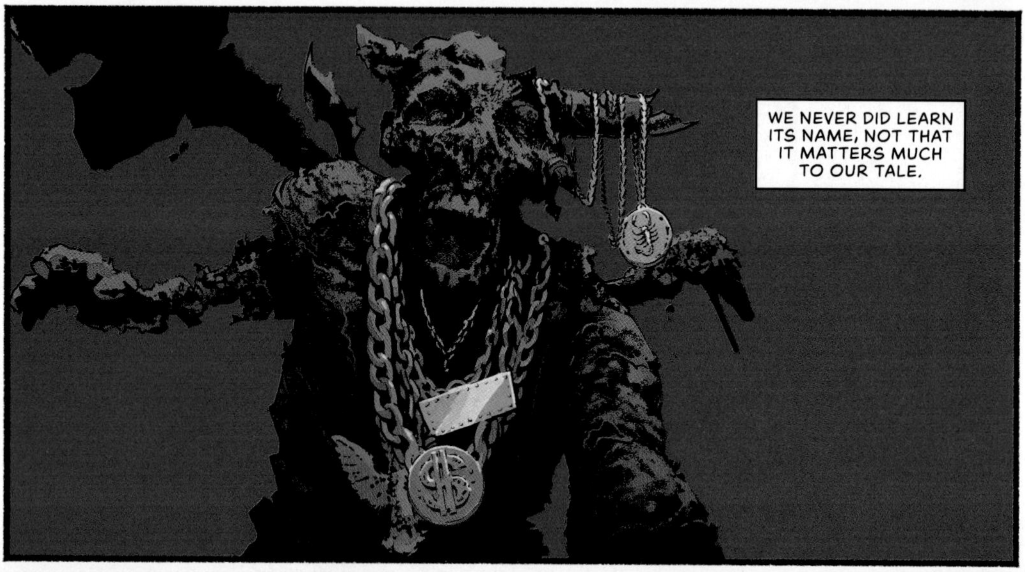
WE NEVER DID LEARN ITS NAME, NOT THAT IT MATTERS MUCH TO OUR TALE.
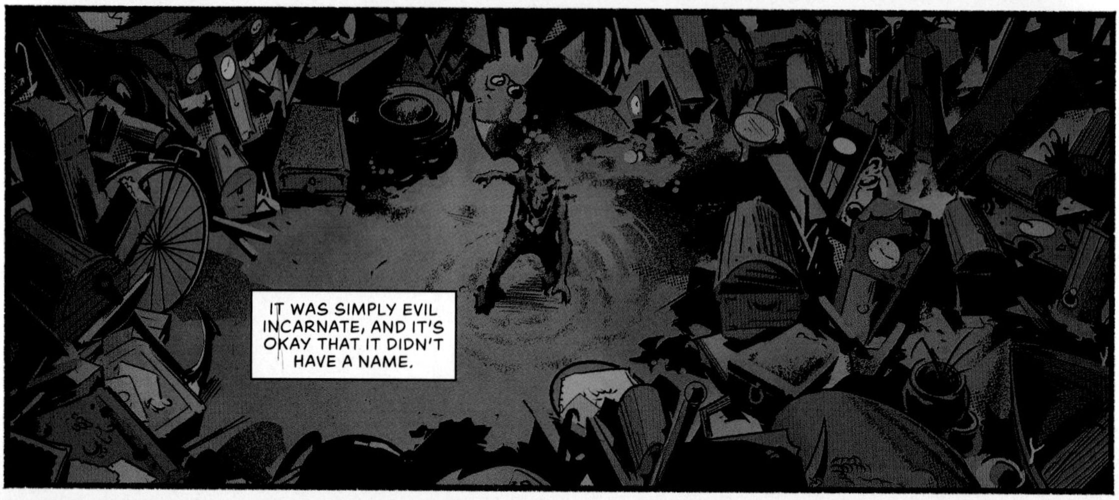
IT WAS SIMPLY EVIL INCARNATE, AND IT'S OKAY THAT IT DIDN'T HAVE A NAME.
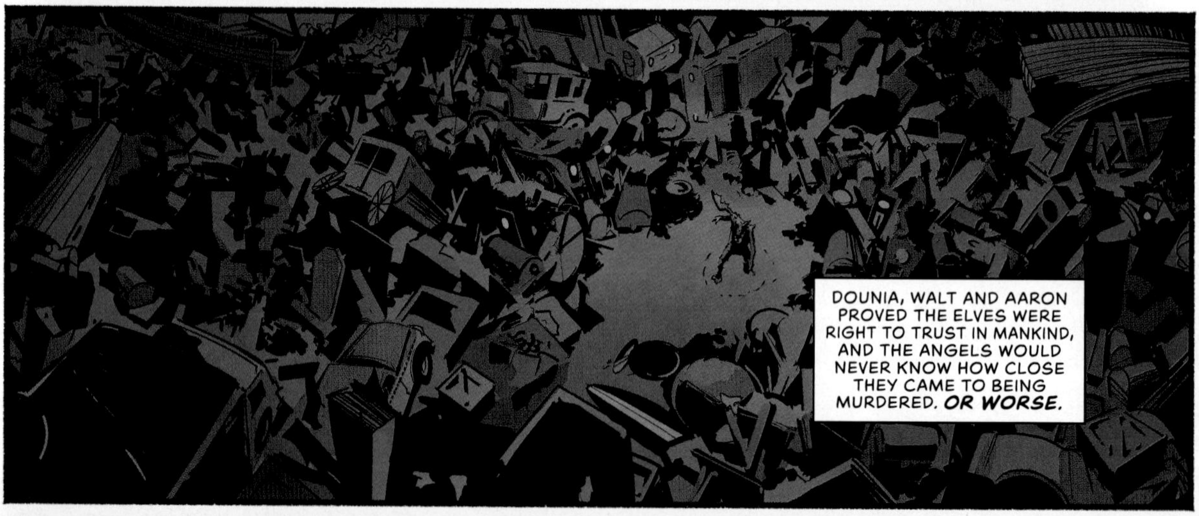
DOUNIA, WALT AND AARON PROVED THE ELVES WERE RIGHT TO TRUST IN MANKIND, AND THE ANGELS WOULD NEVER KNOW HOW CLOSE THEY CAME TO BEING MURDERED. ***OR WORSE.***
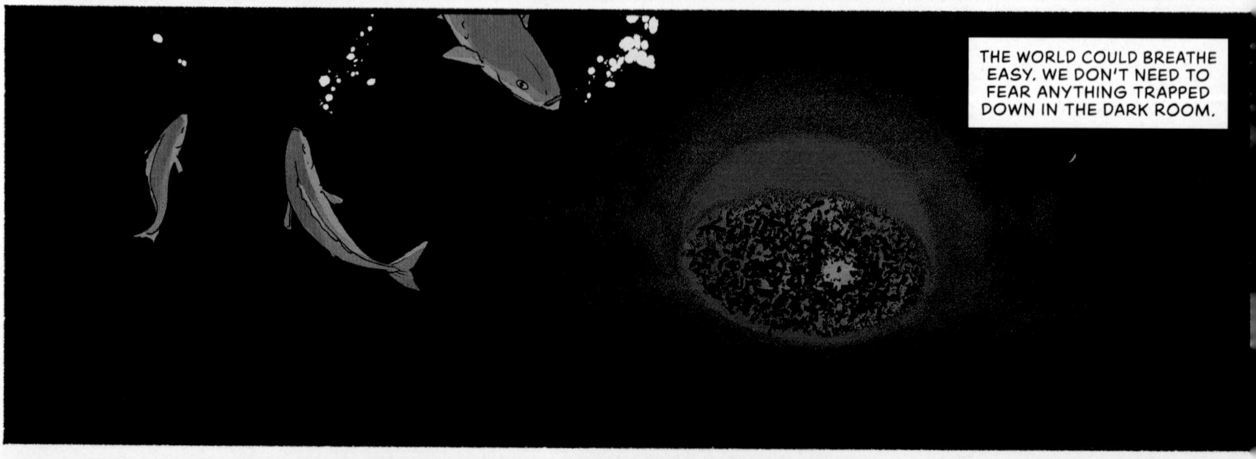
THE WORLD COULD BREATHE EASY. WE DON'T NEED TO FEAR ANYTHING TRAPPED DOWN IN THE DARK ROOM.

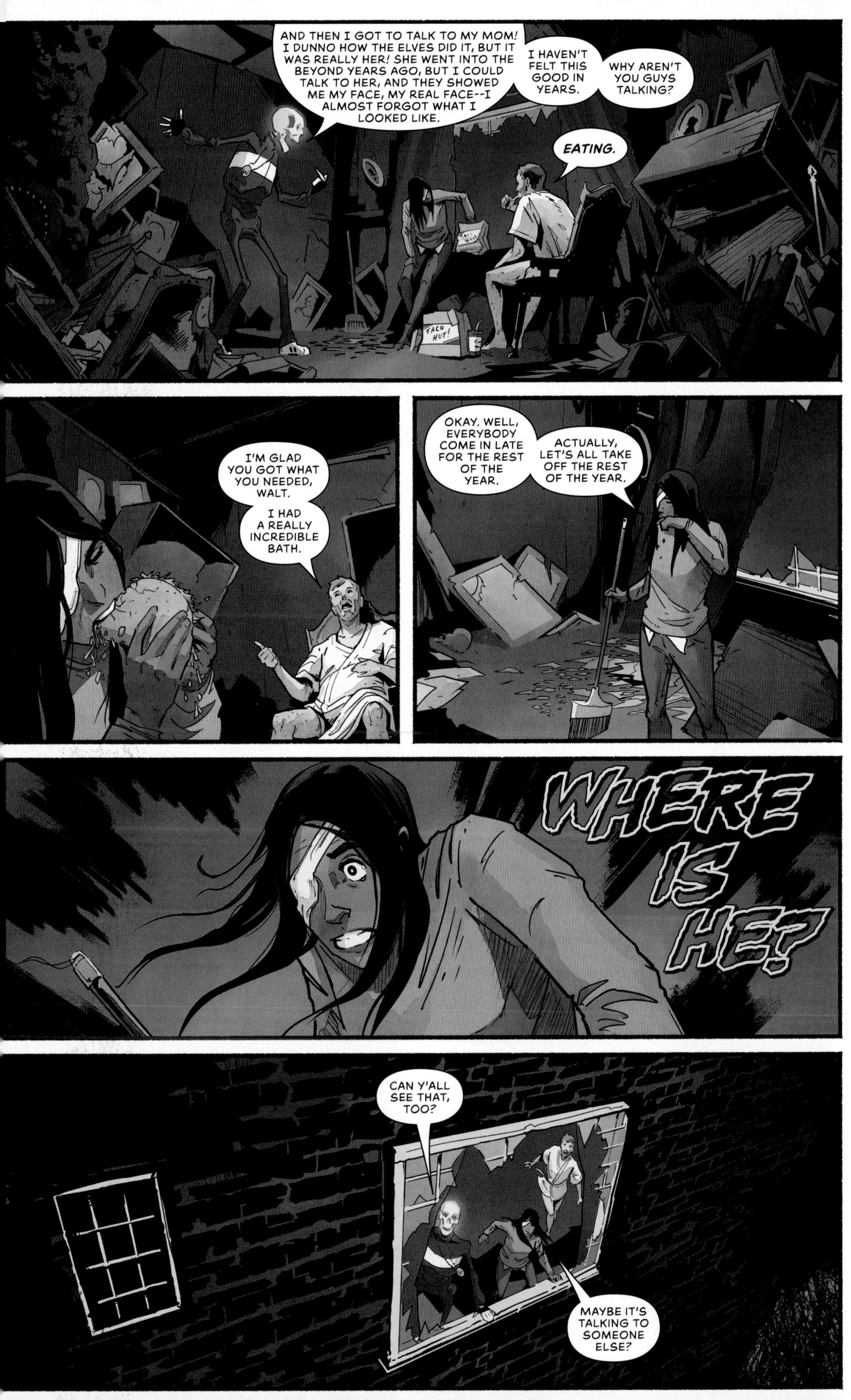
AND THEN I GOT TO TALK TO MY MOM! I DUNNO HOW THE ELVES DID IT, BUT IT WAS REALLY HER! SHE WENT INTO THE BEYOND YEARS AGO, BUT I COULD TALK TO HER, AND THEY SHOWED ME MY FACE, MY REAL FACE--I ALMOST FORGOT WHAT I LOOKED LIKE.
I HAVEN'T FELT THIS GOOD IN YEARS.
WHY AREN'T YOU GUYS TALKING?
EATING.
TACO HUT!
I'M GLAD YOU GOT WHAT YOU NEEDED, WALT.
I HAD A REALLY INCREDIBLE BATH.
OKAY. WELL, EVERYBODY COME IN LATE FOR THE REST OF THE YEAR.
ACTUALLY, LET'S ALL TAKE OFF THE REST OF THE YEAR.
WHERE IS HE?
CAN Y'ALL SEE THAT, TOO?
MAYBE IT'S TALKING TO SOMEONE ELSE?

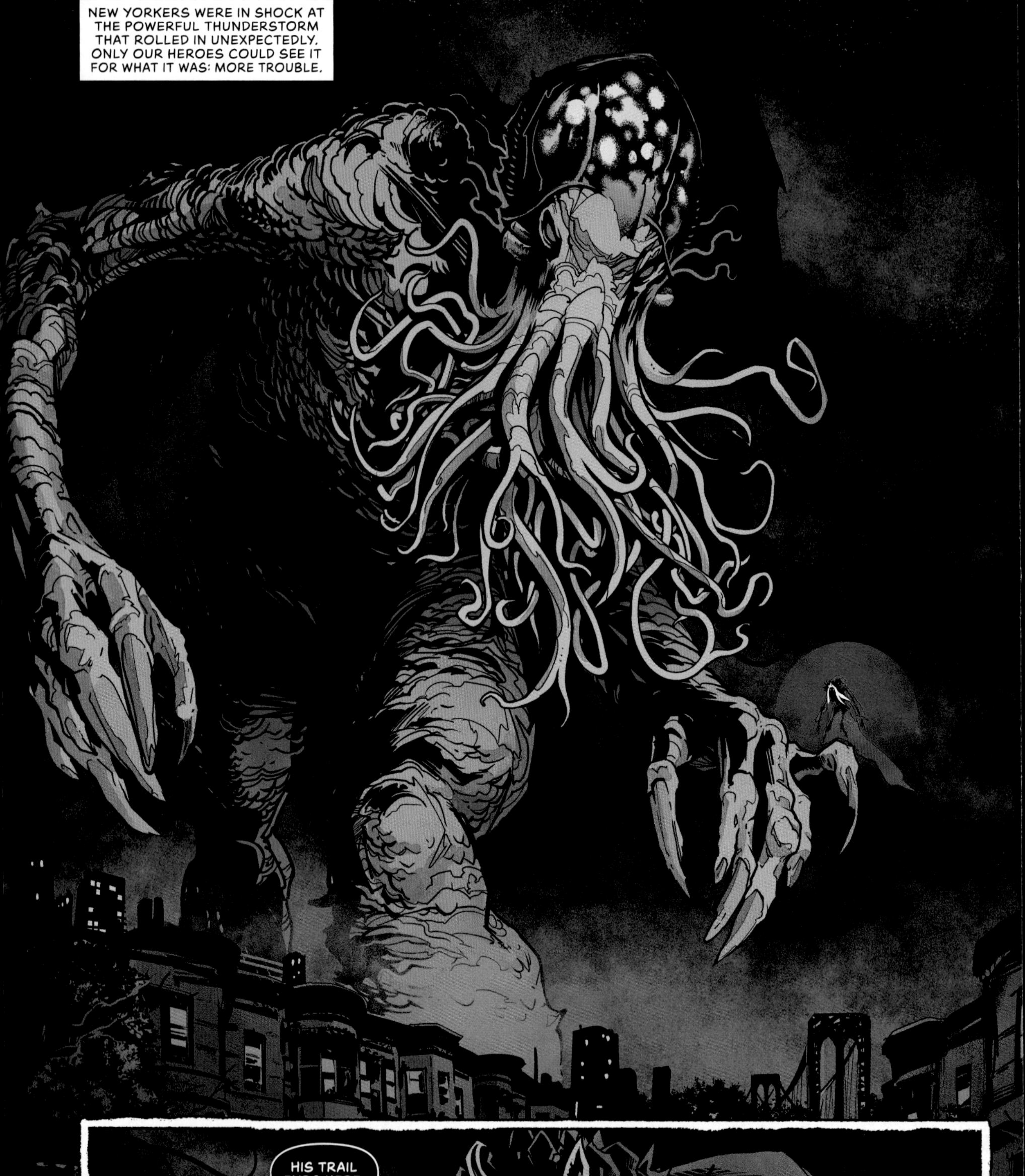
NEW YORKERS WERE IN SHOCK AT THE POWERFUL THUNDERSTORM THAT ROLLED IN UNEXPECTEDLY. ONLY OUR HEROES COULD SEE IT FOR WHAT IT WAS: MORE TROUBLE.

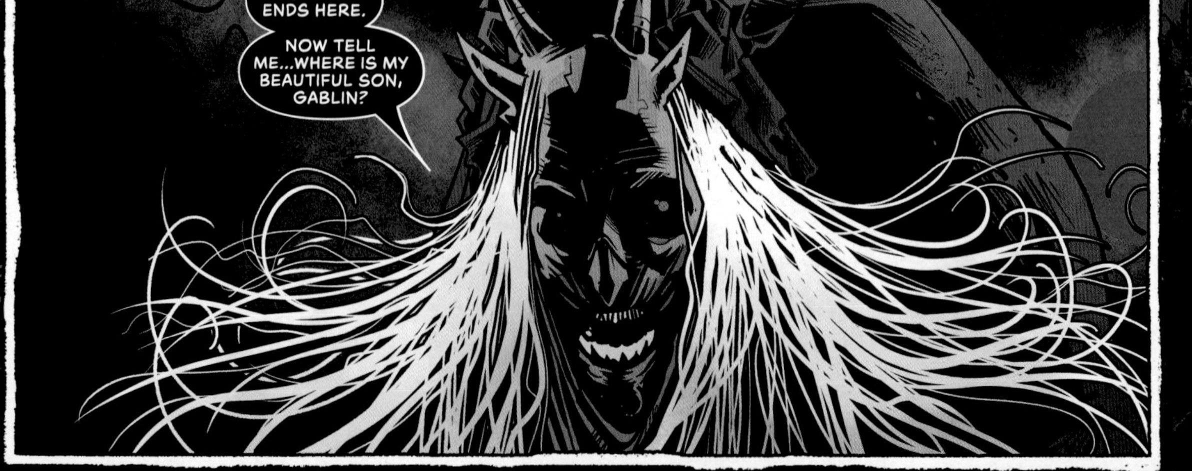
HIS TRAIL ENDS HERE.
NOW TELL ME...WHERE IS MY BEAUTIFUL SON, GABLIN?

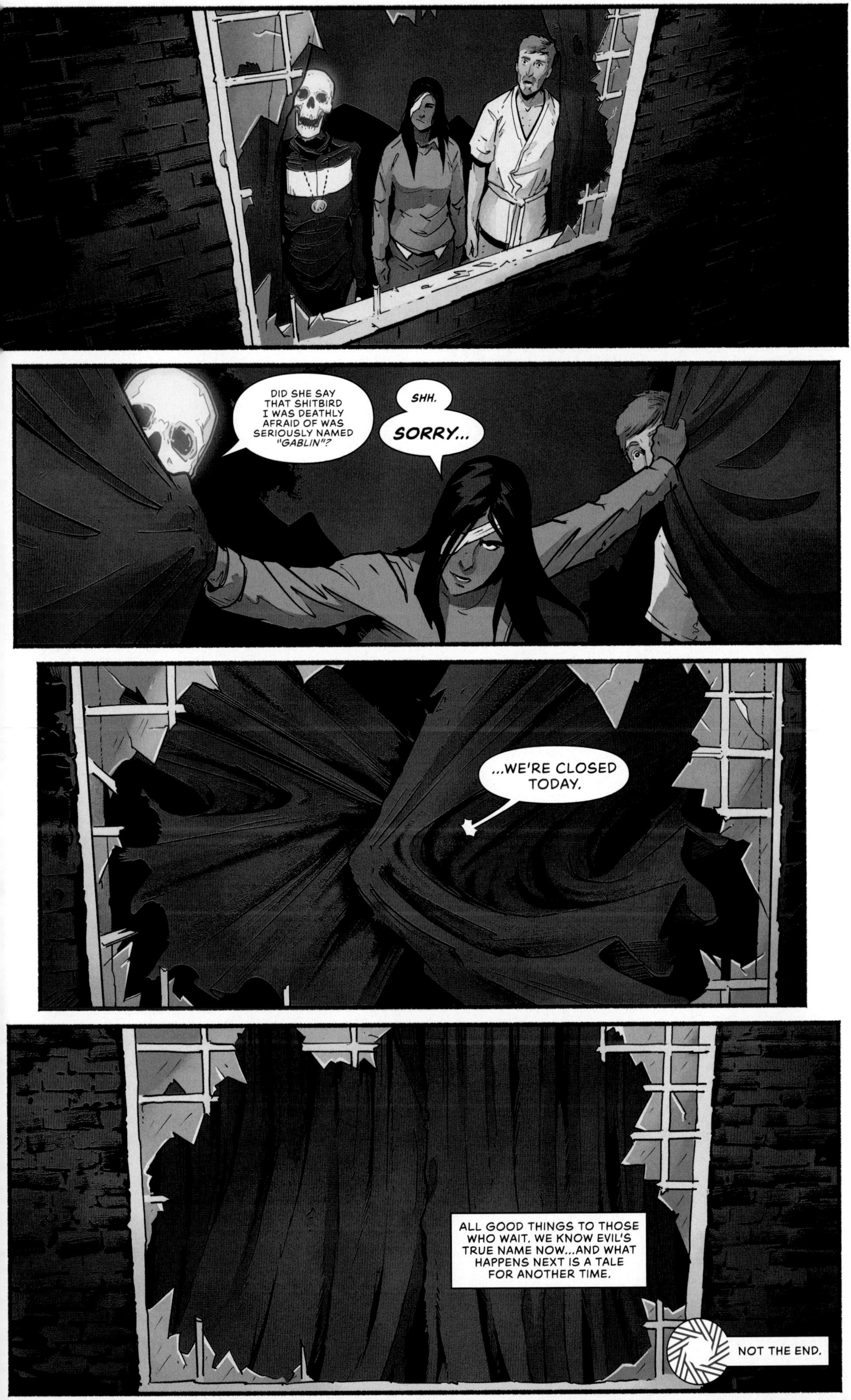
DID SHE SAY THAT SHITBIRD I WAS DEATHLY AFRAID OF WAS SERIOUSLY NAMED "GABLIN"?
SHH.
SORRY...
...WE'RE CLOSED TODAY.
ALL GOOD THINGS TO THOSE WHO WAIT. WE KNOW EVIL'S TRUE NAME NOW...AND WHAT HAPPENS NEXT IS A TALE FOR ANOTHER TIME.
NOT THE END.

The comic we hope you just enjoyed wouldn't exist without our friend Neil Mahoney. If you knew Neil, he made you laugh a lot, but if you don't know Neil he almost assuredly has made you laugh with his work as a writer, director and editor. They say "Never meet your heroes" but Neil met a bunch of his, and they all hired him, because he made them look great and was a blast to hang out with along the way.

In 2018 Neil asked me if I'd be willing to take a look at his friend's portfolio. Scott Buoncristiano was hoping to bring his talent into comic books. I told Neil the truth: I'd do anything for him, including looking at his bum pal's portfolio. Neil's the type of friend that I would still help move, if he would ask, but he's such a good friend, he would never have asked me to help him move. But I would have. If he asked.

I warned Neil, that it'd be unlikely his friend would be ready to start jamming on a comic, but that I've gotten pretty good at providing helpful critiques for folks trying to break in. To my surprise and delight...

...Scott Buoncristiano was ready. And ready in a way I found shocking. A lot of artists can draw amazing illustrations, but it usually takes an artist a decent number of years to flex the kind of sequential storytelling needed to make comics. Not Scott. He has it.

Neil grew up with Scott on Cape Cod, and while I never discussed the matter with Neil, I suspect he knew he was helping me as much as he'd be helping Scott by introducing us. My philosophy on making comics has not wavered in my twenty years as a writer. I tell a story to my partner, and that partner tells a story to the reader. I show up at the end to crack some jokes, and break some hearts, but let's be honest: it's an artist's medium.

Scott and I came up with a plan and got working. We agreed that after we clocked off our day jobs. we'd enter THE DARK ROOM together. Every independent comic book is a small business, and you don't just do business with anyone off the street. Scott was a joy to collaborate with and I knew immediately why Neil was friends with him.

We set out to make the a horror comic filled with the sorts of the characters and scenarios that Scott would be drawing for himself. I'd brought some horror DNA to my Marvel work over the years, but never got to roll up my sleeves and do it for myself at Image.

I let Neil know the happy news, that Scott and I clicked and we had a direction were already underway, and that his inked pages were incredible. Scott was the most professional rookie I'd worked with. I promised to send him the first pages, and I think I got busy, and it slipped my mind. No big deal, I thought. I have deadlines, but showing Neil pages wasn't one of them. Besides, we'd surely thank him in the book.

Then came the news that suddenly, unfairly, and incomprehensibly...Neil was gone.

Everyone that loved Neil just simply exploded in pain.

During the pandemic that grief has few outlets. Sobbing on damp shoulders was not on the menu when we are meant to stay six feet apart. We called, and zoomed and whatever else.

Neil once threw himself a reverse surprise party, emerging from hiding inside the house packed with his friends. Everyone was silent facing the front door and he struts out behind everyone in a tuxedo. We had some reason to doubt the terrible news, okay?

Not long after Neil died my wife looked at me and said "I would have had Neil's children" and I nodded and said "Me too". And humor definitely helped the shit go down, but shit

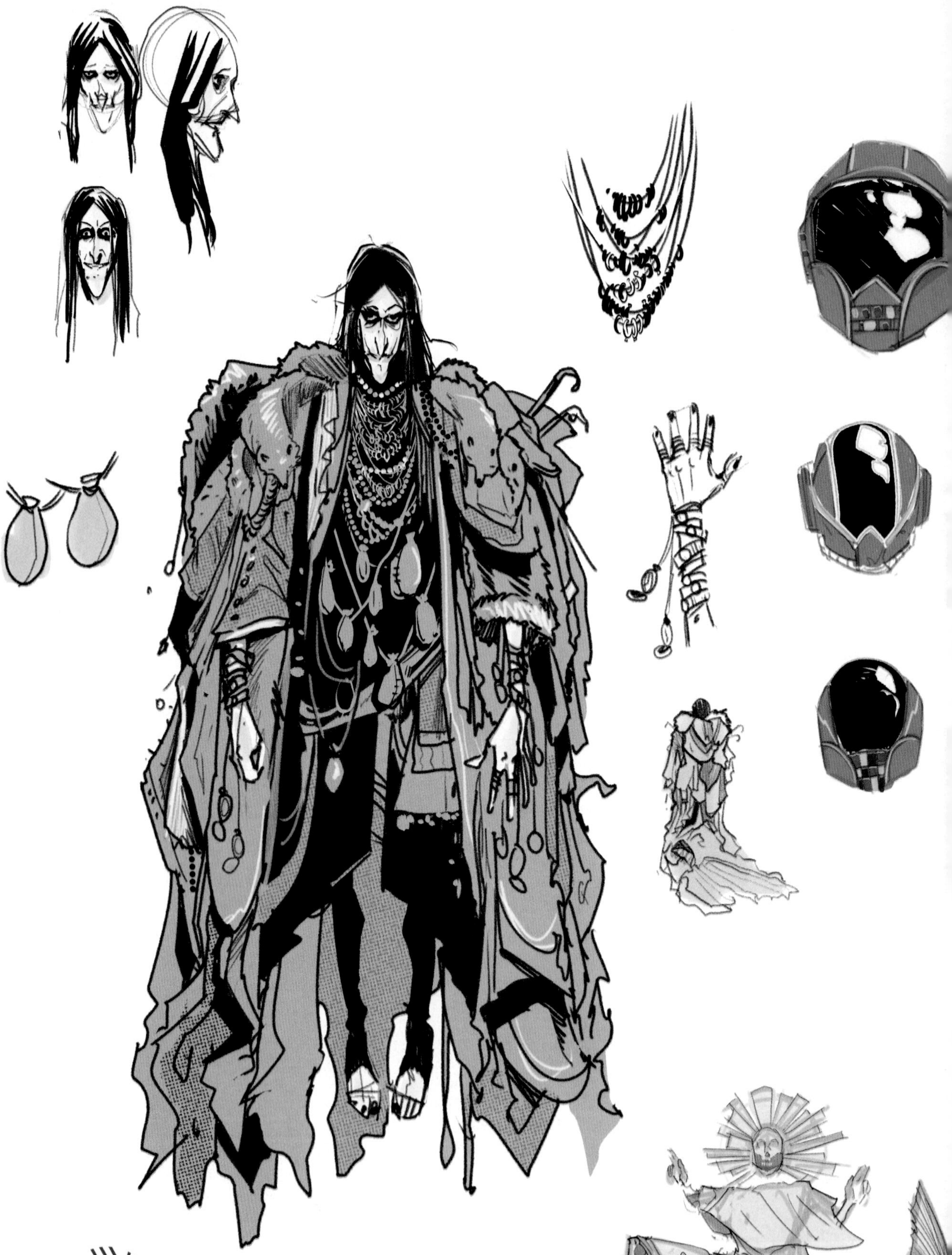

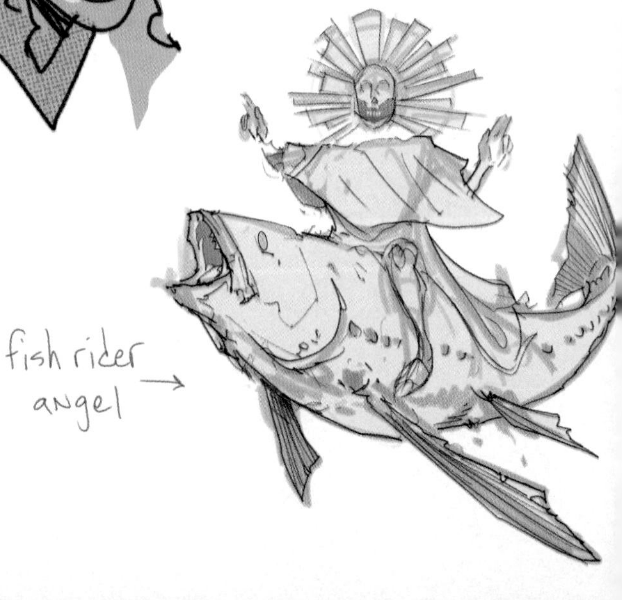
fish rider
angel

SCOTT BUONCRISTIANO
SKETCHBOOK

Vamps

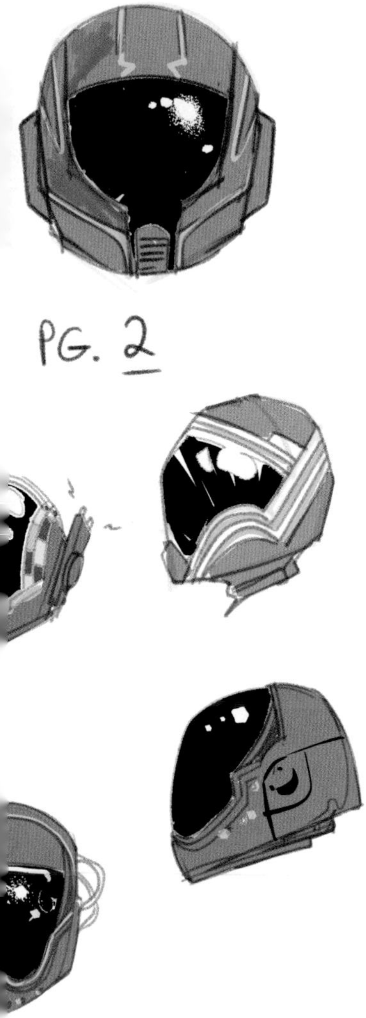

PG. 2

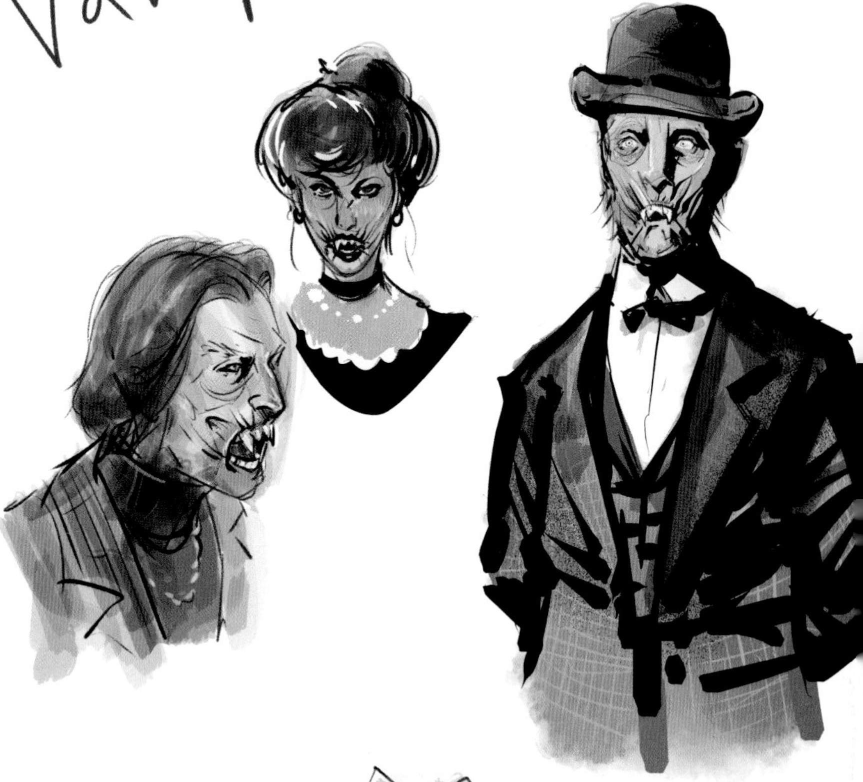

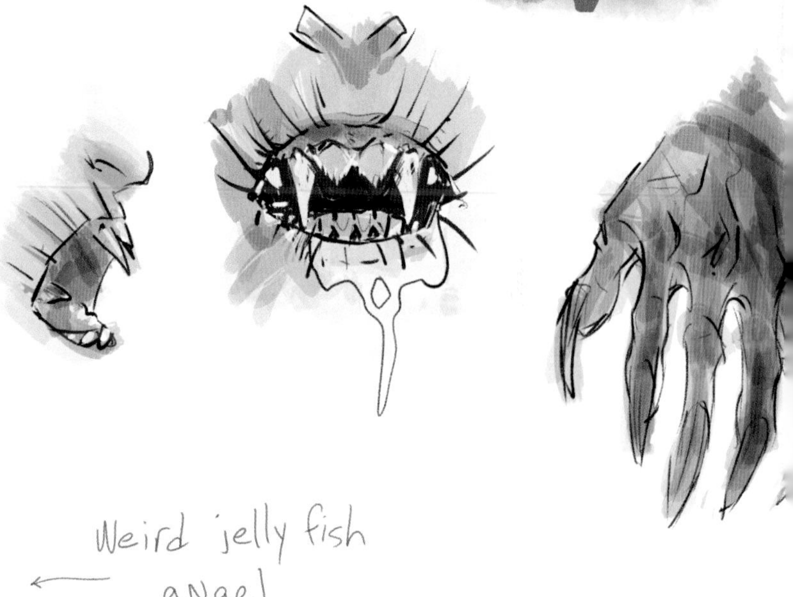

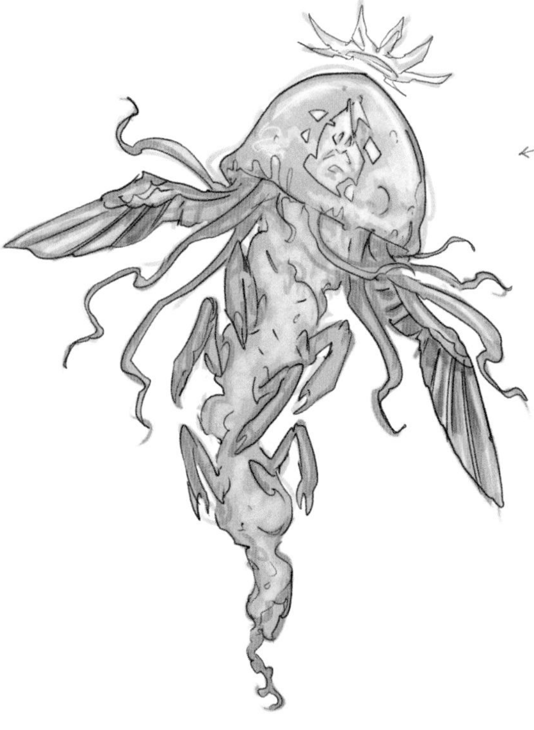

Weird jelly fish angel

(I think I like this the best)

weird creature angel

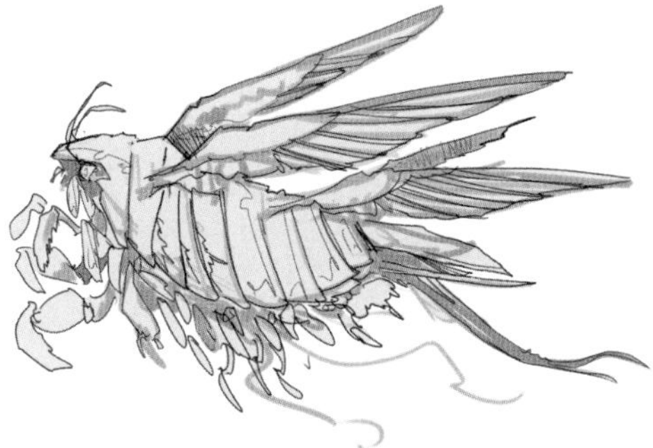

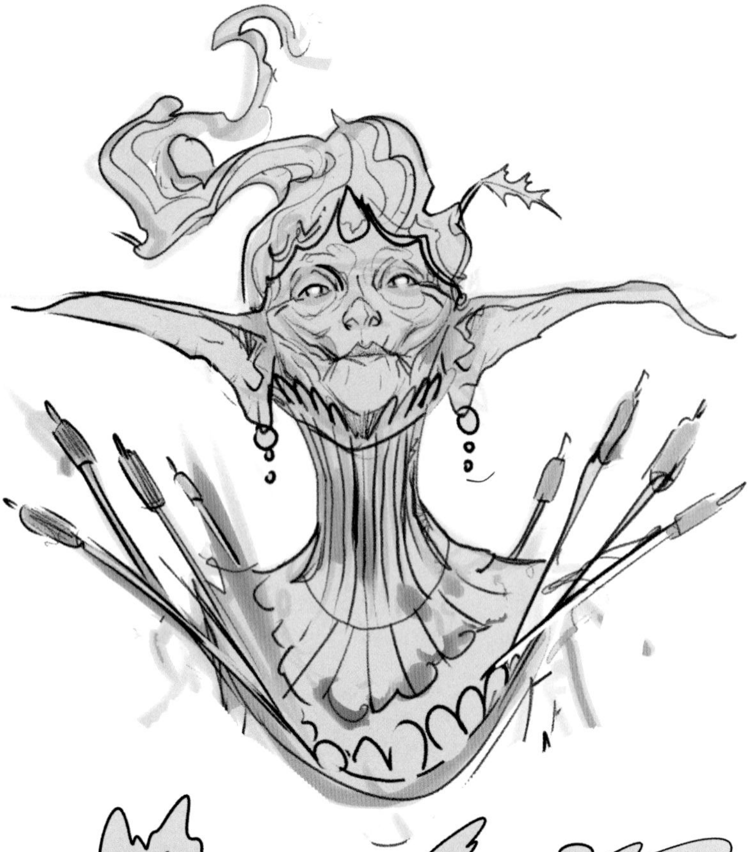
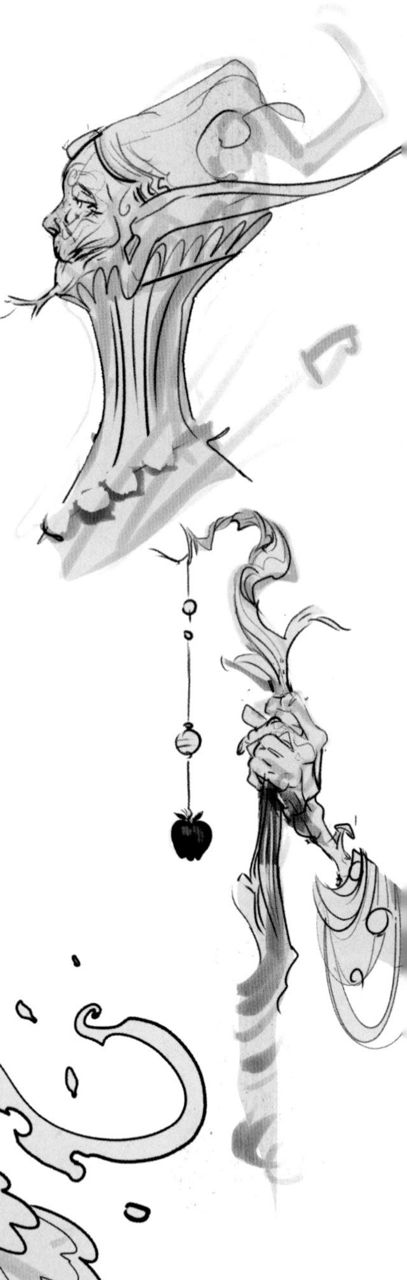
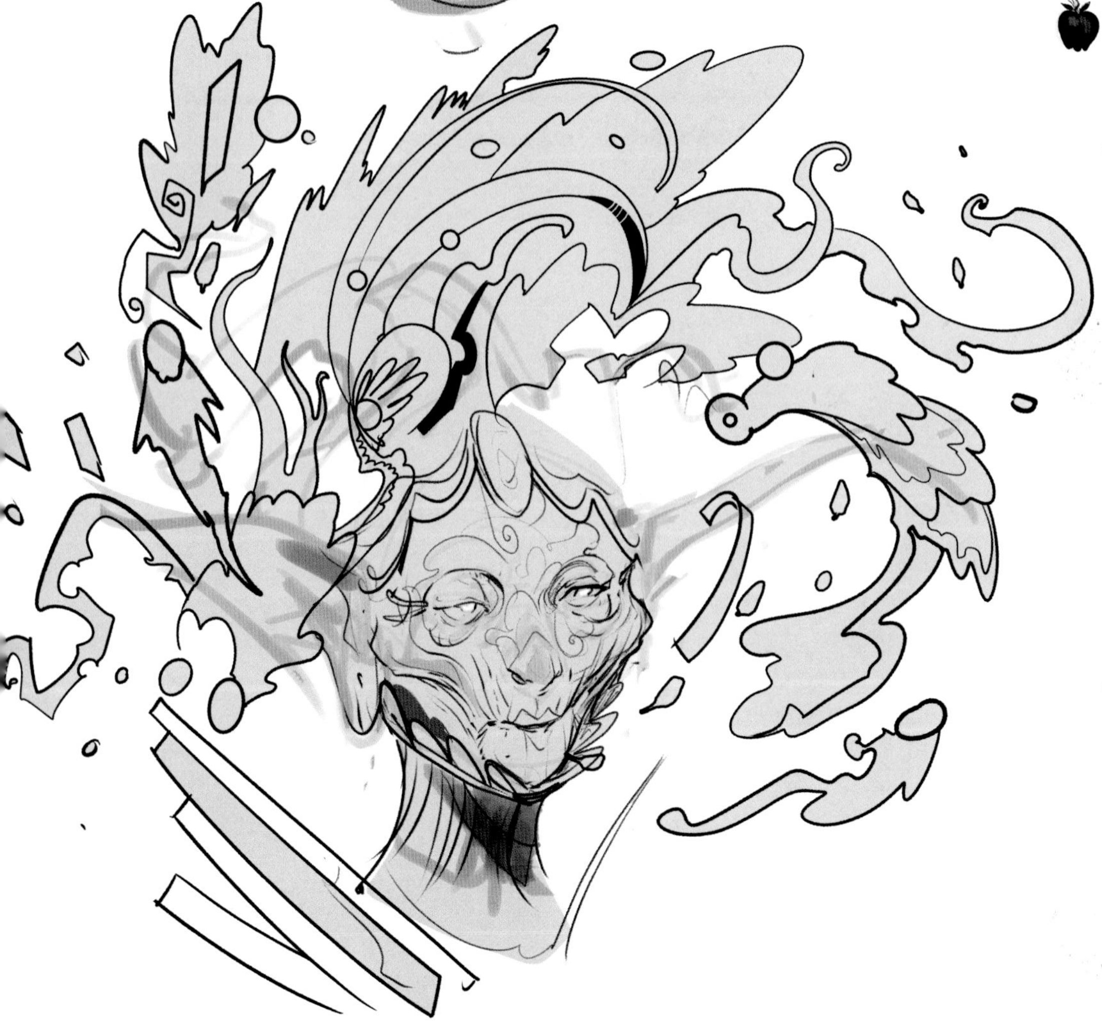

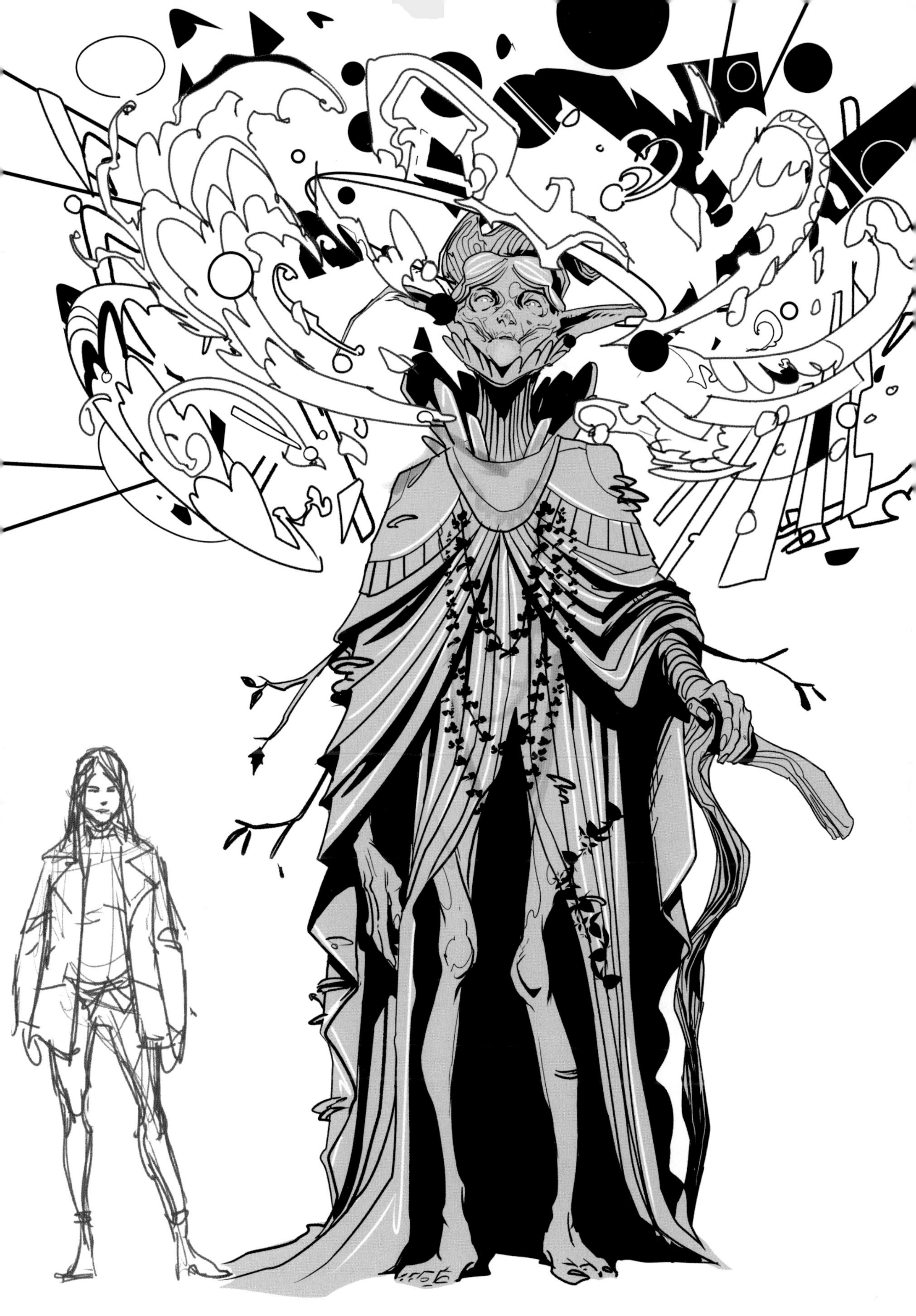

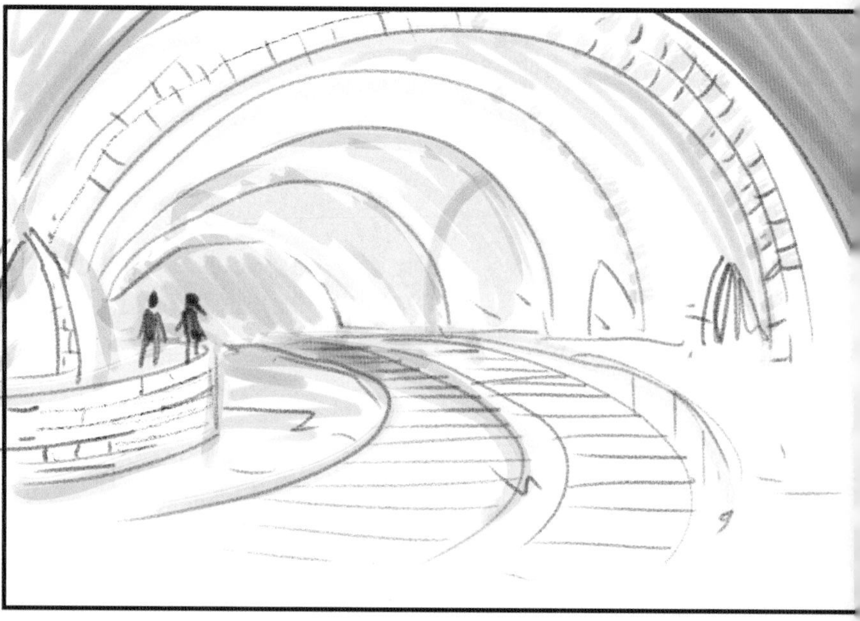

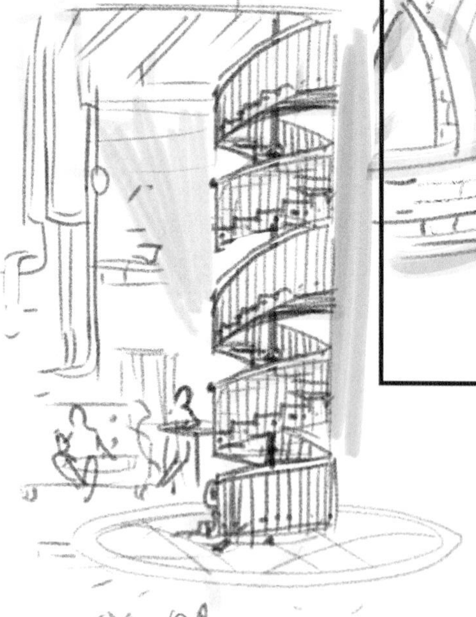

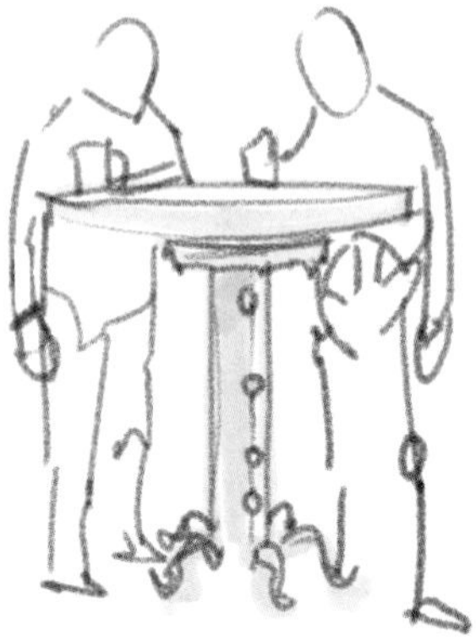

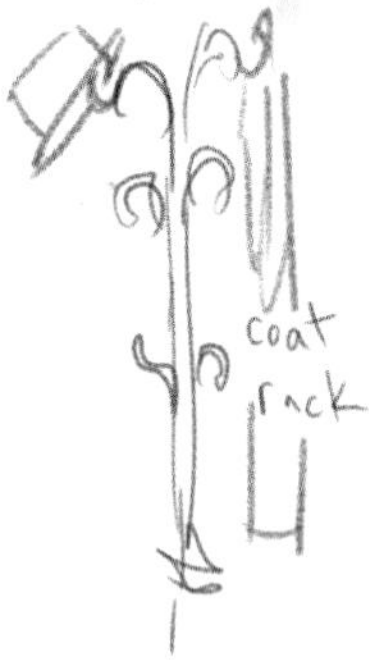
coat rack

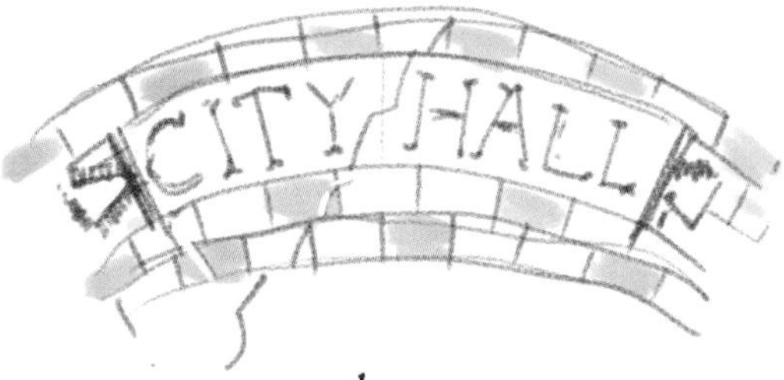
CITY HALL

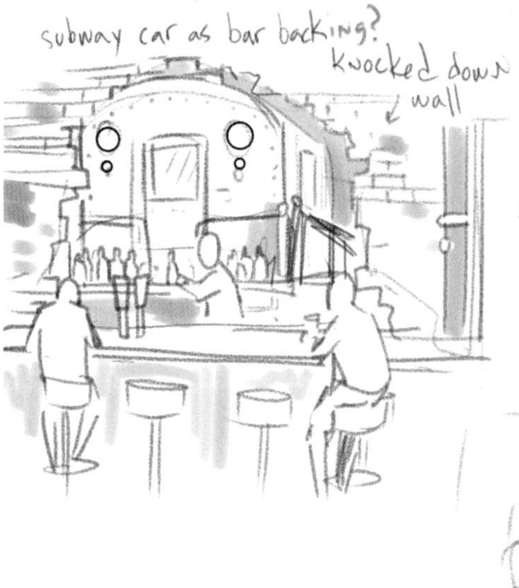
subway car as bar backing?
knocked down wall

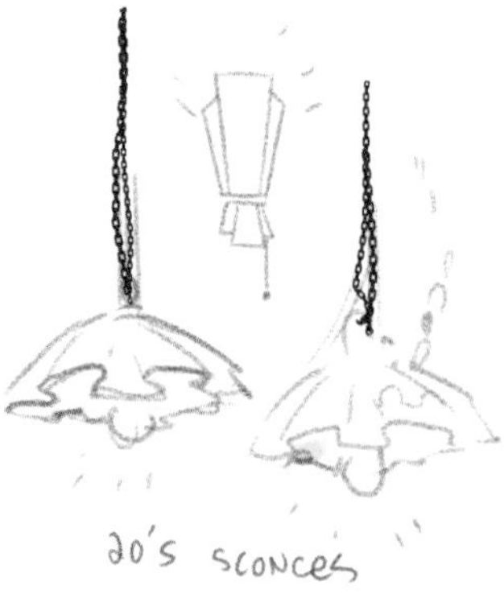
20's sconces

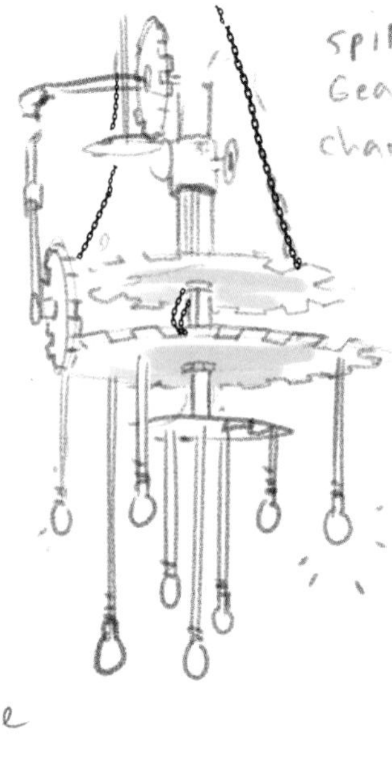
spinning Gear chandelier?

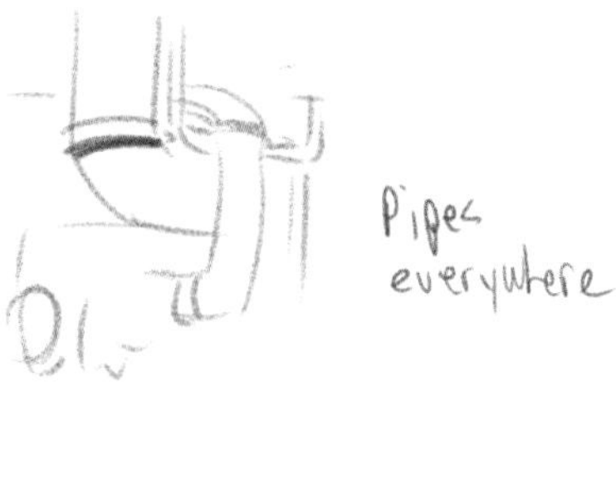
Pipes everywhere

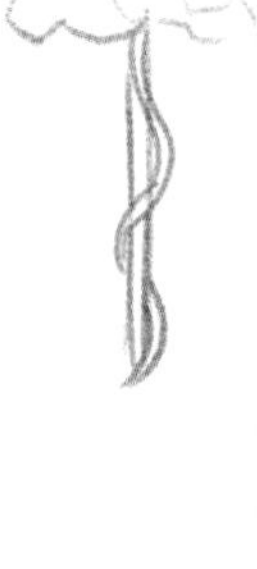

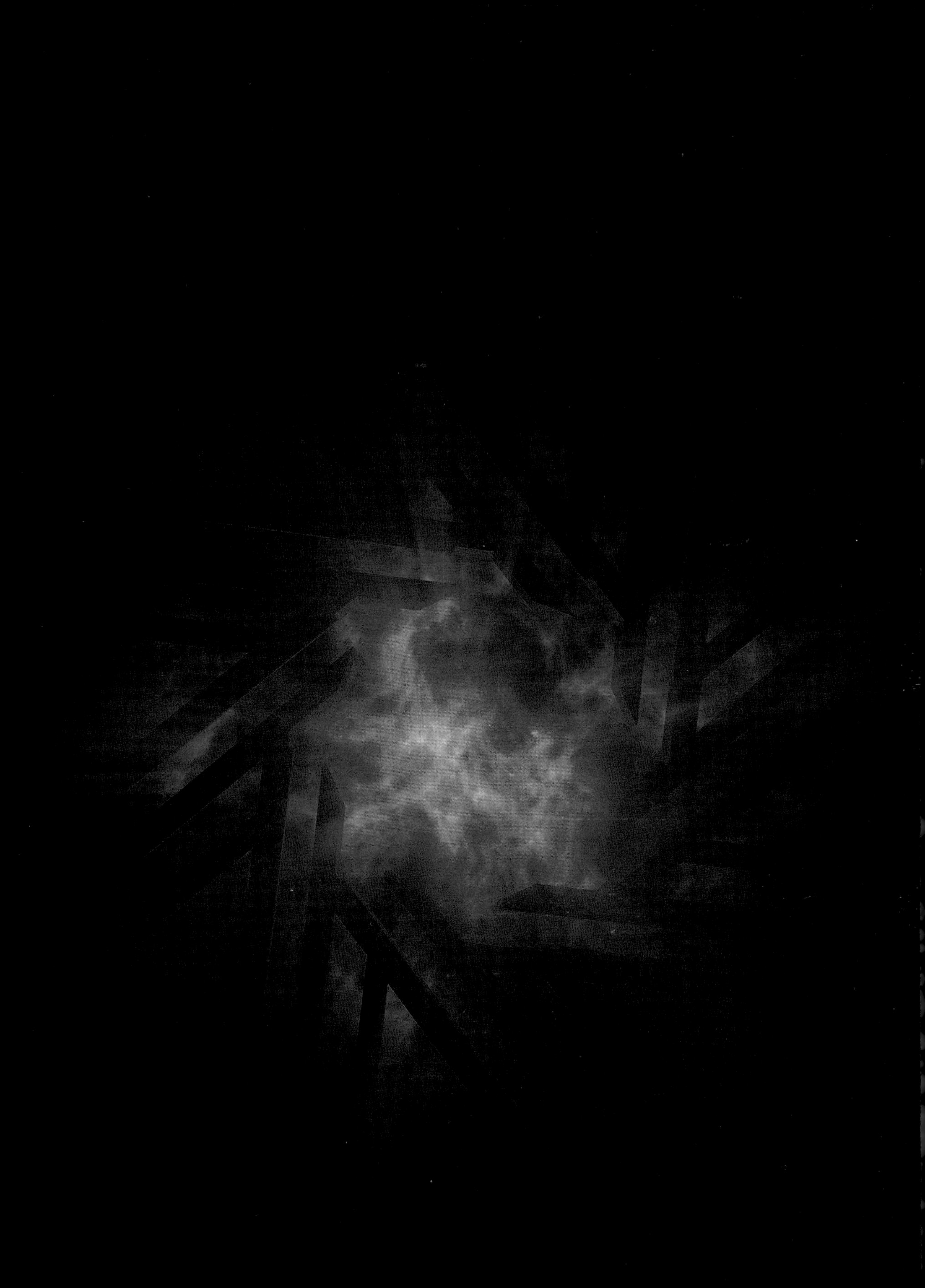

THE DARK ROOM WILL OPEN AGAIN